Contemporary
Japanese

AN INTRODUCTORY LANGUAGE COURSE

Contemporary
Japanese

VOLUME 2

SECOND EDITION

ERIKO SATO

TUTTLE Publishing

Tokyo │ Rutland, Vermont │ Singapore

Contents

Preface

Contemporary Japanese: An Introductory Language Course is designed for beginning students of the Japanese language at the university level. It is a classroom text, but can be an effective self-study text if used with the free online audio recordings and Teacher's Guide. This textbook introduces about 1,000 basic vocabulary words that are essential for daily life and campus life, over 250 basic kanji characters, basic grammar including passive and causative constructions, and basic cultural information that is the key to the understanding of various speech styles and conversational interactions. It helps the students quickly build the foundation necessary for tackling various real-life Japanese-speaking situations in neutral and polite contexts, without overwhelming them with too advanced honorific speech styles, too colloquial potentially-offensive informal speech styles, or too advanced kanji characters. Yet, it provides useful tips and additional information including the modern trend of language use. After completing this textbook, the students are ready to pursue the specific area of their interest while improving their general proficiency in Japanese. This comprehensive textbook is characterized by a unique "multi-vitamin-style" organization and an innovative "Guess and Try" method of learning.

Volume 1 and Volume 2 of this textbook consist of 26 chapters, each of which has a distinct general objective. Each chapter has several lessons, and there are a total of 106 lessons in the entire textbook. Each lesson serves as a nucleus of the textbook, and includes a full course of learning processes (observation, analysis, practice and performance) and the four language skills (speaking, listening, reading and writing), focusing on a single communicative objective. All the materials of each lesson are compactly placed on two facing pages, and are designed to be completed in one (or two) class sessions. This one-lesson-in-one-class format makes the objective of each class clear, and gives the students the feeling of achievement at the end of each class. Furthermore, the students can apply a little bit of all of the four skills in a balanced way in every class, without losing the objective of the class and without being limited to one aspect of language learning. It is like taking a "multi-vitamin" tablet daily, rather than taking vitamin C on Monday and vitamin E on Wednesday. This makes each class period stimulating and multifaceted, and helps the students to stay curious, lively and assertive during the class. As they accumulate a number of completed lessons, they can feel a strong sense of progress. Important points found in the lessons are thoroughly and clearly explained in grammar, usage, culture and writing notes at the end of each chapter, and they are reinforced and integrated in review questions.

Another characteristic of this textbook is found in the innovative and effective way of teaching the rules and facts of the Japanese language. This textbook does not spoonfeed the rules and facts. Instead, it introduces them by a unique method, the "Guess and Try" method. In each lesson, the students first observe a real-life conversation. Translation is highly limited in this program. Then, they are asked to "guess" what was going on in the dialog, using logic and open-mindedness, and to try out what they have guessed. As they work on the "Guess and Try" section, the students become curious, and eventually discover interesting facts and important generalizations themselves, either naturally, or by being surprised at an unexpected fact or generalization. Compared with being spoonfed these rules and facts by hearing a lecture or reading a written explanation, discovering them through guessing and trying makes the learning process fun and extremely challenging, and effective for the students. When one is curious, new information can be absorbed easily, just as when one is hungry, food can be digested easily. As shown in psychological studies, the guessing and trying process minimizes the time needed both for the acquisition and retention of language rules and facts. After the students understand the new rules and facts through "Guess and Try," they proceed to practice them in drill sections, and then to make use of them through a number of interesting communicative tasks, which can be done in pairs, small groups, or as a whole class activity. By performing these tasks, the students can engage in real-life situations for different communicative purposes. At this stage, they can experience the joy of learning Japanese, since Japanese becomes their tool for communication, rather than their master. The advantage of this system is that they can apply their knowledge to real contexts, and experience the delight of using Japanese in every class, or every lesson. In addition, what they do in each class or lesson, namely, continuous observation, guessing, trying, and using what they discover, is what they will be doing when they learn Japanese by being in a Japanese-speaking situation, outside the classroom. The students are encouraged to continue studying Japanese with pleasure, as this book truly makes their learning experience an enjoyable one.

Structure of this Textbook

This textbook has a total of 26 chapters. Volume 1 includes Chapter One to Chapter Fourteen, and Volume 2 includes Chapter Fifteen to Chapter Twenty-Six. Each chapter has sections called "Lessons", "Grammar and Usage", "Culture", "Writing", "Kanji List", "Review" and "Tips and Additional Knowledge", with a few exceptions.

Each lesson is presented on two facing pages as in the illustration, and contains the following:

- "Notes Relating to This Lesson" lists the note numbers and brief titles of all the grammar, usage, culture and writing explanations relevant to each lesson, in a little box located at the upper left corner of the left page.

- The "note-link", in the form of individual note numbers, is specified for each relevant part in the lesson (for example, ②, ❹) for the convenience of the students.

- "Basic Vocabulary and Kanji" introduces the required vocabulary and kanji. The required vocabulary are listed in a three-columned table, where the first column specifies the item in hiragana or katakana. An accent mark is provided for content words. The second column specifies how the item is written in kanji, what its conjugation category is if it is a verb (for example *k*-**u**, *i*-**ru**), and what its basic conjugation forms are if it is a verb or an adjective. The following is the list of verb conjugation category specifications:

e-**ru** : a **ru**-verb whose root ends in the vowel e
i-**ru** : a **ru**-verb whose root ends in the vowel i
r-**u** : an **u**-verb whose root ends in the consonant r
k-**u** : an **u**-verb whose root ends in the consonant k
g-**u** : an **u**-verb whose root ends in the consonant g
s-**u** : an **u**-verb whose root ends in the consonant s
m-**u** : an **u**-verb whose root ends in the consonant m
n-**u** : an **u**-verb whose root ends in the consonant n
b-**u** : an **u**-verb whose root ends in the consonant b
w-**u** : an **u**-verb whose root ends in the consonant w
t-**u** : an **u**-verb whose root ends in the consonant t
irr. : an irregular verb

The third column specifies the item's grammatical category (for example, *n* and *v*), its English translation, and possibly, example phrases. The following is the list of grammatical category specifications:

adj	: adjective		*pn*	: proper noun
adv	: adverb		*pron*	: pronoun
aux	: auxiliary		*prt*	: particle
c	: counter		*q*	: question word
con	: conjunction / connective word		*v*	: verb
cop	: copula		*n*	: noun

interj : interjection

no category mark : phrases, suffixes or prefixes

The kanji found in the second column are not always the required kanji. The required kanji are listed right below the three-columned table, and headed by "Newly introduced kanji". If a particular kanji character is introduced for the very first time, its stroke order is also provided in this section as well as in "Kanji List," but otherwise, its stroke order is found only in "Kanji List".

- "Vocabulary Collection" lists a group of vocabulary relevant to one of the themes of the lesson for optional use.

- "Dialog" provides a short conversation that can be easily memorized and recited by the students. It can be used as a model for skit-creation. All dialogs are recorded in the audio recordings available online.

- "Guess and Try" asks the students to try out what they have discovered after listening to the dialog on the online audio recordings or after observing the dialog recited in the class.

- "Drill" provides simple oral drills. It includes Reading, Repeating, Conjugation, Formation and Mini-Conversation.

- "Task" offers various tasks that train the students' communicative skills. It includes Pair Work, Small Group Work, Classroom Discussion, Classroom Activity, Survey, Skit Performance and Role Play.

- "Short Reading" provides a short passage, often related to the theme of the lesson. It includes kanji characters not previously introduced, so that the students can see how the written forms actually appear in Japanese.

- In "Writing", the students start writing about the related topic using the passage they have seen in "Short Reading" as a model.

Sample Lesson:

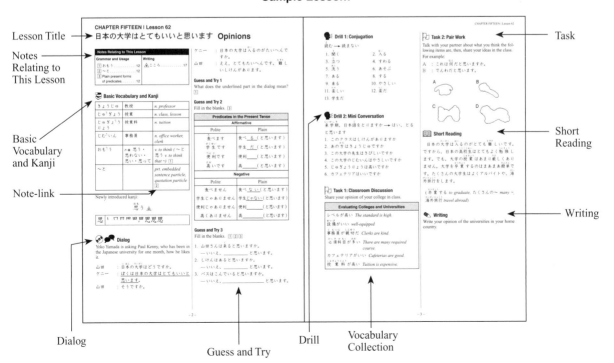

Lesson Title — Notes Relating to This Lesson — Basic Vocabulary and Kanji — Note-link — Dialog — Guess and Try — Drill — Vocabulary Collection — Task — Short Reading — Writing

Orthography

A brief discussion on hiragana, katakana, romaji, and kanji characters is provided in "Introduction" in Volume 1. In Chapter One, hiragana characters are gradually introduced, and the students are expected to be able to read them starting in Chapter Two. Katakana characters are introduced in Chapter Four.

A few new basic kanji words are introduced in each lesson, starting in Chapter Two. They appear in big font, with furigana (hiragana for pronunciation specification) in the "Basic Vocabulary and Kanji" section, and they appear without furigana in the rest of the parts in the same lesson. When they appear in the following lessons, furigana is sparingly provided, wherever it is thought to be helpful for the students, and its use is gradually reduced. In "Short Reading", kanji characters that have never been introduced will also appear, but their first instance will have furigana.

All the kanji words that are introduced in "Basic Vocabulary and Kanji" are listed in "Kanji List" at the end of each chapter. The kanji characters that are listed may be brand new characters for the students or may be previously introduced characters. Each character is provided with its stroke count, reading, meaning, usage example, and stroke order. The kunyomi-reading (Japanese-way of reading) is written in hiragana, and the onyomi-reading (Chinese-way of reading) is written in katakana. Where present, okurigana (the hiragana-written inflectional part that immediately follows a kanji character) is preceded by a dash.

日本の大学はとてもいいと思います **Opinions**

📖 Basic Vocabulary and Kanji

きょうじゅ	教授	n. professor
じゅ⌐ぎょう	授業	n. class, lesson
じゅぎょ⌐う りょう	授業料	n. tuition
じむ⌐いん	事務員	n. office worker, clerk
おも⌐う	r-u 思う・思わない・思い・思って	v. to think (〜と 思う v. to think that 〜) 1
〜と		prt. embedded sentence particle, quotation particle 2

Newly introduced kanji:

思う ⓐ
（おも）

思	丿 冂 冂 用 田 田 甲 思 思 思

💿🗨 Dialog

Yoko Yamada is asking Paul Kenny, who has been in the Japanese university for one month, how he likes it.

山田 ： 日本の大学はどうですか。
　　　　（にほん）（だいがく）
ケニー ： <u>ぼくは日本の大学はとてもいいと 思います。</u>
山田 ： そうですか。

ケニー ： 日本の大学は入るのがたいへんですか。
　　　　　　　　　　　　（はい）
山田 ： ええ、とてもたいへんです。難しいしけんがあります。
　　　　　　　　　　　　　　　（むずか）

Guess and Try 1

What does the underlined part in the dialog mean? 1

Guess and Try 2

Fill in the blanks. 3

Predicates in the Present Tense	
Affirmative	
Polite	Plain
食べます （た）	食べ<u>る</u>（と思います）
学生 です （がくせい）	学生<u>だ</u>（と思います）
便利です （べんり）	便利____（と思います）
高いです （たか）	高____（と思います）
Negative	
Polite	Plain
食べません	食べ<u>ない</u>（と思います）
学生じゃありません	学生<u>じゃない</u>（と思います）
便利じゃありません	便利____（と思います）
高くありません	高____（と思います）

Guess and Try 3

Fill in the blanks. 1 2 3

1. 山田さんは来ると思いますか。
　　　　　　　（く）
　 ― いいえ、_____ と思います。
2. しけんはあると思いますか。
　 ― いいえ、_____ と思います。
3. バスはこんでいると思いますか。
　 ― いいえ、_____ と思います。

🗣 Drill 1: Conjugation

よ
読む ➝ 読まない

1. 聞く
2. 入る
3. 立つ
4. すわる
5. 洗う
6. あそぶ
7. ある
8. する
9. 来る
10. やさしい
11. 楽しい
12. 楽だ
13. 学生だ

🗣 Drill 2: Mini Conversation

らいがっき
来学期、日本語をとりますか ➝ はい、とる
と思います

1. このクラスはしけんがありますか
2. あの方はきょうじゅですか
3. この大学の先生はきびしいですか
4. この大学のじむいんはやさしいですか
5. じゅぎょうりょうは高いですか
6. カフェテリアはいいですか

🏳 Task 1: Classroom Discussion

Share your opinion of your college in class.

Evaluating Colleges and Universities
レベルが高い *The standard is high.*
設備がいい *well-equipped*
事務員が親切だ *Clerks are kind.*
必須科目が多い *There are many required course.*
カフェテリアがいい *Cafeterias are good.*
授業料が高い *Tuition is expensive.*

🏳 Task 2: Pair Work

Talk with your partner about what you think the following items are, then, share your ideas in the class.
For example:

A ： これは何だと思いますか。
B ： でんわだと思います。

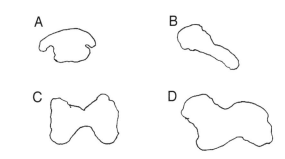

📖 Short Reading

日本の大学は入るのがとても難しいです。ですから、日本の高校生はとてもよく勉強します。でも、大学の授業はあまり厳しくありません。大学を卒業するのはまあまあ簡単です。たくさんの大学生はよくアルバイトや、海外旅行をします。

(卒業する *to graduate*, たくさんの〜 *many 〜*,
海外旅行 *travel abroad*)

✏️ Writing

Write your opinion of the universities in your home country.

たぶん雨がふるでしょう Probabilities

Notes Relating to This Lesson	
Grammar and Usage	**Writing**
4 Temperature 13	あめかんむり 17
5 Interjections. 13	
6 ～でしょう 14	

📖 Basic Vocabulary and Kanji

て￢んき	天気	n. weather
あ￢め	雨	n. rain
ゆき￢	雪	n. snow
く￢も	雲	n. cloud
さむ￢い	寒い・ 寒くない	adj. cold (weather) 4
あつ￢い	暑い・ 暑くない	adj. hot (weather) 4
あたたか￢い	暖かい・ 暖かくない	adj. warm (weather) 4
すずし￢い	涼しい・ 涼しくない	adj. cool (weather) 4
ふ￢る	r-u 降る・ 降らない・ 降り・降って	v. to fall (rain / snow)
はれ￢る	e-ru 晴れる・ 晴れない・ 晴れ・晴れて	v. to become clear (sky)
く も￢る	r-u 曇る・ 曇らない・ 曇り・曇って	v. to become cloudy
た￢ぶん	多分	adv. probably, maybe, perhaps
～でしょう		It is probably the case that ~. (plain form: ～だろう) 6

Newly introduced kanji:

天気・雨・雪・電話・電気・電車

天	一 二 チ 天
気	' 仁 气 气 気 気
雨	一 一 币 币 雨 雨 雨
雪	一 一 户 币 币 币 币 雨 雪 雪 雪
電	一 一 户 币 币 币 币 雨 雷 雷 雷 雷 電

Weather

晴れ *clear weather*	曇り *cloudy weather*
小雨 *drizzle*	大雨 *heavy rain*
霙 *sleet*	大雪 *heavy snow*
雹 *hail*	嵐 *storm*
台風 *typhoon*	風 *wind*
強風 *strong wind*	

💿💬 Dialog

Paul Kenny is inviting Yoko Yamada to play tennis this afternoon.

ケニー　：ごご、テニスをしませんか。

山田　　：ごごはたぶん雨がふるでしょう。

　　　　　ほら、くもがたくさんありますよ。

ケニー　：じゃあ、明日の天気はどうでしょ

　　　　　うか。

山田　　：さあ。

Guess and Try 1

Choose the appropriate option in the parentheses. 5

1. A：スミスさんは来ますか。

　　B：（ほら・さあ）、わかりません。

2. （ほら・さあ）、スミスさんが来ましたよ。

Guess and Try 2

What is the difference between the following two sentences? ⑥

1. 明日クイズがあります。
2. 明日クイズがあるでしょう。

Guess and Try 3

Rephrase the underlined parts using 〜でしょう. ⑥

1. たぶん雪が<u>ふります</u>。
2. ブラウンさんは<u>来ません</u>。
3. よくわかりませんが、テストは<u>難しいです</u>。
4. マイクさんは<u>まじめです</u>。
5. あれはたぶん<u>としょかんです</u>。
6. 明日はたぶん<u>さむくありません</u>。
7. マイクさんはたぶん<u>アメリカ人じゃありません</u>。

Guess and Try 4

What does the underlined part in the dialog mean? ⑥

 **Drill 1: Formation**

Variation 1:
はれる ➞ はれるでしょう

Variation 2:
はれる ➞ はれないでしょう

1. はれている
2. 雨がふる
3. さむい
4. しずかだ
5. いい天気だ
6. 天気がいい
7. およげる

 Drill 2: Mini Conversation

とうきょうは今あついでしょうか ➞
　あつくないでしょう

1. タイワンはすずしいでしょうか
2. 明日は天気がいいでしょうか

3. おみやげはあるでしょうか
4. ボーイフレンドはできるでしょうか
5. サンタクロースは来るでしょうか
6. 社長になれるでしょうか

Task: Pair Work

Ask your partner the current weather of the following places.

1. フロリダ
2. シンガポール
3. シドニー
4. タイワン
5. アラスカ

For example:
A：フロリダはどうでしょう。
B：フロリダは今あたたかいでしょう。

Short Reading

日本は小さいですが、長い国です。最北端は北緯45度、最南端は北緯24度ぐらいです。ですから、場所によって、気候がちがいます。北海道は冬によく雪が降ります。とても寒いです。夏はとても涼しいです。九州はとても暑いです。冬も暖かいです。東京は冬は少し寒いですが、雪はあまり降りません。六月は北海道以外は梅雨で、よく雨が降ります。

(最北端 *northern end*, 北緯 *the north latitude*, 45度 *45 degrees*, 最南端 *southern end*, 場所によって *depending on the place*, 気候 *climate*, 北海道 *Hokkaido (name of a place)*, 九州 *Kyushu (name of a place)*, 〜以外 *other than ~*, 梅雨 *rainy season*)

Writing

Write about the climate in your country.

はいえんかもしれません Possibilities

Notes Relating to This Lesson	
Grammar and Usage	**Writing**
7 〜かもしれません ...15	○c やまいだれ 17

📖 Basic Vocabulary and Kanji

かんじゃ	患者	*n.* patient
びょうき	病気	*n.* sickness, illness
ねつ⌐	熱	*n.* fever, temperature (熱がある *I have a fever.*)
せき⌐	咳	*n.* cough (咳が出る / 咳をする *to cough*)
くしゃみ⌐		*n.* sneeze (くしゃみが出る / くしゃみをする *to sneeze*)
おなか	お腹	*n.* abdomen, stomach
の⌐ど	喉	*n.* throat
で⌐る	**e-ru** 出る・出ない・出・出て	*v.* to come out, to attend, to leave (くしゃみが出る *to sneeze*, セミナーに出る *to attend the seminar*, レストランを出る *to leave the restaurant*)
〜かもしれない		*It may be the case that ~. (polite / neutral form:* 〜かもしれません) 7

Newly introduced kanji:

出る・病気・元気だ (I'm fine)・
病院 (hospital)・痛い (painful) ○c

病	⸍ 亠广广疒疒疒疒病病病
元	一二テ元

院 / 痛

院	⸍ 了 阝 阝' 阝' 阼 阼 阼 院院
痛	⸍ 亠广广疒疒疒疒病病痛痛

💿🗨 Dialog

いしゃ ：どうしましたか。

かんじゃ：せきが出るんです。
　　　　　それに、ねつがあります。

いしゃ ：ああ、そうですか。

かんじゃ：それから、あたまが痛いです。

いしゃ ：のどは。

かんじゃ：のどは痛くありません。

(The doctor checks the patient.)

いしゃ ：かぜかもしれません。でも、肺炎
　　　　　かもしれません。
　　　　　(肺炎 pneumonia)

Guess and Try 1

Explain the difference between the two underlined parts. 7

1. かぜでしょう。うちに帰って、休んでください。

2. かぜかもしれません。でも、はいえんかもしれません。

Guess and Try 2

Rephrase the underlined parts using 〜かもしれません. 7

1. ぜんぜん勉強しませんでした。Fをとります。

2. おなかが痛いんです。クラスに行けません。

3. この薬は高いです。

4. あの人はかんごしです。

5. あの人はいしゃじゃありません。

6. あの病院はこんでいます。

🗣 Drill 1: Formation

Variation 1:

帰る → 帰るかもしれません

Variation 2:

帰る → 帰らないかもしれません

1. 休む
2. 病気だ
3. 胃 *stomach* がわるい
4. しずかだ
5. こんでいる
6. 歩ける

🗣 Drill 2: Mini Conversation

クラスを休みますか → 休まないかもしれません

1. セミナーに出ますか
2. セミナーに出られますか
3. 先生に話しますか
4. この薬はいいですか
5. かぜですか
6. ねつはありますか
7. あの病院はすいていますか

🚩 Task: Pair Work

Pretend that you have one of the sets of symptoms listed in the following table. Try to look like you are sick and suffering, while complaining about the symptoms to your partner, who pretends to be the doctor.

Set 1	Set 2
ねつがある せきが出る のどが痛い	おなかが痛い ねつがある

Set 3	Set 4
くしゃみが出る 鼻水が出る *to have a runny nose*	げりをしている *to have diarrhea* はきけがする *to have nausea*

Possible diagnoses:

もうちょう *appendicitis*, かぜ *cold*,

しょくちゅうどく *food poisoning*,

かふんしょう *hay fever or allergy,*

はいえん *pneumonia*

📖 Short Reading

先月ひどい風邪をひきました。熱があって、ちょっと寒気がしました。のどがとても痛くなりました。それで、病院に行きました。抗生物質を飲みました。それから、オレンジジュースをたくさん飲みました。クラスを三回休みました。一週間ぐらいで治りました。

(先月 *last month,* ひどい *terrible,* 寒気 *chill,* 痛くなる *to become painful,* 抗生物質 *antibiotic,* 一週間 *one week,* 治る *to get better; to be cured of* ~)

✏️ Writing

Write about the last time you became sick.

Illness	
咳が出る *to cough*	花粉症 *hay fever*
くしゃみが出る *to sneeze*	食中毒 *food poisoning*
鼻水が出る *to have a runny nose*	下痢をする *to have diarrhea*
寒気がする *to have the chills*	頭が痛い *to have a headache*
熱がある *to have a fever*	お腹が痛い *to have a stomachache*
鼻が詰まっている *to have a stuffy nose*	吐気がする *to have nausea*
痰が出る *to have phlegm*	盲腸 *appendicitis*
喉が痛い *to have a sore throat*	風邪 *cold*
喘息 *asthma*	アレルギー *allergy*
	インフルエンザ *influenza*

CHAPTER FIFTEEN | Lesson 65

テストはかんたんだったと思います **Previous Test**

Notes Relating to This Lesson	
Grammar and Usage	
8 Plain past forms of predicates 15	

Basic Vocabulary and Kanji

どうし	動詞	*n. verb*
けいよ￢うし	形容詞	*n. adjective*
じょし	助詞	*n. particles*
かつよう	活用	*n. conjugation*
もんだい	問題	*n. question, issue, problem*
ほか	他	*n. others (他の車 other cars)*
う￢まく		*adv. well, skillfully*
きんちょうする	*irr.* 緊張する	*v. to become tense or nervous*
つぎ￢の〜	次の〜	*next 〜*
だいじょ￢うぶです	大丈夫です	*fine, not to worry, all right*

Newly introduced kanji:

問題・質問 (question)・宿題 (homework)

問	丨 冂 冋 冋 冋 門 門 門 問 問 問
宿	丶 宀 宀 宀 宀 宿 宿 宿 宿 宿 宿
質	丿 八 斤 斤 斤 斤 竹 竹 竹 竹 質 質 質 質 質
題	丨 冂 日 日 旦 早 早 昇 是 是 是 題 題 題 題 題 題

Dialog

Mary Carter and John Smith are talking about yesterday's exam in the Japanese class.

カーター ： 昨日のしけんはどうでしたか。

スミス ： きんちょうして、ききとりの問題が、ぜんぜんできませんでした。ほかの問題もあまりできませんでした。

カーター ： そうですか。私はかんたんだったと思いますが。

スミス ： いいえ、難しかったですよ。

(John looks depressed.)

カーター ： だいじょうぶですよ。つぎのしけんはできますよ。

Guess and Try 1

Explain the difference between the sentences below. 8

1. スミスさんはアメリカに帰ったと思います。

2. スミスさんはアメリカに帰ると思います。

Guess and Try 2

Fill in the blanks. 8

Predicates in the Present Tense	
Affirmative	
Polite	Plain
食べます	食べ_る_（と思います）
食べました	食_____（と思います）
学生です	学生_だ_（と思います）
学生でした	学生_____（と思います）
便利です	便利_だ_（と思います）
便利でした	便利_____（と思います）
高いです	高_____（と思います）
高かったです	高_____（と思います）

-8-

Predicates in the Present and Past Tense	
Negative	
Polite	Plain
食べません 食べませんでした	食べ ない (と思います) 食べ なかった (と思います)
学生じゃありません 学生じゃありません でした	学生じゃない (と思います) 学生＿＿＿＿＿(と思います)
便利じゃありません 便利じゃありません でした	便利 じゃない (と思います) 便利＿＿＿＿(と思います)
高くありません （高くないです） 高くありませんでした (高くなかったです)	高＿＿くない ＿(と思います) 高＿＿＿＿＿(と思います)

Guess and Try 3

Fill in the blanks using the adjective いい in an appropriate form. 8

1. 昨日のコンサートはとても ＿＿＿＿＿＿
と思います。

2. 昨日のコンサートはぜんぜん ＿＿＿＿＿
と思います。

Drill 1: Mini Conversation

Variation 1:
難しかったですか ➡ 難しかったと思います

Variation 2:
難しかったですか ➡ 難しくなかったと思います

1. やさしかったですか
2. おもしろかったですか
3. よかったですか
4. かんたんでしたか
5. たいへんでしか
6. きれいでしたか

Drill 2: Mini Conversation

Variation 1:
書きましたか ➡ 書いたと思います

Variation 2:
書きましたか ➡ 書かなかったと思います

1. 書けましたか
2. しましたか
3. うまくできましたか
4. わかりましたか

Task: Survey

Ask three of your classmates how they felt about the last exam. Use the dialog as a model.

私	
さん	
さん	
さん	

Languages and Exams	

聞き取り *listening comprehension*

読み取り *reading comprehension*

選択問題 *multiple-choice questions*

文法 *grammar*　　単語 *vocabulary*

作文 *composition*　　暗記 *memorization*

覚える *to memorize*

Short Reading

昨日は東京の翻訳の会社で面接がありました。社長さんは女の人でした。社長さんと30分ぐらい日本語で話しました。とても、緊張しましたが、まあまあうまく話せたと思います。社長さんは私の日本語は上手だと言いました。その後、翻訳の試験がありました。日本語の取扱説明書や、新聞の記事や、広告などを英語に翻訳しました。広告は意味がぜんぜん分からなくて、困りましたが、他はまあまあ簡単だったと思います。

(翻訳 *translation*, その後 *after that*, 取扱説明書 *instruction manual*, 記事 *article*, 広告 *advertisement*, など *etc.*, 意味 *meaning*, 困る *to get into trouble*)

Writing

Write about the last exam in your Japanese class.

どうして日本語をとっているんですか Asking Reasons

Notes Relating to This Lesson	
Grammar and Usage	**Writing**
⑨ どうして〜んですか …16	⚠ Writing styles …… 17
⑩ 〜から ………… 16	

 ## Basic Vocabulary and Kanji

ぶ￢んか	文化	n. culture
た￢んい	単位	n. (academic) credit
きょ￢うみ	興味	n. interest (〜に興味がある to be interested in 〜)
いけ￢ばな	生け花	n. flower arrangement / flower arranging
いる	r-u 要る・要らない・要り・要って	v. to be required, to be needed (単位がいる (I need credits.)
ど￢うして		q. why ⑨
ほんとうに	本当に	adv. truly
ほんとうです	本当です	It is true.
〜からです		It is because 〜. ⑩

Newly introduced kanji:

文化・本当です

当	丨 丨丶 丷 屵 当 当

 ## Dialog

Two students in a Japanese language class in an American university, John Cohen and Emily Chen, are talking with each other after class.

コーエン ： <u>どうして日本語をとっているんで</u>
<u>すか。</u>

チェン ： <u>外国語のたんいがいるからです。</u>

コーエン ： ああ、そうですか。

チェン ： ジョンさんはどうして日本語を
とっているんですか。

コーエン ： 日本の文化にきょうみがあるから
です。

チェン ： どんな文化にきょうみ
があるんですか。

コーエン ： いけばなです。

チェン ： 本当ですか。

Guess and Try 1

What do the underlined parts in the dialog mean?
⑨ ⑩

Guess and Try 2

Fill in the blanks. ⑨

For example:

おおさかに行きます。

— どうしておおさかに<u>行くんですか</u>。

1. 会社をやめました。

— どうして会社を _____。

2. お金がほしいんです。

— どうしてお金が _____。

3. スミスさんが好きです。

— どうしてスミスさんが _____。

Guess and Try 3

Add 〜からです at the end of the underlined part and make the necessary changes. ⑩

1. どうしてお金がないんですか。

— <u>ようふくを買いました。</u>

2. どうしてスミスさんが好きなんですか。

— <u>やさしいです。</u>

3. どうして山田さんのチケットは安いんですか。

— <u>この大学の学生です。</u>

4. どうしていけばなを習っているんですか。

— <u>好きです。</u>

Guess and Try 4 (Optional)

What do the following sentences mean? ☐10

1. どうしてはしで食べるんですか。
   — 日本人だからです。
2. 日本人だから、はしで食べます。
   （日本人だ。だから、はしで食べる。）
3. 日本人ですから、はしで食べます。
   （日本人です。ですから、はしで食べます。）

Drill 1: Formation

日本語を勉強している ⟶ どうして日本語を勉強しているんですか

1. 田中さんからお金をかりた
2. 社会学をとる　　3. 宿題をしなかった
4. しけんが好きだ　　5. 日本に住みたい

Drill 2: Formation

日本にともだちがいる ⟶ 日本にともだちがいるからです

1. 日本の文化にきょうみがある
2. 食べものがおいしい
3. 日本語はかんたんだ
4. からてを習っている
5. アニメが好きだ

Task: Survey

Ask three of your classmates why they are taking Japanese. Use the dialog as a model.

私	
さん	
さん	
さん	

Reasons for Studying Japanese

空手を習っている *I am learning karate.*

日本人の友達がいる *I have a Japanese friend.*

日本の会社で働きたい *I want to work in a Japanese company.*

日本のアニメが好きだ *I like Japanese animations.*

日本の音楽が好きだ *I like Japanese music.*

日本の食べ物が好きだ *I like Japanese foods.*

必須科目だ　　　　　簡単だ
It is a required course.　It is easy.

Short Reading

僕は台湾で生まれた。台湾は日本に近いから、日本の影響をよく受けた。台湾には日本製の製品がたくさんある。例えば、任天堂のビデオゲームや、ドラえもんの漫画や、ガンダムのアニメーションだ。はじめはゲームをするために、家庭教師と日本語を勉強した。大学に入って、ビデオゲームはもうやめた。でも、日本語の勉強はやめなかった。今、僕はアメリカの大学にいるから、英語も話す。僕は将来、英語と日本語と中国語を使って、貿易の仕事をしたいと思っている。

ジェフリー・リン　21才　学生

(台湾 *Taiwan*, 生まれる *to be born*, 〜の影響を受けた *was influenced by 〜*, 日本製 *made in Japan*, 製品 *product*, 任天堂 *Nintendo (toy company)*, 漫画 *comic book*, はじめは *at the beginning*, 〜ために *in order to 〜*, 家庭教師 *tutor*)

Writing

Write about why you are studying Japanese.

– Grammar and Usage –

① おもう: To think

The verb 思う *to think* is very useful for stating one's opinion in a modest and non-aggressive manner. For example, (a) sounds less assertive than (b):

(a) (私は) アメリカの大学はいいと思います。
I think American universities are good.

(b) アメリカの大学はいいです。
American universities are good.

When the first or second person is the thinker, 思う takes either a simple form (思います) or progressive form (思っています). The latter gives an impression that the idea may be a temporary one. On the other hand, when the third person is the thinker, only the progressive form (思っています) can be used. Thus, sentences (c) to (f) are grammatical, but (g) is not.

(c) 私はスミスさんは来ると思います。
I think Mr. Smith will come.

(d) 私はスミスさんは来ると思っています。
I think Mr. Smith will come, (at least now).

(e) あなたはどう思いますか。
What do you think?

(f) 父はスミスさんは来ると思っています。
My father thinks Mr. Smith will come.

(g) 父はスミスさんは来ると思います。（✖）
(Ungrammatical)

Either the main verb (思う) or embedded verb may be negated. The following two sentences are almost synonymous.

(h) 私はスミスさんは来ると思いません。
I do not think Mr. Smith will come.

(i) 私はスミスさんは来ないと思います。
I think Mr. Smith will not come.

② ～と: That ～ [Embedded sentence marker]

English verbs such as "to think" and "to say" can be followed by a sentence that indicates the content of thinking or saying. Such a sentence is called an "embedded sentence" since it is embedded in another sentence. In English, an embedded sentence can be introduced by the word "that" (for example, I think **that** Mr. Smith will go to Japan; Mr. Brown said **that** Mr. Smith would go to Japan). In Japanese, embedded sentences are marked by the particle と, which is placed right after them, and they are placed before the verb such as "to think" and "to say".

(a) 私はスミスさんは日本に行くと思います。
I think that Mr. Smith will go to Japan.

(b) ブラウンさんはスミスさんは日本に行くと言いました。
Mr. Brown said that Mr. Smith would go to Japan.

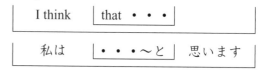

Unlike "that" in English, the particle と is not optional. The verbs and adjectives of an embedded sentence must be in the plain form, unless the embedded sentence is a direct quotation marked by a pair of quotation marks, "「" and "」", as in the following sentence.

(c) ブラウンさんは 「スミスさんは日本に行きます。」 と言いました。
Mr. Brown said, "Mr. Smith will go to Japan."

③ Plain present forms of predicates

Plain forms are not only informal speech forms. They must be used before some suffixes, particles and phrases, regardless of the speech style. For example, the following two sentences take the polite / neutral speech style, but the verb 食べる is in the plain form.

(a) スミスさんはすしを食べると思います。
(I) think Mr. Smith will eat sushi.

(b) 今晩はすしを食べるつもりです。
(I) plan to eat sushi tonight.

The plain and polite forms in the present tense are summarized in the following table.

Verbs and Adjectives in the Plain and Polite Forms in the Present Tense		
Affirmative		
	Polite	Plain
Verbs	食^たべます	食^たべる
Noun + copula	学生^{がくせい}です	学生^{がくせい}だ
Na-type adjectives	便利^{べんり}です	便利^{べんり}だ
I-type adjectives	高^{たか}いです	高^{たか}い
Negative		
	Polite	Plain
Verbs	食べません	食べない
Noun + copula	学生じゃ ありません	学生じゃない
Na-type adjectives	便利じゃ ありません	便利じゃない
I-type adjectives	高くありま せん	高くない

*じゃ in the phrases above may be replaced by では.
**ありません can be ないです.

4　Temperature

Japanese has different adjectives for temperature, depending on whether it is air temperature (for example, room temperature and weather) or solid / liquid temperature (for example, shower, coffee, body parts and food).

	Air temperature	Solid / liquid temperature
Hot	熱^{あつ}い	熱^{あつ}い
Warm	暖^{あたた}かい	温^{あたた}かい
Cool	涼^{すず}しい	ぬるい (*only for liquids)
Cold	寒^{さむ}い	冷^{つめ}たい

5　Interjections (あっ, ほら, etc.)

Interjections such as あっ and ほら do not have a concrete meaning, but have a specific function in conversations. The following table lists some examples.

Some Interjections in Japanese	
Interjections	Function and Examples
ああ	Used for acknowledging information. (*I see.*) For example: A: お金^{かね}がないんです。 *I do not have money.* B: ああ。 *Oh, I see.*
あっ	Used when you notice or remember something or when you are surprised. (*Oh!*) For example: あっ、すみません。 *Oh, I'm sorry.*
あのう	Used when you are about to tell something. (*Ummm ...*) For example: あのう、車^{くるま}をかりたいんです が。 *Ummm ..., I'd like to borrow your car.*
あれ	Used when you have noticed that there is something wrong or something has been forgotten. (*Wait a minute.*) For example: あれ。スミスさんがいませんよ。 *Wait a minute. Mr. Smith is not here.*
ええと	Used when you need time to figure out the right expression or response. (*Well...*) For example: A: だれが来^きますか。 *Who is coming?* B: ええと。スミスさんと、 リーさんが来ます。 *Well, Mr. Smith and Mr. Lee are coming.*

Some Interjections in Japanese	
Interjections	**Function and Examples**
さあ	Used for showing that you do not know or care about something. It corresponds to the shrugging gesture for the Westerners. (*I have no idea.*) For example: A: スミスさんは来ますか？ *Is Mr. Smith coming?* B: さあ。 *I have no idea.*
ちょっと	Used when you want to get attention from someone. (*Hey!*) For example: ちょっと、すみません。 *Excuse me.*
ほら	Used when you want to show something. (*Look! You see?*) For example: ほら、あそこにスミスさんがいますよ。 *Look, Mr. Smith is over there.*

6 ～でしょう: It is probably the case that ～ ; I guess ～ [Likeliness]

～でしょう follows a sentence, and shows that the statement is based on a subjective guess. For example, 明日クイズがあるでしょう means *It is probably the case that there will be a quiz tomorrow* or *I guess there will be a quiz tomorrow.* ～でしょう is most appropriate for describing the situation over which the speaker does not have control (for example, the weather and future economy). ～でしょう follows a verb or an adjective in the plain form, but だ, which appears in a copula and a na-type adjective in their plain present affirmative forms, must be deleted before でしょう, as in 学生だ / 学生でしょう and 便利だ / 便利でしょう.

(a) たぶん雨がふるでしょう。
It will probably rain.

(b) ブラウンさんは来るでしょう。
(Probably) Mr. Brown will come.

(c) テストは難しいでしょう。
The exam is (probably) difficult.

(d) マイクさんはまじめでしょう。
(I guess) Mike is studious.

(e) よくわかりませんが、あれはたぶんとしょかんでしょう。
I am not really sure, but that one is probably a library.

(f) スミスさんはたぶんわからないでしょう。
I guess Mr. Smith would not understand it.

(g) 明日はたぶんさむくないでしょう。
Probably, it will not be cold tomorrow.

(h) マイクさんはたぶんアメリカ人じゃないでしょう。
Probably, Mike is not an American.

(i) スミスさんはお金がないでしょう。
(Probably), Mr. Smith does not have money.

When でしょう is used with a question word and / or the question particle か, as in どうでしょうか, どうでしょう or 来るでしょうか, it shows that the speaker wonders about something and wants to hear what the listener thinks.

(j) 明日の天気はどうでしょうか。
I wonder how tomorrow's weather will be. What do you think?

(k) 明日の天気はどうでしょう。
I wonder how tomorrow's weather will be. What do you think?

(l) ブラウンさんは来るでしょうか。
I wonder whether Mr. Brown will come. What do you think?

The plain form of でしょう is だろう:

(m) たぶん雨がふるだろう。
It will probably rain.

7　～かもしれません: It is possibly the case that ～ [Possibility]

～かもしれません is added at the end of a sentence and shows that the situation stated in the statement is just a possibility. It follows verbs and adjectives in the plain form, as in 食べるかもしれません and 食べないかもしれません. だ that appears in a copula and na-type adjective in their plain present affirmative forms must be deleted before かもしれません, as in 学生だ / 学生かもしれません and 便利だ / 便利かもしれません.

Unlike ～でしょう, which expresses the probable situation, ～かもしれません expresses the possible situation. For example, sentence (a) can be used only when the probability of a cold is higher than 50%, but sentence (b) can be used even when the probability of a cold is just 1%.

(a) かぜでしょう。
Probably, it is a cold.

(b) かぜかもしれません。
It may be a cold.

The following are additional examples.

(c) よくわかりませんが、あの人はあまりまじめじゃないかもしれません。
I am not very sure, but that person may not be very studious.

(d) ぜんぜん勉強しませんでした。Fをとるかもしれません。
I didn't study at all. I may get an F.

(e) ねつがあるんです。クラスに行かないかもしれません。
I have a fever. I may not go to class.

(f) このセーターはきれいですね。高いかもしれません。でも、今日はセールです。ですから、高くないかもしれません。
This sweater is beautiful, isn't it? It may be expensive. But it is on sale today. So, it may not be expensive.

(g) あの人ははしで食べていますよ。日本人かもしれません。
That person is eating with chopsticks. He may be a Japanese.

8　Plain past forms of predicates

The plain past affirmative form of a verb can be created by replacing the vowel **e** at the end of its te-form with the vowel **a**. For example, the te-form of the verb "to eat" is 食べて (tabete), and its plain past affirmative form is 食べた (tabeta).

The plain past affirmative form of a copula and na-type adjectives can be created by replacing だ at the end of their present forms with だった, as in 学生だ / 学生だった and 便利だ / 便利だった.

And the plain past affirmative form of an i-type adjective is created by replacing an い at the end of the present form with かった, as in 高い / 高かった. The adjective いい conjugates irregularly and the plain past form of いい is よかった.

The plain past negative form of all the predicates is created by replacing ない at the end of their present forms with なかった, as in 食べない / 食べなかった, 学生じゃない / 学生じゃなかった, 便利じゃない / 便利じゃなかった and 高くない / 高くなかった.

These are summarized in the following table.

Verbs and Adjectives in the Plain and Polite Forms			
Affirmative			
		Polite	Plain
Verbs	Present	食べます	食べる
	Past	食べました	食べた
Noun + copula	Present	学生です	学生だ
	Past	学生でした	学生だった
Na-type adjectives	Present	便利です	便利だ
	Past	便利でした	便利だった
I-type adjectives	Present	高いです	高い
	Past	高かったです	高かった

Verbs and Adjectives in the Plain and Polite Forms			
Negative			
		Polite	Plain
Verbs	Present	食べません	食べない
	Past	食べません でした	食べなかっ た
Noun + copula	Present	学生じゃあり ません	学生じゃない
	Past	学生じゃあり ませんでした	学生じゃな かった
Na-type adjectives	Present	便利じゃあり ません	便利じゃない
	Past	便利じゃあり ませんでした	便利じゃ なかった
I-type adjectives	Present	高くありませ ん	高くない
	Past	高くありません でした	高くなかった

*じゃ in the phrases above may be replaced by では.
** ありません can be ないです, and ありません でした can be なかったです.

The following sentences contain plain past forms:

(a) スミスさんはアメリカに帰ったと思 います。
I think Mr. Smith went back to the United States.

(b) スミスさんはアメリカに帰ると思います。
I think Mr. Smith will return to the United States.

(c) 昨日のコンサートはとてもよかったと思い ます。
I think that yesterday's concert was very good.

(d) 昨日のコンサートはぜんぜんよくなかった と思います。
I think that yesterday's concert was not good at all.

(e) テストはかんたんだと思いました。
I thought the exam was easy.

⑨ どうして〜んですか: Why 〜?
[Asking reasons and causes]

For asking a "why" question using the question word どうして *why*, the question must end in

〜んですか. Remember to replace だ at the end of the copula or a na-type adjective with な, when it comes before 〜んですか, as in 学生だ / 学生な んですか and 便利だ / 便利なんですか.

(a) どうして薬をのむんですか。
Why do you take medicine?

(b) どうして会社をやめたんですか。
Why did you quit the company?

(c) どうしてあたまが痛いんですか。
Why do you have a headache?

(d) どうしてスミスさんが好きなんですか。
Why do you like Mr. Smith?

(e) どうして田中さんはへんな人なんですか。
Why (do you think) Mr. Tanaka is a weird person?

なぜ can also be used instead of どうして in relatively formal contexts or written forms.

⑩ 〜から: Because 〜 [Reasons]

The typical answer to the "why question" (どう して〜んですか) takes the form of 〜からです. 〜からです means *It is because ....* The verbs and adjectives right before 〜からです must be in the plain form.

(a) どうしてそうじをするんですか。
Why do you clean?
— おきゃくさんが来るからです。
— Because a guest is coming.

(b) どうしてお金がないんですか。
Why don't you have money?
— ようふくを買ったからです。
— Because I bought clothes.

(c) どうして買ったんですか。
Why did you buy (it)?
— 安かったからです。
— Because (it) was cheap.

(d) どうして田中さんはよく勉強するんですか。
Why does Mr. Tanaka study very well.
— まじめだからです。
— Because he is studious.

(e) どうしてはしで食べるんですか。
Why do you eat with chopsticks?
— 日本人だからです。
— *Because I am a Japanese.*

The particle から can follow a sentence and create an adverbial sentence that expresses the reason for the following main sentence. The predicate before から can be either in the plain or polite form.

(f) あたまが痛いから、薬をのみます。
Since I have a headache, I will take medicine.

(g) あたまが痛いですから、薬をのみます。
Since I have a headache, I will take medicine.

When two sentences are independent sentences, use the connective word ですから or だから.

(h) あたまが痛いです。ですから、薬をのみます。
I have a headache. So, I will take medicine.

(i) あたまが痛いです。だから、薬をのみます。
I have a headache. So, I will take medicine.

− Writing −

ⓐ こころ

心	こころ *heart, mind*
	Example: 思う *to think*, 悲しい *sad*, 意志 *intention*, 息 *breath*

ⓑ あめかんむり

雨	あめかんむり *rain / weather / atmosphere / electricity*
	Example: 雪 *snow*, 雲 *cloud*, 電話 *telephone*, 雷 *thunder and lightning*, 電気 *electricity*

ⓒ やまいだれ

疒	やまいだれ *sickness / pain*
	Example: 病気 *sickness*, 痛い *pain*, 疲れる *to get tired*

ⓓ Writing styles: ですます-style, だ-style and である-style

There are three writing styles in Japanese: ですます-style, だ-style and である-style. If you want to add a spoken tone and politeness to your essay and personal letters, use the ですます-style, which is equivalent to the polite / neutral speech style. If you want to omit the politeness effect and add simple and clear impression as well as the spoken tone, use the だ-style, which is equivalent to the plain / informal speech style. For academic papers and very formal written documents, use the である-style. Do not mix different writing styles in one essay. The examples are as follows:

Writing Styles
ですます-style
〜です
〜ではありません
（〜じゃありません）
〜でした
〜ではありませんでした
（〜じゃありませんでした）
For example:
日本は小さい国です。大きい国ではありません。
Japan is a small country. It is not a big country.
だ-style
〜だ
〜ではない（〜じゃない）
〜だった
〜ではなかった（〜じゃなかった）
For example:
日本は小さい国だ。大きい国ではない。
Japan is a small country. It is not a big country.
である-style
〜である
〜ではない
〜であった
〜ではなかった
For example:
日本は小さい国である。大きい国ではない。
Japan is a small country. It is not a big country.

– Kanji List –

思う・天気・雨・雪・電話・電気・
電車・出る・病気・元気だ・病院・痛
い・問題・質問・宿題・文化・本当だ

思 おも-う・シ think	丶 冂 冂 四 用 田 甲 思 思 思 [9]
	Example: 思う *to think*

天 あめ・あま・テン weather, sky	一 二 チ 天 [4]
	Example: 天気 *weather*, 天国 *heaven*

気 キ spirit, mind, air, atmo-sphere	丶 ニ 气 気 気 [6]
	Example: 病気 *sickness*, 元気だ *healthy, fine*, 天気 *weather*

雨 あめ・ウ rain	一 一 币 币 币 雨 雨 雨 [8]
	Example: 雨 *rain*

雪 ゆき・セツ snow	一 二 戸 币 币 币 雨 雨 雪 雪 雪 [11]
	Example: 雪 *snow*

電 デン electricity	一 二 戸 币 币 币 雨 雨 雨 雪 雪 雪 電 [13]
	Example: 電車 *electric train*, 電気 *electricity*, 電話 *telephone*

話 はな-す・はなし・ワ talk	丶 二 二 言 言 言 言 話 話 話 話 [13]
	Example: 話す *to speak*, 電話 *telephone*

車 くるま・シャ car	一 厂 戸 百 百 亘 車 [7]
	Example: 車 *car*, 電車 *train*

出 で-る・だ-す・シュツ／シュッ come, go out	丨 屮 屮 出 出 [5]
	Example: 出る *to come out*, 出す *to hand in, to take out*

病 ビョウ sick	丶 一 广 广 广 疒 疒 疠 病 病 [10]
	Example: 病気 *sickness*, 病院 *hospital*

元 みなもと・ゲン・ガン origin, base, source	一 二 テ 元 [4]
	Example: 元気だ *healthy, fine*

院 イン institute, hall, house	' ３ ｹ ｹ' ｹ' 阝 阡 陀 陀 陀 院 [10]
	Example: 大学院 *graduate school*, 病院 *hospital*

痛 いた-い・いた-む・ツウ pain	丶 一 广 广 广 疒 疒 疒 疠 疠 痏 痛 [12]
	Example: 痛い *painful*

問 と-う・モン inquire, question	丨 冂 冂 冂 冂 門 門 門 門 問 問 [11]
	Example: 問題 *question, problem*, 質問 *question*

題 ダイ *title, theme*	丨 冂 日 日 旦 早 早 昇 是 是 是 是 題 題 題 題 題 題 [18]
	Example: 問題 *question, problem*, 宿題 *homework*

質 シツ *quality, question*	' ｒ ｒ ｒ ｒ' 所 所 所 所 質 質 質 質 質 [15]
	Example: 質問する *to ask a question*

宿 やど・シュク lodging, dwelling	｀ ｀ 宀 宀 宀 宀 宿 宿 宿 宿 [11]
	Example: 宿題 homework

文 ブン・モン・ (ふみ) pattern, letter, sentence	｀ 一 ナ 文 [4]
	Example: 文 a sentence, 作文 composition, 文学 literature, 文法 grammar, 文化 culture

化 ば-ける・ カ change, -ization	ノ イ イ 化 [4]
	Example: 文化 culture, 化学 chemistry

本 もと・ホン root, origin, true, main	一 十 オ 木 本 [5]
	Example: 本 book, 日本 Japan, 本当 truth

当 あ-たる・ トウ hit, concerned	｀ ｀ ｀ 当 当 当 [6]
	Example: 本当です It is true., 本当に truly

– Review –

Q1. *Make sentences using the following words and state what they mean.*

1. 思う 2. ふる

3. ねつ 4. せき

Q2. *Write the pronunciation of the following kanji characters and state what is common among the members of each set.*

1. 雨・雪・電話・電気・電車

2. 病気・病院・痛い

3. 間・問題・質問・時間・聞く

4. 本・本当に・日本・一本・二本・三本

Q3. *Modify the phrases in the parentheses appropriately.*

1. あの人は (学生です) と思います。

2. 弟は宿題を (しませんでした) と思います。

3. 来年は日本に (行きます) んです。

4. どうしてお金がないんですか。
   — コンサートのチケットを (買いました) からです。

5. スミスさんは (来ません) でしょう。

6. あの人は (日本人です) でしょう。

7. 明日雨が (ふります) かもしれません。

8. このコンピューターは (べんりです) かもしれません。

Q4. *Modify the underlined parts by using one of the items in the box appropriately.*

～つもりです	～かもしれません
～と思います	～んですか
～でしょう	～からです

1. 明日はたぶん雨が<u>ふります</u>。

2. よくわかりませんが、<u>はいえんです</u>。
   (はいえん pneumonia)

3. あのクラスは難しいですよ。
   — そうですか。私は<u>かんたんです</u>。

4. どうして日本に<u>行きますか</u>。

5. どうしてこのじしょを買ったんですか。
   — <u>安いです</u>。

6. 明日セミナーに出ますか。
   — <u>出ます</u>。

Q5. *Fill in the blanks.*

1. どうしてレストランに行かないんですか。
   —＿＿＿＿＿＿＿＿＿＿＿＿＿＿＿＿ からです。

2. どうして ＿＿＿＿＿＿＿＿＿＿＿＿＿ んですか。
   — あたまが痛かったからです。

3. どうして ＿＿＿＿＿＿＿＿＿＿＿＿ んですか。
   — 難しいからです。

Q6. *Answer the following questions in Japanese. Use*
   〜つもりです, 〜と思います, 〜でしょう *or*
   〜かもしれません *appropriately.*

1. 来年日本に行きますか。
2. 来年も日本語をとりますか。
3. 日本語の先生はやさしいですか。
4. 日本の車は高いですか。

Tips and Additional Knowledge: Doctor's Office

You do not need to make an appointment to visit a doctor's office in Japan. You can always walk in, although you may have to wait for a long time in a waiting room. At a large hospital, many people come in early in the morning, get a number ticket, go home, and come back again around the time their turn comes. Almost all Japanese have a government health insurance plan and foreigners can also have it. The following are the terms for medical specialties.

内科
internal medicine

小児科
pediatrics

歯科
dentistry

眼科
ophthalmology

皮膚科
dermatology

整形外科
orthopedics

耳鼻咽喉科
otolaryngology

精神科
psychiatry

産婦人科
obstetrician and gynecologist

スリッパをはいてもいいですか Etiquette

📖 Basic Vocabulary and Kanji

きょうしつ	教室	n. classroom
たたみ	畳	n. straw mat
じゅ￢うたん		n. carpet
スリ￢ッパ		n. slippers Ⓐ
こま￢る	r-u 困る・困らない・困り・困って	v. to be in trouble 1
きをつける	気をつける	to be careful (車に気をつける to watch out for cars) 2
ぜったい(に)	絶対 (に)	adv. absolutely (絶対にいけません absolutely not permitted)

Newly introduced kanji:

教 室・気をつける・困る・
部屋 (room) Ⓐ Ⓑ・〜屋 (store)

室	' ' 宀 宀 宏 宏 宏 室 室
困	一 冂 冂 用 用 用 困
部	' 一 ナ ナ 立 立 咅 咅 咅 部 部
屋	一 コ コ 尸 尸 尼 居 居 屋 屋

💿 💬 Dialog 1

Mark Baker is going to visit a Japanese person's house for the very first time. Yoko Yamada gives him some advice.

山田 ： 日本のうちではくつをはいてはいけませんよ。気をつけてくださいね。

ベーカー ： はい。うちの中はスリッパですね。

山田 ： ええ。でも、たたみの部屋はスリッパで入ってはいけませんよ。

ベーカー ： じゃあ、じゅうたんの部屋はスリッパで入ってもいいですか。

山田 ： ええ、いいですよ。

Guess and Try 1 3

1. Ask whether it is OK to eat in the classroom.
   教室で ＿＿＿＿＿＿＿＿＿＿＿＿＿ 。

2. Answer the above question.
   はい、＿＿＿＿＿＿＿＿＿＿＿＿ 。
   いいえ、＿＿＿＿＿＿＿＿＿＿＿ 。

💿 💬 Dialog 2

Mark Baker is asking Yoshio Tanaka whether he can smoke in his room.

ベーカー ： すみません。タバコをすってもいいですか。

田中 ： あのう、ちょっと困るんですが。

Guess and Try 2

What does 困る mean in the above dialog? 1

Guess and Try 3

How would you say "No" when your friend asks you
この車を使ってもいいですか？ **B**

🗣 Drill 1: Formation

Variation 1:
食べる ➞ 食べてもいいですよ

Variation 2:
食べる ➞ 食べてはいけません

1. 休む　　　　　　2. すわる
3. ねる　　　　　　4. およぐ
5. 帰る

🗣 Drill 2: Mini Conversation

教室で食べてもいいですか ➞ いいえ、食べて
はいけません

1. ビールを飲んでもいいですか
2. テレビを見てもいいですか
3. 車を使ってもいいですか
4. ゲームセンターに行ってもいいですか
5. マンガを読んでもいいですか

🏴 Task 1: Classroom Discussion

Discuss whether the following are allowed in your
home country or in some of the countries that the
teacher picks.

1. 授業中にコーヒーを飲む
   to drink coffee in the classroom during the class
2. 授業中に足をくむ
   *to cross one's legs in the classroom during the
   class*
3. ? ? ? (Question of your choice)

For example:

A : アメリカでは電車の中でタバコをすって
　　もいいですか。
B : わかりません。でも、いいと思います。/
　　ぜったいにいけません。

Taboos in Japan

ハンカチで鼻をかむ *to blow one's nose using
a handkerchief*

プレゼントの包み紙をやぶく *to rip the wrapping paper of a present*

電車の中で大きい声で話す *to talk loudly
in a train*

レストランで携帯電話を使う *to use a
cellular phone in a restaurant*

人の引出しを勝手に開ける *to open someone
else's drawer without his / her permission*

スーパーマーケットで商品を食べる *to eat
the food for sale in a supermarket*

人の給料をきく *to ask about other
people's salary*

仕事中にガムをかむ *to chew gum during
work*

🏴 Task 2: Survey

Find out how many people in the class enter their
houses with their shoes on. Ask everyone one by one.

For example:

A : Bさんのうちはくつで入ってもいいですか。
B : ええ、いいですよ。/ いいえ、いけません。

📖 Short Reading

　日本人は温泉が好きです。お湯の中では髪
や身体を洗ってはいけません。それから、お
湯の中にタオルを入れてはいけません。お湯の
中でゆっくりリラックスします。とても気持ち
がいいです。

(温泉 *hot spring,* お湯 *hot water,* 髪 *hair,* 身体
body, タオル *towel,* …に〜を入れる *to put ~ in
...,* 気持ちがいい *to feel great*)

✏ Writing

Write about some interesting etiquette found in your
country.

じきゅうが安くてもいいですか　Working Condition

Notes Relating to This Lesson

Grammar and Usage	Writing
④ ～てもいい / 　～てはいけない... 29	Ⓒ のぎへん........ 30

📖 Basic Vocabulary and Kanji

じきゅう	時給	n. payment by the hour
ざんぎょう	残業	n. overtime work
さらあ⌐らい	皿洗い	n. dish-washing
せわ⌐	世話	n. care, aid (～の世話をする to take care of ~)
つうきん	通勤	n. travel to work, commute
おぼえ⌐る	e-ru 覚える・覚える・覚えない・覚え・覚えて	v. to memorize
しんぱいする	irr. 心配する	v. to worry (about ~)

Newly introduced kanji:

覚える・仕事 (job)・便利だ (convenient)

Ⓒ・不便だ (inconvenient)

覚	、　` ゛ ゛゛ ゛゛ ゛゛ ゛゛ 学 学 労 労 労 労 労 覚 覚
仕	ノ イ イ 什 仕
事	一 一 一 写 写 写 事
便	ノ イ 亻 佢 佢 佢 佢 便 便
利	、 二 千 チ 禾 利 利
不	一 ブ 不 不

💿🗨 Dialog

Mark Baker is attending a job interview in Japanese at a Japanese company.

会社の人：きんむ時間がちょっと長くてもいいですか。(勤務時間 working hours)

ベーカー　：はい、いいです。

会社の人：ああ、そうですか。よかった。じゃあ、明日からおねがいします。

ベーカー　：ああ、…あのう、カタカナとひらがなをまだ覚えていないんですが。

会社の人：ああ、それはだいじょうぶです。しんぱいしないで下さい。

ベーカー　：ああ、そうですか。じゃあ、よろしくおねがいします。

会社の人：はい。じゃあ、ここに名前を書いて下さい。

ベーカー　：ローマ字でもいいですか。

会社の人：いいえ、ローマ字ではいけません。カタカナで書いて下さい。

Guess and Try

Fill in the blanks and state what the sentences mean. ④

For example:　　つうきんが不便ですよ。
　　　　　　　— 不便<u>でも</u>いいです。

1. これはじてん車ですよ。
　　—じてん車 _____ いいですよ。

2. これは古いですよ。
　　—古 _____ いいですよ。

3. これは子供の本ですよ。
　　—子供の本 _____ いけません。

4. これは小さいですよ。
　　—小 _____ いけません。

5. これは新しくありませんよ。
　　—新しく _____ いいですよ。

🗣 Drill: Mini Conversation

難しいですよ ➡ 難しくてもいいです

1. つまらないですよ   2. とおい
3. つうきんが不便ですよ 4. きたないですよ
5. じきゅうがわるいですよ
6. ざんぎょうが多いですよ
7. たいへんな仕事ですよ
8. 仕事がたいへんですよ

📢 Task: Group Work

Pretend that everyone in the group must select one of the jobs listed below. Ask your group members which job they pick.

テレビ スタジオ TV studio	有名な芸能人 (famous entertainer) と話せる。おもしろい。 日曜日 – 7 a.m. – 4 p.m. 電車で2時間 800円 / 時間
すし屋 sushi restaurant	さらあらい。とても楽なしごと。 月火水木 – 6 p.m. – 8 p.m. 歩いて5分 800円 / 時間 – 食事つき with meals
工場 factory	とてもたいへんだ。目がつかれる。 月水金 – 10 p.m. – 5 a.m. 地下鉄で25分 2,000円 / 時間
英語学校 English school	会話を教える。 月水金 – 6 p.m. – 8 p.m. 1,000円 / 時間
近所のうち houses in the neighborhood	5オのわんぱくな (naughty) 男の子と、大きい犬の世話をする 月水金 – 10 a.m. – 5 p.m. 歩いて5分 800円 / 時間 – 食事つき with meals

For example:

A： Bさんはどの仕事がいいですか。
B： 私はテレビスタジオの仕事がいいです。
C： でも、じきゅうがわるいですよ。
B： じきゅうがわるくてもいいです。
D： でも、とおくて、不便ですよ。
B： ええ、不便でもいいです。
A： どうしてですか。
B： おもしろい仕事だからです。

Working Conditions	
給料 *pay*	時給 *hourly pay*
月給 *monthly pay*	ボーナス *bonus*
残業 *overtime work*	通勤 *travel to work*
交通費 *transportation expenses*	
休日出勤 *working on a holiday*	
夜勤 *night duty, night shift*	

📖 Short Reading

私はアメリカ人の学生です。今日本の大学で日本語と人類学を勉強しています。今、アルバイトを探しています。給料は安くてもいいです。楽しくて、おもしろい仕事がいいです。レストランのウエイターもおもしろいと思います。いろいろな人を観察できるからです。それから、英語の教師もおもしろいと思います。日本人と仲良くなれるからです。私は車がありません。ですから、便利なところがいいです。

(人類学 *anthropology*, 探す *to look for; to search*, いろいろな *various*, 観察する *to observe*, 仲良くなる *to become close*)

✏ Writing

Write about the jobs you would like to get in the future.

しずかじゃなくてはいけませんか　Living Conditions

📖 Basic Vocabulary and Kanji

まいにち	毎日	n. every day
まいしゅう	毎週	n. every week
まいつき	毎月	n. every month
まいとし	毎年	n. every year
だいどころ	台所	n. kitchen
ふろ⌐・おふ⌐ろ	風呂・お風呂	n. bath
ト⌐イレ		n. toilet
さがす	s-u 探す・探さない・探し・探して	v. to search ~, to search for ~, to look for ~
～までに		by ~ (deadline) (9 時までに帰ります I will return by 9 o'clock.) 6

Newly introduced kanji:

毎日（まいにち）・毎週（まいしゅう）・毎月（まいつき）・
毎年（まいとし）・探す（さが）d

毎	丿 𠂉 𠂉 듀 듀 毎
週	丿 门 月 門 用 用 周 周 ˋ周 调 週
探	一 十 扌 扌 扌 扩 护 护 护 探 探

🔊💬 Dialog

Jason Chen is looking for an apartment. He asks John Smith for some information

チェン　：　今（いま）アパートを探しているんです。

スミス　：　今のアパートは？

チェン　：　今のアパートは来月（らいげつ）の 20 日（はつか）までに出（で）なくてはいけないんです。

スミス　：　ああ、それはたいへんですね。

チェン　：　ええ。

スミス　：　どんなアパートがいいんですか。

チェン　：　そうですね。んん…

スミス　：　やちんが安（やす）くなくてはいけませんか。

チェン　：　いいえ、安くなくてもいいですよ。

スミス　：　しずかじゃなくてはいけませんか。

チェン　：　いいえ、しずかじゃなくてもいいです。

スミス　：　ルームメートがいてもいいですか。

チェン　：　はい、いてもいいですよ。

スミス　：　じゃあ、ぼくのアパートはどうですか。

Guess and Try　5

1. Ask whether it is required to memorize kanji characters (for the course):

   _____

2. Answer the above question:

   はい、_____。

   いいえ、_____。

3. Fill in the blanks appropriately, using the following items: (広（ひろ）い・きれい (な)・ちかい)
   私はアパートを探さなくてはいけません。

   _____。

   (It does not have to be spacious.) _____

_____。

(It does not have to be clean.) でも、大学から

_____。

(But it has to be near the university.)

🗣 Drill 1: Formation

Variation 1:

食_たべる ➝ 食べない

Variation 2:

食べる ➝ 食べなくてはいけません

1. 探す　　　　　　2. そうじする
3. 広_{ひろ}い　　　　　　4. 近_{ちか}い
5. いい　　　　　　6. 便利_{べんり}だ
7. きれいだ

🗣 Drill 2: Mini Conversation

毎日そうじをする ➝

S 1: 毎日そうじをしなくてはいけませんか

S 2: いいえ、しなくても いいですよ

1. だいどころがある　　2. おふろがある
3. しずかだ　　　　　　4. きれいだ
5. 広い

🏁 Task: Group Work

Pretend that everyone in the group must find an apartment. Ask each other the following questions.

1. きれいじゃなくてはいけませんか。
2. しずかじゃなくてはいけませんか。
3. やちんは安くなくてはいけませんか。
4. 大学から近くなくてはいけませんか。
5. だいどころがなくてはいけませんか。
6. かぐ (furniture) がなくてはいけませんか。
7. ルームメート (roommate) がいてもいいですか。

📖 Short Reading

　今_{いま}、アパートを探しています。家賃_{やちん}は少_{すこ}し高_{たか}くてもいいです。台所_{だいどころ}がなくてもいいです。小_{ちい}さくてもいいです。でも、大学から遠_{とお}くてはいけません。大学から近_{ちか}くなくてはいけません。私は車_{くるま}がないからです。それから、ルームメートがいてはいけません。

✏️ Writing

Pretend that you must find a new apartment. Write about the minimum requirements for your new apartment. Write the reasons, too.

– Grammar and Usage –

1 こまる (困る): To be in trouble

困る literally means *to be in trouble*, but it also means *to be concerned* or *No*, depending on the context:

(a) 今お金がなくて、困っています。
I do not have money now, and I am in trouble.

(b) ちょっと困っているんです。たすけてください。
I am in trouble. Please help me.

(c) 主人が残業をやめないので、困っています。
Since my husband does not stop working over-time, I am very concerned.

(d) ここでタバコをすってもいいですか。
Is it okay to smoke here?

— いいえ、困ります。
— *No, please don't.*

2 き (気): Spirit

Japanese has many idioms that have the word 気, which means *attention*, *spirit* or *feelings*.

～に気がつく to notice ~	あの人は鈍感で、何も気がつかないんです。 *That person is insensitive and doesn't notice anything.*
～に気をつける to be cautious or careful for ~	車が来ましたよ。気をつけてくださいね。 *A car is coming. Be careful!*
～が気に入る to become fond of ~	このアパートは明るくて、気に入りました。 *This apartment is bright, and I became fond of it.*
気が緩む to be too relaxed, not alert enough, careless, or not attentive	また、遅刻ですか。気が緩んでいますね。 *You were late again. You are too relaxed.*

気が弱い to be timid or weak-willed	私は気が弱いから、そんなこと言えません。 *I'm timid, so I cannot say such a thing.*
気が強い to be strong-willed, tough, or hard-headed	あき子さんは気が強いから、だれとでも喧嘩をします。 *Akiko is strong-willed, so she fights with anyone.*
気が短い to be impatient	兄は気が短いから、つりには向いていません。 *My brother is impatient, so he is not suited for fishing.*
気が長い to be patient	まだ、彼女の返事を待っているんですか。気が長いですね。 *You are still waiting for her reply? You are so patient.*

3 ～てもいい / ～てはいけない [Permission / prohibition]

You can express permission by combining a conditional phrase in the form of ～ても *even if ~* and an agreement phrase such as いいです *it is fine*. For example, テレビを見てもいいです literally means that *even if you watch TV, it is fine*, which actually means that *you may watch TV*.

(a) 歩いてもいいです。
You may walk.

(b) 教室で食べてもいいですか。
Is it okay to eat in the classroom?

— はい、食べてもいいですよ。
— *Yes, it is okay.*

(c) タバコをすってもいいですか。
May I smoke?

— はい、いいですよ。
— *Yes, go ahead.*

On the other hand, prohibition is expressed by combining a conditional phrase in the form of ～ては *if ~* and a disagreement phrase such as いけません *it is bad*. For example, テレビを見てはいけません

literally means that *if you watch TV, it is bad*, which actually means that *you may not watch TV*.

(d) 歩いてはいけません。
You must not walk.

(e) 教室で食べてもいいですか。
Is it okay to eat in the classroom?

— いいえ、教室で食べてはいけません。
— *No, you may not eat in the classroom.*

(f) タバコをすってもいいですか。
May I smoke?

— いいえ、タバコをすってはいけません。
— *No, you may not smoke.*

(g) じしょを見てもいいですか。
May I look at the dictionary?

— いいえ、いけません
— *No, you may not.*

4 ～てもいい / ～てはいけない
[Permissible / impermissible]

The constructions ～てもいい and ～てはいけない can be used not only with a verb, but also with a copula and an adjective. In such cases, they express whether a given item or a property is permissible or impermissible.

(a) これは古いですよ。 *This is old.*
— 古くてもいいですよ。
— *An old one is fine.*

(b) これは新しくありませんよ。
This is not new.
— 新しくなくてもいいですよ。
— *It is okay not to be new.*

(c) これはとても不便ですよ。
This is very inconvenient.
— 不便でもいいですよ。
— *It is fine even if it is inconvenient.*

(d) これはじてん車ですよ。
This is a bicycle.
— じてん車でもいいですよ。
— *A bicycle is fine.*

(e) これは子供の本ですよ。
This is a children's book.
— 子供の本ではいけません。
— *A children's book is not good.*

(f) これは小さいですよ。 *This is small.*
— 小さくてはいけません。
— *A small one is not okay.*

5 ～なくてはいけない / ～なくてもいい
[Obligation / discretion]

Obligation is expressed by combining a negative conditional phrase in the form of ～なくては *if you do not ~* and a disagreement phrase like いけません *it is bad*. For example, 宿題をしなくてはいけません literally means that *if you do not do your homework, it is bad*, which actually means that *you must do your homework*.

(a) 毎日クラスに出なくてはいけません。
You must attend the class every day.

(b) 漢字を覚えなくてはいけませんか。
Do I have to memorize kanji?
— はい、覚えなくてはいけません。
— *Yes, you have to.*

Discretion can be expressed by combining a negative conditional phrase ～なくても *even if you do not ~* and an agreement phrase like いいです *it is fine*. For example, 宿題をしなくてもいいです literally means that *even if you do not do your homework, it is fine*, which actually means that *you do not have to do your homework*.

(c) 毎日クラスに出なくてもいいです。
You don't have to attend the class every day.

(d) 漢字を覚えなくてはいけませんか。
Do I have to memorize kanji?
— いいえ、覚えなくてもいいです。
— *No, you don't have to.*

These constructions can be used with adjectives and nouns also.

(e) 安くなくてはいけません。
It has to be cheap.

(f) 安くなくてもいいです。
It doesn't have to be cheap.

(g) 日本語の教師は日本人じゃなくてはいけません。

Japanese language teachers have to be Japanese.

(h) 日本語の教師は日本人じゃなくてもいいです。

Japanese language teachers do not have to be Japanese.

(i) 広くなくてもいいです。

It doesn't have to be spacious.

(j) きれいじゃなくてもいいです。

It doesn't have to be clean / pretty.

(k) 大学から近くなくてはいけません。

It has to be near the university.

Occasionally, 〜なければ is used instead of 〜なくては. For example, 見なければいけません and 見なくてはいけません are more or less synonymous, and mean that *(I) have to see (it)*. In addition, いけません can be replaced by なりません in this construction. They are almost synonymous, but なりません gives the impression that the obligatory situation is somewhat inevitable and has arisen naturally.

6 〜までに: By 〜 [Deadline]

The combination of two particles までに (まで and に) expresses the deadline when used with time phrases.

(a) 5時までに帰ります。

(I) will return by 5 o'clock.

(b) 5時に帰ります。

(I) will return at 5 o'clock.

– Culture –

Ⓐ スリッパ: Slippers

You must take off your shoes before entering Japanese houses. Guests are offered slippers at the foyer. But their slippers are only for wood floor or carpeted areas, and may not be used in *tatami* floor rooms. Tatami are thick mats of braided straw, and they are easily damaged by the hard surface of slip-pers. Toilet rooms in Japanese houses have their own special slippers. So, guests must take off their regular slippers in the hallway, in front of the toilet room, then enter the toilet room and put on the toilet room slippers.

Ⓑ Expressing prohibition

Expressing prohibitions straightforwardly may insult other people and so it must be done mildly. For example, you can ask someone not to smoke, using the following expressions:

(a) あのう、タバコはちょっと…。

Well, cigarettes are a bit ...

(b) あのう、タバコはちょっと困るんですが。

Well, cigarettes are a bit troublesome here.

(c) あのう、タバコはほかの部屋ですって下さいませんか。

Well, could you smoke in a different room?

(d) あのう、すみませんが、タバコはほかの部屋で おねがいします。

Well, I'm sorry, but please smoke in a different room.

– Writing –

ⓐ おおざと

阝	おおざと *village*
	Example: 部 *club; division*, 都 *capital city*, 郡 *county; township*, 郵便局 *post office*

ⓑ しかばね

尸	しかばね *corpse, building*
	Example: 本屋 *bookstore*, 郵便局 *post office*, 居間 *living room*

ⓒ のぎへん

禾	のぎへん *rice, grain, soft*
	Example: 私 *I; me*, 便利 *convenient*, 稲 *rice*, 和 *harmony*, 秋 *autumn*

ⓓ てへん

扌	てへん *hand, arm*
	Example: 探す *to search*, 持つ *hold*, 指 *fingers*, 折る *to fold*, 払う *to pay*, 押す *to push*, 投げる *to throw*, 打つ *to hit*

– Kanji List –

教室・気をつける・困る・部屋・
〜屋・覚える・仕事・便利だ・不便
だ・毎日・毎週・毎月・毎年・探す

教	一 十 土 耂 耂 孝 孝 教 教 [11]
おし-える・キョウ *education, teach, religion*	Example: 教室 *classroom*, 教える *to teach*
室	丶 宀 宀 宔 宔 宔 宔 室 [9]
シツ *room, house*	Example: 教室 *classroom*
気	ノ 卜 气 气 気 気 [6]
キ *spirit, mind, air, atmosphere*	Example: 病気 *sickness*, 元気だ *healthy, fine*, 天気 *weather*
困	丨 冂 冂 困 困 困 困 [7]
こま-る・コン *trouble*	Example: 困る *to be in trouble*
部	丶 亠 亠 立 立 咅 咅 咅 部 部 [11]
ブ・(ヘ) *department, part, section, club*	Example: 部屋 *room*

屋	一 コ 尸 尸 尸 层 层 屋 屋 [9]
や・オク *roof, shop, house*	Example: 部屋 *room*, 本屋 *bookstore*
覚	丶 ⺌ ⺌ ⺌ 学 学 学 覚 覚 覚 覚 [12]
おぼ-える・さ-める・さ-ます・カク *awake, sense*	Example: 覚える *to memorize*
仕	ノ イ 仁 什 仕 [5]
つか-える・シ *serve*	Example: 仕事 *job, work*
事	一 戸 戸 写 写 写 事 [8]
こと・ごと・ジ *affair, fact, engagement*	Example: 仕事 *job, work*, 食事 *meal*
便	ノ イ 仁 仁 佢 佢 佢 便 便 [9]
たよ-り・ベン・ビン *current, traffic, convenience*	Example: 便利だ *convenient*, 不便だ *inconvenient*
利	ノ 二 千 禾 禾 利 利 [7]
き-く・リ *profit, proficient*	Example: 便利だ *convenient*
不	一 プ ア 不 [4]
フ・ブ *un-, in-, not*	Example: 不便だ *inconvenient*
毎	ノ 𠂉 乍 乍 毎 毎 [6]
マイ *every*	Example: 毎日 *every day*
日	丨 冂 日 日 [4]
ひ・び・ニチ・ニ・ジツ *sun, day*	Example: 日本 *Japan*, 毎日 *every day*

週 シュウ week	) 刀 月 門 冃 冃 用 周 周 ` 凋 週 週 [11]
	Example: 毎週 *every week*, 来週 *next week*
月 つき・ゲツ・ガツ *moon, month*	) 刀 月 月 [4]
	Example: 一月 *January*, 一ヶ月 *one month*, 毎月 *every month*
年 とし・ネン *year, age*	' ケ ヒ ヒ 三 年 [6]
	Example: 来年 *next year*, 毎年 *every year*, 一年生 *first grade*
探 さが-す・さぐ-る・タン *search, probe*	一 十 寸 扌 扩 扩 扞 挥 挥 採 探 [11]
	Example: 探す *to search, to look for*

– Review –

Q1. *Write the reading of the kanji characters in the following sentences.*

1. このじしょは便利です。でも、あのじしょは不便です。
2. 毎週新しい漢字を習います。
3. 毎日仕事があります。
4. 毎月おおさかに行きます。

Q2. *Translate the following sentences into English.*

1. ミーティングに出てもいいです。(ミーティングに出る *to attend the meeting*)
2. ミーティングに出てはいけません。
3. ミーティングに出なくてもいいです。
4. ミーティングに出なくてはいけません。
5. 明日はクラスに出なくてはいけませんか。
6. 日本語のクラスでかんこく語を話してもいいですか。
7. ひこうきの中でシートベルトをしなくてもいいですか。
8. 今日勉強しなくてもいいですか。

Q3. *Say the following in Japanese.*

1. I must go to class tomorrow.
2. I have to take an exam tomorrow. (しけんをうける)
3. May I smoke here?
   — Yes, you may.
4. Can I drink some tea?
   — Sure, you can.
5. Is it OK if I go home?
   — Yes, it is fine.
6. Do I have to do homework?
   — No, you do not have to.

Tips and Additional Knowledge: Looking for an Apartment

When you look for an apartment, go to a realtor and tell him / her what kind of apartment you are looking for. The following are some related terms you should know.

ようしつ 洋室	Western-style room	わしつ 和室	Japanese-style room
しんしつ 寝室	bedroom	ベランダ	veranda
おしいれ 押入	closet, storage	げんかん 玄関	(front) entrance, foyer
だいどころ 台所 / キッチン	kitchen		
よくしつ　ふろば 浴室 / 風呂場	bath		
トイレ / ダブルシー W C	toilet room		
ユービー U B / ユニットバス	unit bath		
ディーケー D K	dining kitchen (eat-in-kitchen)		

さんディーケー 3 D K	three bedrooms and a dining kitchen (an eat-in-kitchen)
さんエルディーケー 3 L D K	three bedrooms, a living room, a dining kitchen (an eat-in-kitchen)
じょう ～ 帖	counter for たたみ 畳 (a straw mat approximately 3' x 6')
とほ　　ふん 徒歩 15 分	15 minutes walking distance
やちん 家賃	rent
しききん 敷金	deposit
れいきん 礼金	fee to the house owner

きょうとえき
JR 京都駅
徒歩 15 分
家賃　　　72,000 円
敷金　　 210,000 円
礼金　　 150,000 円

CHAPTER SEVENTEEN
Comparison

どちらの方が広いですか **Comparison**

Notes Relating to This Lesson	
Grammar and Usage	
① どちら 42	③ おなじぐらい 42
② ～より 42	④ ～ほど (･･･ ない) .42

📖 Basic Vocabulary and Kanji

ほっか^ヿいど う	北海道	pn. Hokkaido (name of a Japanese island)
ほ^ヿんしゅう	本州	pn. Honshu (name of a Japanese island)
きゅ^ヿうしゅ う	九州	pn. Kyushu (name of a Japanese island)
しこく	四国	pn. Shikoku (name of a Japanese island)
とち	土地	n. land
じんこう	人口	n. population
ぶっか	物価	n. prices of things in general
ずっと		adv. by far
おなじ	同じ	same ③
～ほう	～方	side, direction ①
～より		prt. than ②
～ほど(･･･な い)		prt. (not) as ... as ~ ④

Newly introduced kanji:

北海道・本州・九州・四国・
（ほっかいどう・ほんしゅう・きゅうしゅう・しこく）
土地・地下 (basement)・人口・同じ・
（とち・ちか・じんこう・おな）
～の方・森田 (surname)
（ほう・もりた）

海	丶 氵 氵 氵 汒 洰 海 海 海
州	丶 丿 丿 州 州 州
地	一 十 土 均 圵 地
同	丨 冂 冂 同 同 同

🔊 💬 Dialog

Jeff Brown is asking Kaori Morita about Japanese islands.

ブラウン ： 九州と、四国と、どちらの方が広_{ひろ}
いですか。

森田 ： 九州の方が四国より広いです。

ブラウン ： 九州は北海道と同じぐらい広_{ひろ}いで
すか。

森田 ： いいえ、九州は北海道ほど広くあ
りません。

ブラウン ： どちらの方が人口が多いですか。

森田 ： よくわかりませんが、同じぐらい
でしょう。

Guess and Try 1

Make a question that asks which is larger, China or
the United States. ①

Guess and Try 2

Fill in the blanks by looking at the illustration that
follows, and translate the sentences into English. ①
② ③ ④

1. けい子さんと、よう子さんと、_____
_____ 背_せが高_{たか}いですか。

2. けい子さんはよう子さん _____ 背が高いです。

3. けい子さんはアンさん _____ 背がひくいです。

4. けい子さんはアンさん _____ 背が高くありません。

5. マリーさんはけい子さん ____ 背が高いです。

ようこ　けい子　マリー　アン

🗣 Drill 1: Mini Conversation

<ruby>中国<rt>ちゅうごく</rt></ruby>・日本・広いです ⟶

S 1: 中国と、日本と、どちらの方が広いですか。

S 2: 中国の方が (ずっと) 広いです。

1. 中国・インド・人口が<ruby>多<rt>おお</rt></ruby>いです。

2. アパート・りょう・しずかです。

3. とうきょう・おおさか・土地が高いです。

4. とうきょう・マンハッタン・ぶっかが高いです。

🗣 Drill 2: Formation

日本・フランス・<ruby>広<rt>ひろ</rt></ruby>くありません ⟶ 日本はフランスほど広くありません

1. フランス・日本・人口が多くありません。

2. なりた・とうきょう・にぎやかじゃありません。

3. ニューヨーク・アラスカ・さむくありません。

4. とうきょう・きょうと・古くありません。

🏴 Task 1

Complete the sentences based on the given information, using the adjective 広い. Conjugate it appropriately.

Area (1,000 km²)		Area (1,000 km²)	
ポーランド	323	日本	378
中国	9,597	インド	3,288
ペルー	1,285	アメリカ	9,364
フィリピン	300	オーストラリア	7,741

1. ペルーは日本 _____。

2. オーストラリアはアメリカ _____ _____。

3. 中国はアメリ _____。

4. インドは中国 _____。

5. 日本は _____ 同じ _____ _____。

🏴 Task 2: Pair Work

Pretend that you and your partner are going to live in the same city. Pick two cities, compare them, and decide which one you would like to live in.

For example:

A : <ruby>東京<rt>とうきょう</rt></ruby>はサンフランシスコよりおもしろいですよ。

B : でも、東京はサンフランシスコよりやちんが高いですよ。ぶっかも高いですよ。

📖 Short Reading

私は<ruby>東京<rt>とうきょう</rt></ruby>に<ruby>住<rt>す</rt></ruby>んでいます。東京は人口が<ruby>多<rt>おお</rt></ruby>くて、土地がとても<ruby>高<rt>たか</rt></ruby>いです。<ruby>物価<rt>ぶっか</rt></ruby>も高いです。<ruby>家賃<rt>やちん</rt></ruby>もとても高いです。マンションの家賃は2DKで<ruby>一ヶ月<rt>いっかげつ</rt></ruby>に 15 <ruby>万円<rt>まんえん</rt></ruby>ぐらいです。3LDK では一ヶ月に 20 万円ぐらいです。<ruby>駐車場<rt>ちゅうしゃじょう</rt></ruby>も高いです。一ヶ月 3 万円ぐらいです。

(マンション *a modern style condominium or apartment in Japan*, 2DK: *two bedrooms, a dining room and a kitchen*, 3LDK: *three bedrooms, a living room, a dining room and a kitchen*)

✏ Writing

Write about your area, discussing the cost of living and housing conditions.

プールで泳ぐ方が海で泳ぐより好きです　Preferences

Notes Relating to This Lesson	
Grammar and Usage	
5 〜の 42	6 〜も 43

📖 Basic Vocabulary and Kanji

かわ	川	n. river
みずう み	湖	n. lake
あんぜん (な)	安全だ・安全じゃない	adj. safe
あぶない	危ない・危なくない	adj. dangerous
はし る	r-u 走る・走らない・走り・走って	v. to run

Newly introduced kanji:

川（かわ）・　湖（みずうみ）　・海（うみ）(sea, ocean)・泳（およ）ぐ (to swim)

湖	` `´ ⺍ ⺡ 汁 汁 洁 洁 浏 湖 湖
泳	` `´ ⺍ ⺡ 汀 汀 汾 泳

💿 🗨 Dialog

Jeff Brown and Kaori Morita are talking about swimming.

ブラウン　：海で泳ぐのと、プールで泳ぐのと、どちらの方が好（す）きですか。

森田　：<u>どちらも好きです。</u>ジェフさんは。

ブラウン　：もちろん、プールで泳ぐ方（ほう）が海で泳ぐより好きですよ。

森田　：どうしてですか。

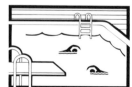

ブラウン　：プールはくらげがいないからです。

（くらげ jellyfish）

Guess and Try 1

Fill in the blanks with the particle の, if necessary. 5

A　：はしる ＿＿＿と、泳ぐ ＿＿＿と、どちら（の方）が好きですか。

B　：泳ぐ ＿＿＿ 方が、はしる ＿＿＿ より好きです。泳ぐ ＿＿＿ は、はしる ＿＿＿ よりおもしろいです。

Guess and Try 2

What does the underlined part in the dialog mean? 6

🗣 Drill 1: Formation

はしる・泳ぐ ⟶ はしるのと、泳ぐのと、どちら（の方）が好きですか

1. レストランで食べる・うちで食べる
2. スニーカーをはく・くつをはく
3. 本を読（よ）む・えいがを見る
4. スポーツをする・スポーツを見る

🗣 Drill 2: Formation

話（はな）す・聞（き）く・難（むずか）しいですか ⟶ 話すのと、聞くのと、どちら（の方）が難しいですか

1. 教（おし）える・習（なら）う・かんたんですか
2. はしる・泳ぐ・好きですか
3. フットボールをする・サッカーをする・あぶないですか
4. ひこうきに乗（の）る・車に乗る・あんぜんですか

⊓ Task: Classroom Activity

Each student is assigned to conduct a survey on one of the following questions in the classroom. Ask all of your classmates the question assigned to you, and report the result to your teacher (for example, レポートを書く方が好きな人は 5 人いました。しけんをうける方が好きな人は 8 人いました). More than a student may be assigned to the same question.

1. レポートを書くのと、しけんをうけるのと、どちら (の方) が好きですか。
2. よる 勉 強 するのと、昼 (daytime) 勉強するのと、どちら (の方) が好きですか。
3. えいがかんでえいがを見るのと、うちで DVD でえいがを見るのと、どちら (の方) が好きですか。
4. りょうりを作る (to cook) のと、さらをあらう (to wash dishes) のと、どちら (の方) が好きですか。
5. 朝 シャワーをあびるのと、よるシャワーをあびるのと、どちら (の方) が好きですか。
6. スポーツをするのと、スポーツを見るのと、どちら (の方) が好きですか。
7. ？？？ (Your choice!)

📖 Short Reading

　私は生まれてから、 大学までずっと家族と住んでいました。いつも一人暮らしをしたいと思っていました。

　日本の大学を 卒 業 して、アメリカの大学に留学し、大学院生になりました。はじめは寮 に入りましたが、ルームメートに気をつかうのが嫌で、アパートを借りて一人暮らしを始めました。一人暮らしは、とても自由でよかったです。しかし、 冬休みには大学の友達はみんな家族のところに帰りました。そうすると、キャンパスは 急 に寂しくなりました。

　ずっと一人暮らしをしたいと思っていましたが、 今は家族と住む方が寂しくなくて楽しいかもしれないと思います。

山 北のり子　23 歳

(生まれてから since (I) was born, ずっと continuously, 一人暮らしをする to live alone, 卒 業 する to graduate, 留 学する to study abroad, 大学院 生 graduate student, 気をつかう to care about, 〜が嫌です to dislike ~ing, 始める to start, 自由 (な) free, しかし but (cf. でも), 冬 休み winter recess, 急 に suddenly, 寂しくなる to become lonesome)

✎ Writing

Write about how you want to live.

きせつでは何が一番好きですか Your Favorite

Notes Relating to This Lesson	
Grammar and Usage	**Writing**
⑦ いちばん 43	ⓐ さかなへん 44

 Basic Vocabulary and Kanji

せ￣かい	世界	*n. world*
き￣せつ	季節	*n. season*
にく￣	肉	*n. meat*
さかな	魚	*n. fish*
やさい	野菜	*n. vegetable*
くだ￣もの	果物	*n. fruit*

Newly introduced kanji:

肉・魚 ⓐ・色 (color)・
一番 (the most, the best)

肉	丨 冂 内 内 内 肉
魚	ノ ク ⼟ 凸 冎 角 缶 魚 魚 魚 魚
色	ノ ク ⼎ 刍 刍 色
番	ノ ⼎ 丷 ⼧ 平 乎 来 采 番 番 番

 Dialog 1

Kyungtaek Park and Ichiro Minami are talking about their family.

パーク : 南さんのお父さんと、お母さんと、お兄さんの中では、だれが一番やさしいですか。

南 : 兄が一番やさしいです。

パーク : ああ、そうですか。じゃあ、南さんのうち (の中) では、だれが一番こわいですか。

南 : 母です。

Note: の中 is optional.

Guess and Try 1 ⑦

Choose the appropriate option in the parentheses.

1. 山田さんと、川口さんと、田中さんの中では、(どちら・だれ・どこ・何) が一番背が高いですか。

2. クラスの中では、(どちら・だれ・どこ・何) が一番背が高いですか。

Guess and Try 2 ⑦

Choose the appropriate option in the parentheses.

1. 本州と、北海道と、九州の中では、(どちら・どれ・だれ・どこ) が一番あついですか。

2. 日本の中では、(どちら・何・だれ・どこ) が一番あついですか。

 **Dialog 2**

Kyungtaek Park and Ichiro Minami are talking about seasons.

南 : 春と、秋と、夏の中では、どれが一番好きですか。

パーク : 秋が一番好きです。

南 : じゃあ、きせつの中では、何が一番好きですか。

パーク : 冬が一番好きです。スキーができますから。

Guess and Try 3 ⑦

Complete the following table based on the above facts.

Question Words Used for Comparison			
	People	Location	Others
Two items	どちら	どちら	どちら
Three or more items	だれ		どれ
Set		どこ	

Guess and Try 4 [7]

Choose the appropriate option in the parentheses.

1. ねこと、犬と、さるの中では、(どれ・何・どちら) が一番好きですか。(さる monkey)

2. どうぶつでは、(どれ・何) が一番好きですか。

3. くだものの中では、(どれ・何) が一番好きですか。

4. ねるのと、食べるのと、あそぶのでは、(どれ・何) が一番楽しいですか。

5. 今、(どれ・何) が一番したいですか。

🗣 Drill 1: Formation

魚 —→ 魚 (の中) では、何が一番好きですか

1. 飲みもの
2. 肉
3. 色
4. きせつ
5. くだもの
6. テレビドラマ

🗣 Drill 2: Formation

肉・魚・やさい —→ 肉と、魚と、やさい (の中) では、どれが一番好きですか

1. ワイン・おさけ・ビール
2. テニス・スキー・スケート
3. じてん車・バス・電車・車
4. すし・すきやき・てんぷら

🏳 Task: Survey

Ask three people what they like the best among the following sets of things. Who is most similar to you?

For example:

A : アイスクリーム (の中) では何が一番好きですか。

B : バニラが一番好きです。

	アイスクリーム ice cream	色 color	きせつ season	ペット pet	??? (Your choice)
私					
さん					
さん					
さん					

📖 Short Reading

日本では血液型で性格を占うのがはやっています。A型と、B型と、O型と、AB型があります。A型は一番まじめで他人のことをよく考えます。B型は一番ユニークで創造力があります。O型は勇気があって寛大です。AB型は合理的です。日本人の中ではA型が一番多いです。手相占いや、星占いもありますが、血液型占いが一番人気があります。

(血液型 blood type, 占う tell fortunes, 性格を占う to tell personality, はやっている to be popular, ～型 type, 他人 other people, 考えます to consider, 創造力 creativity, 勇気 courage, 寛大 generous, 合理的 practical, 手相占い palm reading; palmistry, 星占い horoscope, 人気 popularity)

✏ Writing

What is the most popular form of fortune-telling in your country? Which one do you believe in?

– Grammar and Usage –

1 どちら: Which one of the two? [A question word for two-item-comparison]

For asking a question that compares two items as in, *Which one is more ...?*, place the two items that are to be compared, as X と、Y と at the beginning of the sentence and use どちら *which one*. Most Japanese add 〜の方 *~'s side* at the end of どちら, as in どちらの方:

(a) 漢字と、カタカナと、どちら (の方) が
　　難しいですか。

　　Which is more difficult, kanji or katakana?

The variations for "X と、Y と" are "X と、Y では" and "X と、Y とでは". So, (b) and (c) are also acceptable.

(b) 漢字と、カタカナでは、どちら (の方) が
　　難しいですか。

(c) 漢字と、カタカナとでは、どちら (の方)
　　が難しいですか。

The answer to a どちら -question starts from 〜の方が , as in (d):

(d) 漢字と、カタカナと、どちら (の方) が難
　　しいですか。
　　Which is more difficult, kanji or katakana?
　　— 漢字の方が難しいです。
　　— *Kanji is more difficult (than katakana).*

The informal version of どちら is どっち.

2 〜より: Than 〜 [Comparing two items]

To express comparison, there is no need to conjugate adjectives or adverbs in Japanese. If you are comparing two items, just add the particle 〜より *than* to the item with which the topic item is compared. For instance, スミスさんはリーさんよりやさしいです means *Mr. Smith is kinder than Mr. Lee.*

(a) アメリカは日本より広いです。
　　America is larger than Japan.

(b) スミスさんはチェンさんよりよく勉強
　　します。
　　Mr. Smith studies harder than Mr. Chen.

(c) 犬はねこより速く走れます。
　　Dogs can run faster than cats.

(d) この本はあの本より高いですか。
　　Is this book more expensive than that book?

3 おなじぐらい: As 〜 as ... [Equivalence]

Using the phrase 〜と同じぐらい, we can express the equivalence. For example, 私は兄と同じぐらい背が高いです means *I am as tall as my older brother.*

(a) マリーさんはけい子さんと同じぐらい背
　　が高いです。
　　Mary is as tall as Keiko.

(b) 私は兄と同じぐらいよく勉強します。
　　I study as hard as my older brother.

(c) ねこは犬と同じぐらいかわいいです。
　　Cats are as cute as dogs.

4 〜ほど (…ない): Not as... as 〜 [Unreachable]

To express that the degree of some property of one item "does not reach" the one of the other item, use the particle ほど along with a **negative** adjective or verb. For example, 私は兄ほど背が高くありません means that *I am not as tall as my brother.*

(a) けいこさんはアンさんほど背が高くあり
　　ません。
　　Keiko is not as tall as Ann.

(b) 私は兄ほど勉強しません。
　　I do not study as much as my older brother.

(c) 私はあなたほど頭がよくありません。
　　I am not as smart as you are.

5 〜の [Noun-maker used in comparative sentences]

When comparing activities using verbs, the verbs that occur right before a particle such as が、は

and で must be followed by the noun-maker の. However, の is not used when a verb occurs right before より, ほど and 方.

(a) 漢字を書くのはひらがなを書くより難しいです。

Writing kanji is more difficult than writing hiragana.

(b) ピアノをひくのはうたをうたうのと同じぐらい楽しいです。

Playing the piano is as fun as singing a song.

(c) 勉強するのと、遊ぶのでは、どちら(の方)が好きですか。

Which do you like better, studying or playing?
— 遊ぶ方が勉強するより好きです。

— I like playing better than studying.

(d) 話すのは書くほど難しくありません。

Speaking is not as difficult as writing.

6 ～も: Both, all

When the particle も follows a question word such as どちら or どの～, it means *both* or *all*.

(a) どちらも好きです。

I like both.

(b) どちらもきらいです。

I hate both.

(c) どの学生も来ました。

All the students came.

It means *either*, *neither* or *no (none)*, if the verb or adjective of the sentence is negative.

(d) どちらも好きじゃありません。

I like neither of them.

(e) どの学生も来ませんでした。

No student came.

7 いちばん: The most ～
[Superlative comparison]

一番 literally means *the first*, *the best* or *the most*. You can express the superlative comparison using 一番 without conjugating the adjective at all. For

instance, 私は背が高いです means *I am tall*, but 私は一番背が高いです means *I am the tallest (among some members understood in the context)*. The basis of superlative comparison can be a list of items or set, and it is marked by the particle で. ～の中 is optionally added.

(a) 兄と姉と私(の中)では、兄が一番よく勉強します。

Among my brother, my sister and I, my brother studies the hardest.

(b) うち(の中)では、兄が一番よく食べます。

My brother eats the most in my family.

(c) ロシアと、カナダと、中国(の中)では、ロシアが一番広いです。

Among Russia, Canada and China, Russia is the largest.

(d) 世界(の中)では、ロシアが一番広いです。

Russia is the largest in the world.

For superlative comparison questions, どちら cannot be used. Use だれ for people, and どこ for locations.

(e) ジョンさんと、マイクさんと、ビルさん(の中)では、だれが一番背が高いですか。

Who is the tallest, John, Mike or Bill?

(f) クラス(の中)では、だれが一番背が高いですか。

Who is the tallest in the class?

(g) 図書館と、寮と、ラボ(の中)では、どこが一番静かですか。

Which is the quietest, the library, dormitory or lab?

(h) 大学(の中)では、どこが一番静かですか。

Which is the quietest (place) in the university?

For other items, use どれ or 何. If they are listed, use どれ, and if they are treated as a set, use 何.

(i) 猫と、犬と、猿(の中)では、どれが一番好きですか。

Which one do you like the best, cats, dogs or monkeys.

(j) 動物（の中）では、何が一番好きですか。

What do you like the best among animals?

(k) ピザと、ハンバーガーと、すし（の中）では、どれが一番好きですか。

Among pizza, hamburger and sushi, which one do you like the best?

(l) 食べもの（の中）では、何が一番好きですか。

Among foods, what do you like the best?

(m) 寝るのと、食べるのと遊ぶのでは、どれが一番楽しいですか。

Which one is most fun, sleeping, eating or playing?

(n) 今、何が一番したいですか。

What do you like to do the most now?

The choice of question words used for comparison is summarized in the following table.

Question Words Used for Comparison			
	People	Location	Others
Two items	どちら	どちら	どちら
Three or more items	だれ	どこ	どれ
Set	だれ	どこ	何

– Writing –

Ⓐ さかなへん

魚	さかなへん *fish*
	Example: 鯖 *mackerel*, 鱈 *codfish*, 鰻 *eel*, 鯛 *red snapper*, 鱒 *trout*, 鰹 *bonito*

– Kanji List –

北海道・本州・九州・四国・土地・地下・人口・同じ・〜の方・森田・川・湖・海・泳ぐ・肉・魚・色・一番

北 きた・ホク・ホッ north	一 十 寸 北 北 [5]
	Example: 北 *north*, 北海道 *Hokkaido*
海 うみ・カイ sea	丶 冫 氵 汀 泎 洵 海 海 [9]
	Example: 海 *sea, ocean*, 北海道 *Hokkaido*
道 みち・ドウ street, way	丶 丷 斗 产 首 首 首 首 道 道 [12]
	Example: 道 *street, road*, 北海道 *Hokkaido*
本 もと・ホン root, origin, true, main	一 十 才 木 本 [5]
	Example: 本州 *Honshu*
州 シュウ state	丶 ナ 丬 州 州 州 [6]
	Example: 九州 *Kyushu*, ニューヨーク州 *New York state*
九 ここの-つ・キュウ・ク nine	ノ 九 [2]
	Example: 九 *nine*, 九つ *nine pieces*, 九州 *Kyushu*
四 よっ-つ・よん・よ・シ four	丨 冂 匹 四 四 [5]
	Example: 四時 *4 o'clock*, 四国 *Shikoku*
国 くに・コク country	丨 冂 冂 冃 冃 国 国 国 [8]
	Example: 四国 *Shikoku*, 国 *country*
土 つち・ド・ト soil	一 十 土 [3]
	Example: 土地 *land*, 土曜日 *Saturday*
地 チ・ジ ground, land	帷 幄 幃 幀 幊 幗 [6]
	Example: 土地 *land*, 地下 *basement*, 地下鉄 *subway*

下 した・さ-がる・くだ-る・カ・ゲ under, down	一 丁 下 [3]
	Example: 地下 basement, 下 under

人 ひと・ジン・ニン man, person	ノ 人 [2]
	Example: 人口 population, 男の人 man

口 くち・ぐち・コウ mouth	丨 冂 口 [3]
	Example: 人口 population, 口 mouth

同 おな-じ・ドウ same	丨 冂 冂 同 同 同 [6]
	Example: 同じ the same

方 かた / がた・ホウ direction, way, means	` 一 方 方 [4]
	Example: ～の方 ~'s side

森 もり・シン forest	一 十 オ 木 木 本 秣 森 森 森 森 [12]
	Example: 森田 Mr./Ms. Morita (surname)

田 た・だ・デン rice field	丨 冂 冊 田 田 [5]
	Example: 森田 Mr./Ms. Morita (surname) 山田 Mr./Ms. Yamada (surname)

川 かわ・がわ・セン river	ノ 丿 川 [3]
	Example: 川 river

湖 みずうみ・コ lake	` ミ ミ シ 汁 汁 汁 沽 沽 湖 湖 湖 湖 [12]
	Example: 湖 lake

泳 およ-ぐ・エイ swim	` ミ ミ ジ 氵 汃 泋 泳 [8]
	Example: 泳ぐ to swim

肉 ニク flesh, meat	丨 冂 冂 内 肉 肉 [6]
	Example: 肉 meat

魚 さかな・うお・ギョ fish	ノ ク ⺈ 冇 伯 角 角 角 魚 魚 魚 [11]
	Example: 魚 fish

色 いろ・ショク color, feature	ノ ク ⺈ 刍 刍 色 [6]
	Example: 色 color

一 ひと-つ・イチ one	一 [1]
	Example: 一番 the first, the most, the best

番 バン number, order	ノ ⺍ ⺪ 平 平 乎 来 来 番 番 番 [12]
	Example: 一番 the first, the most, the best

– Review –

Q1. *State what is common among the members of each set.*

1. 泳・海・漢・湖   2. 色・魚

3. 森・林・校・枚

Q2. *Choose the appropriate option in the parentheses.*

1. (やさい・くだもの) の中ではバナナが一番
　好きです。

2. (魚・きせつ) の中では夏が一番好きです。

3. (海・山) で泳ぎます。

4. 九州は (本州・四国) より広いです。

Q3. *Fill in the blanks with appropriate question words.*

1. ねこと、犬と、＿＿＿＿＿ がかわいいですか。

2. 日本では、＿＿＿＿＿ が一番にぎやかですか。

3. クラスでは、＿＿＿＿＿ が一番背が高いですか。

4. 食べものでは、＿＿＿＿＿ が一番おいしい
　ですか。

5. 春と、秋と、夏では、＿＿＿＿＿ が一番好き
　ですか。

Q4. *Make a sentence using the items in each set, then, state what it means.*

1. ～より・高い　　　2. ～ほど・大きい

3. 同じぐらい　　　　4. 一番・どれ

5. ねる・どちら・好きです

Q5. *Compare your city and Tokyo, and answer the following questions.*

1. どちらの方が人が多いですか。

2. どちらの方が車が多いですか。

3. どちらの方がやちんが高いですか。

4. どちらの方があんぜんですか。

Tips and Additional Knowledge:
くだもの (fruits) in Japan

Fruits in Japan are expensive in general, but they are produced under high standards of quality control. For example, the size and shape of strawberries and apples are amazingly uniform, and they are often attractively packed. They also produce volleyball-sized watermelons, which are very convenient to carry home and put in the refrigerator. They even produced a square watermelon!

いちご *strawberry*

りんご *apple*

すいか *watermelon*

CHAPTER EIGHTEEN
When to Do What?

今お食事をしているところですか Unexpected Guest

📖 Basic Vocabulary and Kanji

しょくじ	食事	*n. meal, dining* (食事をする *to dine*)
えんりょ	遠慮	*n. hesitation, reservation* (遠慮 (を) する *to hesitate*)
おわる	*r-u* 終わる・終わらない・終わり・終わって	*v. to be over, to end*
か⌐えす	*s-u* 返す・返さない・返し・返して	*v. to return*
でかける	*e-ru* 出かける・出かけない・出かけ・出かけて	*v. to go out*
でき⌐る	*i-ru* できる・できない・でき・できて	*v. to be made, to be completed, to be able to do ~* ①
とつぜん	突然	*adv. suddenly, abruptly*
ごめんくだ さ⌐い		*Hello!* (*used when one knocks on the door*) ②
ま⌐あ		*interj. Oh dear!* (*used by female*)
ところです		*It is at the moment when ~.* (今食べてい〜るところです *I am in the middle of eating now.*) ③

〜だけです		*It's just that ~.* (ちょっと会いたかっただけです *I just wanted to see you.*) ④

Newly introduced kanji:

食事・出かける

💿 🗨 Dialog

Ben Lee stops by at Yoko Yamada's house at 7 p.m. Yoko's mother, Mrs. Yamada, answers the door.

リー ： (At 7 p.m., knocking on the door.) ごめんください。

山田 ： (Opening the door.) はい。ああ、リーさん、こんばんは。

リー ： とつぜん、すみません。お食事はおわりましたか。

山田 ： いいえ、今からするところです。いっしょに食べませんか。今、てんぷらができたところですから。

リー ： いいえ。私はこの本をかえしたかっただけですから。

山田 ： まあ、えんりょしないで下さい。

リー ： ああ、どうも。でも、うちに帰らなくてはいけませんから。

山田 ： ああ、そうですか。…じゃあ、また今度ね。

Guess and Try 1

What is the function of ごめんください in the above dialog? ②

Guess and Try 2

What do the underlined parts in the above dialog mean? ③

Guess and Try 3

Fill in the blanks. ③

A. 　　B. 　　C.

A. _____ ところです。

B. _____ ところです。

C. _____ ところです。

Drill 1: Formation

食べる → 食べるところです

1. てんぷらを作る　　2. てんぷらを作っている
3. てんぷらを作った　4. シャワーをあびる
5. シャワーをあびている　6. シャワーをあびた
7. 宿題をする　　8. 宿題をしている
9. 宿題をした

Drill 2: Formation

今、食べています → 今、食べているところです

1. 今、食事をしています　2. 今、電話をしています
3. 今、出かけます　4. 今、ねます
5. 今、宿題がおわりました　6. 今、おきゃくさんが帰りました

Task 1: Role Play

(Use the dialog as a model.)
A: You are on the way home, and you happen to be near your friend's apartment. You have not seen him / her for a few weeks, and you decided to say hello to him / her.

B: It is 6 p.m. on Friday. You are about to prepare your supper, when you hear someone knocking on the door.

Reasons for Visiting Someone

ちょっと顔を見たかっただけです。
I just wanted to see your face.
ちょっとあいさつをしたかっただけです。
I just wanted to say hello.
ちょっと寄っただけです。*I just stopped by.*
ちょっと聞きたいことがあるんです。
I have something I want to ask you about.
どうしているかなと思ったんです。
I was wondering how you are doing.

Task 2: Role Play

A: It is Saturday afternoon. You feel like inviting someone out to have supper. You call your friend, ask what he / she is doing and try to make an arrangement for supper.

B: Your friend calls and asks you what you are doing now.

For example:

A ： もしもし、A ですが。
B ： ああ、A さん。
A ： 今いそがしいですか。
B ： いいえ。今、テレビを見ていたところです。

Short Reading

　私の兄は今小説を書いています。今、300ページぐらい書いたところです。もうすぐ終わるところです。私の姉はフランス語を習っています。今、単語を30ぐらい覚えたところです。まだ、本は読めません。友達の明子さんはバイオリンを習っています。今、キラキラ星を練習しているところです。

(小説 *novel*, もうすぐ *soon*, キラキラ星
Twinkle, Twinkle, Little Star (Name of a song))

Writing

Write about what you are into currently.

食べる時に「いただきます。」と言います **Time**

📖 Basic Vocabulary and Kanji

ち｀ず	地図	*n. map*
きっぷ	切符	*n. ticket*
き｀ぶん	気分	*n. feeling（気分がいい to be in a good mood, 気分がわるい to be in a bad mood）*
めんど｀う（な）	面倒だ・面倒じゃない	*adj. troublesome*
ねむい	眠い・眠くない	*adj. sleepy*
もらう	*w-u* もらう・もらわない・もらい・もらって	*v. to receive*
いただきま｀す	頂きます	*a set phrase used right before eating* 5
ごちそうさま	ご馳走様	*a set phrase used right after eating* 5
いってきま｀す	行ってきます	*a set phrase used before leaving one's home for work or school*
ただいま	只今	*a set phrase used when one gets home*
おやすみなさい	お休みなさい	*Good night!*
〜とき（に）	〜時（に）	*at the time of 〜* 6

Newly introduced kanji:

地図 ・〜時 ・新聞 (newspaper)
（ち ず）（とき）（しんぶん）

💿🗨 Dialog

Ben Lee and Kaori Morita are about to eat lunch together.

リー ： 日本では、食べる時に何か言いますか。

森田 ： ええ。食べる時には「いただきます。」
と言います。

リー ： じゃあ、食べおわった時は。
（食べおわる *to finish eating*）

森田 ： 食べおわった時には「ごちそうさま。」
と言います。

リー ： ちょっとめんど
うですね。

Guess and Try 1

Fill in the blanks in the following passage, and interpret it. 7

出かける時に、「いってきます。」＿＿＿＿ 言います。
（で）

帰った時は、「ただいま。」＿＿＿＿ 言います。
（かえ）

Guess and Try 2

Explain the difference between the two sentences in each set. 6

1. A. 日本に行く時に、地図を買います。
（か）

   B. 日本に行った時に、地図を買います。

2. A. バスに乗る時に、きっぷを買いました。
（の）

   B. バスに乗った時に、きっぷを買いました。

Guess and Try 3

Look at the following sentences, and state what forms you need before 時. 6

1. ひまな時に、新聞を読みます。
（よ）

   When I'm free, I read the newspaper.

2. 高校生(こうこうせい)の時に、テニスをしました。
When I was a high school student, I played tennis.

3. おなかが痛(いた)い時に、薬(くすり)をのみます。
When my stomach hurts, I take medicine.

🗣 Drill 1: Formation

食べる・「いただきます。」 ➡ 食べる時に、「いただきます。」と言います

1. 出かける・「いってきます。」
2. うちに帰(かえ)った・「ただいま。」
3. ねる・「おやすみなさい。」
4. 人に会(あ)った・「こんにちは。」
5. ノックする・「ごめんください。」
6. 何かもらった・「ありがとう。」

🗣 Drill 2: Formation

しずかだ・勉強(べんきょう)します ➡ しずかな時に、勉強します

1. きぶんがいい・そうじをします
2. さびしい・テレビを見ます
3. テストだ・勉強します
4. わからない・質問(しつもん)します
5. りょこうに行く・地図を買(か)います
6. お金がない・アルバイトをします
7. ねむい・コーヒーを飲(の)みます

📱 Task 1: Classroom Discussion

Do you have set phrases that are used at specific time in your native language or your parents' language? Share them with your classmates.

📱 Task 2: Survey

Ask three of your classmates what they do to stay up when they feel very sleepy.

For example:

A ： ねむい時には、何をしますか。

B ： コーヒーを飲(の)みます。

私	
さん	
さん	
さん	

📱 Task 3: Pair Work

Ask your partner when he / she does the following.

1. ムッとする (to get upset / to feel being annoyed)
2. 泣(な)く (to cry / to weep)
3. ニコニコする (to smile)

For example:

A ： Bさんはどんな時に、ムッとしますか。

B ： 私は、バスが来(こ)ない時に、ムッとします。

📖 Short Reading

私は三ヶ月前(さんかげつまえ)にサンフランシスコに来(き)ました。今(いま)、大学で英語(えいご)を勉強(べんきょう)しています。英語はまだ下手(へた)です。ですから、まだ友達(ともだち)があまりいません。私のボーイフレンドは日本にいます。最近(さいきん)あまり手紙(てがみ)が来ません。さびしい時はよく海(うみ)を見(み)ます。そして、日本のことを思(おも)い出(だ)します。早(はや)く卒業(そつぎょう)して、日本に帰(かえ)って、家族(かぞく)や友達(ともだち)に会(あ)いたいです。

斎藤恵子(さいとうけいこ) 21才(さい)

(三ヶ月前(さんかげつまえ) *three months ago,* 思(おも)い出(だ)す *to recall*)

✏️ Writing

Write what you usually do when you feel lonesome. Or, write about your experience of homesick if you had any in the past.

卒業する前に、仕事を探しますか **Before or After**

Notes Relating to This Lesson

📖 Basic Vocabulary and Kanji

そつぎょうする	irr. 卒業する	v. to graduate
にゅうがくする	irr. 入学する	v. to enter a school, to be admitted to a school
なくな¬る	r-u なくなる・なくなる・なくならない・なくなり・なくなって	v. to disappear, to run out
それと¬も		con. alternatively (cf. それか) 8
～まえ(に)	～前(に)	before ~ 9
～あと(に)	～後(に)	after ~ 9
～あいだ(に)	～間(に)	during ~ 9
～から		prt. after ~ 9

Newly introduced kanji:

卒業する・入学する・前・後・
後ろ (behind) Ⓐ・午前 (a.m.)・午後 (p.m.)

卒	` 亠 亢 亡 卆 卒 卒
業	` ` ` ` 丱 丱 丱 丱 丵 丵 業 業 業
後	` ク イ イ 仁 产 待 後 後
午	ノ 匕 二 午

💿 🗨 Dialog

John Smith is checking with Yoko Yamada when the Japanese college students start looking for a job.

スミス : 日本の大学生は、卒業する前に仕事を探しますか。それとも、卒業した後に仕事を探しますか。

山田 : もちろん、卒業する前に探しますよ。

スミス : ああ、そうですか。

山田 : ええ。卒業した後はちょっと難しくなります。

（難しくなる to become difficult）

Guess and Try 1

Choose the appropriate option in the parentheses. 8

1. すしを食べますか。(それとも・それか)、さしみを食べますか。
2. すしを食べます。(それとも・それか)、さしみを食べます。

Guess and Try 2

Choose the appropriate option in the parentheses, and state what each sentence means. 9

1. 晩ごはんを (食べる・食べて・食べている・食べた) 前に、父に話しました。
2. 晩ごはんを (食べる・食べて・食べている・食べた) 後に、父に話しました。
3. 晩ごはんを (食べる・食べて・食べている・食べた) 間に、父に話しました。
4. 晩ごはんを (食べる・食べて・食べている・食べた) から、父に話しました。
5. 食事の (前・間・後) に、「いただきます。」と言います。
6. 食事の (前・間・後) に、テレビは見ません。
7. 食事の (前・間・後) に、「ごちそうさま。」と言います。

🗣 Drill 1: Formation

食べる ⟶ 食べる前と、食べた後

1. 飲む
2. 働く
3. テレビを見る
4. シャワーをあびる

🗣 Drill 2: Formation

食べる・はをみがきます ⟶ 食べる前に、はを
みがきます

1. おきゃくさんが来る・そうじをします
2. 出かける・シャワーをあびます
3. 食べものがなくなる・スーパーマーケット
   に行きます
4. 卒業する・りょこうをします

🗣 Drill 3: Formation

食べた・はをみがきます ⟶ 食べた後に、はを
みがきます

1. 入学した・せんこうをきめます
2. きゅうりょうが出た・買いものをします
3. 働いた・スナックを食べます
4. 宿題をした・テレビを見ます

🚩 Task 1: Classroom Activity

Complete your schedule in the table, pretending that
you do these activities in a specific order: 新聞を読
む・スナックを食べる・としょかんに行く・仕
事に行く. Don't show your schedule to others. Your
teacher will then pick one of you and let the rest of
you ask him / her questions. Only それとも questions may be asked. The first to identify the complete
order of the student's schedule wins. Your teacher
will repeat the activity with different students.

For example:

A : Bさんは新聞を読んだ後に、仕事に行きま
    すか。
    それとも、新聞を読む前に、仕事に行きま
    すか。
B : 新聞を読んだ後に、仕事に行きます。
C : Bさんは、仕事に行った後に、スナック
    を食べますか。

それとも、仕事に行く前に、スナックを
食べますか。

B : 仕事に行く前にスナックを食べます。

1. おきる
2.
3.
4.
5.
6. ねる

🚩 Task 2: Classroom Activity

In which order do you perform the following routines
in the morning? (シャワーをあびる・朝ごはん
を食べる・ようふくを着る・はをみがく) Find
the people who do these in the same order as yours.

📖 Short Reading

　お好み焼きの作り方：小麦粉と、卵と、水
をよく混ぜる。それから、千切りキャベツを入
れる。えびや、たこや、いかを入れてもいい。
それを鉄板の上で焼く。
焼く前に鉄板をよくあた
ためる。両面がだいた
い焼けた後に、ソースを
塗って、鰹節と青海苔
をかける。紅しょうがをのせてもいい。

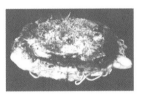

(お好み焼き *Japanese pancake*, 作り方 *recipe*,
小麦粉 *flour*, 卵 *egg*, 水 *water*, 混ぜる *to mix*,
千切りキャベツ *(finely) shredded cabbage*, えび
shrimp, たこ *octopus*, いか *squid*, 入れる *to put;
to add*, 鉄板 *iron plate*, 焼く *to cook*, あたため
る *to warm*, 両面 *both sides*, だいたい *mostly*,
焼ける *to be cooked*, 塗る *to spread*, 鰹節 *dried
bonito flakes*, 青海苔 *green laver*, かける *to
sprinkle*, 紅しょうが *(shredded) red pickled ginger*, のせる *to put something on*)

✏️ Writing

Write how you make pizza. Or, write how you make
your favorite dish.

食べながら、話します
Doing Two Activities at the Same Time

Notes Relating to This Lesson	
Grammar and Usage	
10 ～ながら 58	

 Basic Vocabulary and Kanji

ぎょうぎ	行儀	*n. manners, behavior*
ぎょうぎよ⌐く	行儀よく	*adv. with good manners*
しゅ⌐じん・ごしゅ⌐じん	主人・御主人	*n. husband*
のんび⌐りする	*irr.* のんびりする	*v. to relax*
～たち	～達	*plural suffix for nouns (that denote people and animals)* (私達 *we,* 学生達 *students*)
～ながら		*prt. while doing ~* 10

Newly introduced kanji:

主人・お酒 (rice wine, alcoholic beverage) ・
ご飯 (meal, cooked rice)

主	`ヽ 一 十 キ 主
酒	`ヽ ぃ ジ ジ 汀 沂 沔 洒 洒 酒
飯	ノ ハ ゕ 今 今 今 宦 宦 飣 飯 飯

 Dialog

Two housewives are chatting.

林 ：石田さんのむすこさんたちはぎょうぎよくご飯を食べますか。

石田：いいえ、健一はテレビを見ながら食べるんです。健二はマンガを読みながら食べるんですよ。

林 ：ご主人は。

石田：主人は新聞を読みながら食べます。

林 ：ああ、そうですか。

Guess and Try 1
Complete the following sentences. 10
1. 父は ＿＿＿＿＿＿ながら車を運転します。
2. 私は ＿＿＿＿＿＿ながら漢字を覚えます。

Guess and Try 2
For each of the following sentences, state what is the major activity that Kenichi is doing now, and what is the accompanying activity. 10
1. 健一はテレビを見ながら食べています。
2. 健一は食べながらテレビを見ています。

Drill 1: Conjugation

歩く ⟶ 歩きながら

1. 食べる　　　　2. 見る
3. 遊ぶ　　　　4. 読む
5. 話す　　　　6. しゃべる
7. はしる　　　　8. 運転する

Drill 2: Formation

歩きます・話します ⟶ 歩きながら話します
1. 歩きます・漢字を覚えます
2. おんがくを聞きます・食べます
3. うたをうたいます・シャワーをあびます

4. テレビを見ます・のんびりします

5. たばこをすいます・勉強_{べんきょう}します

6. お酒を飲_のみます・えいがを見ます

Task 1

Tell what each of the following people is doing.
(For example: … さんは … ながら … しています)

ピーター　　メイリン　　よし子

Task 2: Classroom Activity

Your teacher pretends to be doing two activities at the same time. He / she shows you some gestures very briefly (for about 2 seconds) without saying anything. Guess what he / she is doing.

Task 3: Group Work

Share your idea of saving time by doing two activities at the same time.

Short Reading

私はいつも忙_{いそが}しいです。試験_{しけん}の前_{まえ}は特_{とく}に忙しいです。よく、いろいろなことをいっしょにします。例_{たと}えば、歯_はを磨_{みが}きながら洋服_{ようふく}を着_きます。宿題_{しゅくだい}をしながら朝_{あさ}ごはんを食_たべます。歩_{ある}きながらテープをきいて、日本語の単語_{ごたんご}を覚_{おぼ}えます。図書館_{としょかん}でアルバイトをしながら勉強_{べんきょう}をします。よく寝_ねながら、考_{かんが}え事_{ごと}をします。ですから、よく忘_{わす}れ物_{もの}をします。

(特_{とく}に *especially*, いろいろなこと *various things*, 考_{かんが}え事_{ごと}をする *to think (about something)*, 忘_{わす}れ物_{もの}をする *to forget things*)

Writing

Write how you save your time when you are very busy.

– Grammar and Usage –

1 できる: To be able to do / to be completed / to be made

The verb できる means *to be able to do, to be completed* or *to be made*.

(a) テニスができます。
(I) can play tennis.

(b) 宿題ができました。
My homework has finished.

(c) てんぷらができました。
The tempura is done.

(d) 酒はお米からできています。
Sake is made from rice.

(e) このかばんは革でできています。
This bag is made of leather.

2 ごめんください: Hello! Is anyone there? / Goodbye!

ごめんください is a set phrase used when one knocks on the door, trying to get the attention of a person in the building. Women often say ごめんください when they are about to leave someone's house, or when they are about to hang up the telephone in a polite / formal context.

3 ～ところです: It is at the moment when ～

～ところです follows a verb in the plain form, and means *it is at the moment when ～*. Depending on the tense of the verb, the interpretation differs.

(a) 今、食べるところです。
I am just about to eat now.

(b) 今、食べているところです。
I am in the middle of eating now.

(c) 今、食べたところです。
I have just finished eating.

Eating

食べる　　　食べている　　　食べた
ところです　ところです　　　ところです

4 ～だけです: It is just that ～

～だけです is placed at the end of a sentence, and it means *It's just ..., and nothing more than that*. The verbs and adjectives that precede だけ must be in the plain form, except that だ that occurs as an ending part of a na-type adjective or a copula must be changed to な.

(a) よく勉強したんですか。
Did you study well?
— いいえ、テキストを読んだだけです。
— No, I just read the text.

(b) 東京で食事をするんですか。
Will you dine in Tokyo?
— いいえ、買物をするだけです。
— No, I will just go shopping there.

(c) 山田さんのアパートはいいですね。
Ms. Yamada, your apartment is great, isn't it?
— いいえ、通勤が便利なだけですよ。
— No, it's just that it's convenient for commuting.

(d) だいじょうぶですか。
Are you okay?
— はい、ちょっと頭が痛いだけです。
— Yes, it is just a headache.

(e) あの人はりっぱな人ですね。
That person is a great person.
— いいえ、ちょっと金持ちなだけです。
— No, it is just that he is a little bit rich.

(f) どうぞ入って下さい。
Please come in.
— いいえ、この本を返したかっただけです。
— No, I just wanted to return this book to you.

5 いただきます and ごちそうさま [Before and after eating]

When a group of Japanese people is going to eat at a table, they usually wait for the host or hostess to ask them to start eating by saying, for example, どうぞ *please*. They say いただきます right before they start eating. When they finish eating, they say ごちそうさま or ごちそうさまでした. Leaving the table without saying ごちそうさま is considered extremely rude in Japan.

6 ～とき (に): At the time when ～

The time of an event can be specified by a simple time expression such as 月曜日に and 明日, as you know.

(a) 月曜日に話します。

(I) will tell (him) on Monday.

(b) 明日話します。

(I) will tell (him) tomorrow.

The time of an event can also be specified by a time adverbial phrase with 時. 時 means *time*, and when it follows another phrase, it means *at the time of ...* or *at the time when ....* The preceding phrase must be in the pre-nominal form since 時 is a noun. The particle に is optional after 時.

(c) 食事の時 (に)、話します。

(I) will tell (him) at mealtime.

(d) しずかな時 (に)、話します。

(I) will tell (him) (at the time) when it is quiet.

(e) 気分がいい時 (に)、話します。

(I) will tell (him) (at the time) when (I) am feeling good.

(f) バスが来ない時 (に)、イライラします。

When the bus does not come, I get irritated.

(g) 食べている時 (に)、話します。

(I) will tell (him) when we are eating.

(h) 食べた時 (に)、話します。

(I) will tell (him) when we finish eating.

(i) 食べる時 (に)、話しました。

(I) told (him) at the time when we were about to eat.

When 時 follows a verb, the precise point of time depends on the tense of the verb. For example, 食べる時 (に) means *when one is about to eat*, 食べている時 (に) means *when one is eating*, and 食べた時 (に) means *when one finishes eating*.

As in sentence (h) and sentence (i), the tense of the verb in the adverbial phrase and the tense of the main verb may be different.

7 Direct quote

A direct quote is marked by a pair of quotation marks 「 and 」 and a quotation particle ～と.

山田さんは「私はまじめですよ」と言いました。

Ms. Yamada said, "I'm serious."

The phrase or sentence that appears between the quotation marks is what was actually said or written, and the verb or adjective in it does not have to be in the plain form.

8 それとも: Alternatively [Alternative yes-no questions]

The sentence connective word それとも is used when there are two yes-no questions, and it means *alternatively*, or *or*.

(a) すしを食べますか。それとも、さしみを食べますか。

Will you eat sushi? Or, will you eat sashimi?

(b) えいがを見ましょうか。それとも、テニスをしましょうか。

Shall we watch a movie? Or, shall we play tennis?

To connect two sentences that are not questions, use それか instead of それとも.

(c) すしを食べます。それか、さしみを食べます。

I will eat sushi. Or, I will eat sashimi.

(d) えいがを見ましょう。それか、テニスをしましょう。

Let's watch a movie. Or, let's play tennis.

9 Adverbial phrases for periods of time (～まえに, etc.)

We can create a time adverbial phrase using the nouns 前 *beforehand*, 後 *afterward* and 間 *during*. 前, 後 and 間 can follow a noun plus の or a verb in the plain form:

(a) 食事の前に話します。

I will tell you before the meal.

(b) 食事の後に話します。
I will tell you after the meal.

(c) 食事の 間 に話します。
I will tell you during the meal.

(d) 食べる前に話します。
I will tell you before eating.

(e) 食べた後に話します。
I will tell you after eating.

(f) 食べている 間 に話します。
I will tell you during eating time.

Importantly, the verb that precedes 前 must be in the present form (for example, 〜する前に), the verb that precedes 後 must be in the past form (for example, 〜した後に), and the verb that precedes 間 must be in the progressive form (for example, 〜している 間 に), regardless of when the event takes place.

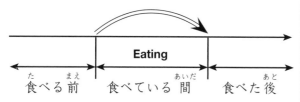

~する時 (に) and ~した時 (に) only specify the time close to the event, but ~する前に and ~した後に can specify not only the time close to the event, but also a wider range of time before or after the event. For example, when one studies Japanese three days before his going to Japan, both (g) and (h) are appropriate. By contrast, when one studies Japanese three years before his going to Japan, (g) is appropriate but (h) is not.

(g) 日本に行く前に日本語を勉 強します。
I will study Japanese before going to Japan.

(h) 日本に行く時 (に) 日本語を勉強します。
I will study Japanese at the time that I go to Japan.

~した後に and ~ (て) から (te-form plus the particle から) can be interchangeably used.

(i) 卒 業 してから、仕事を探します。
I will look for a job after I graduate.

(j) 卒業した後に、仕事を探します。
I will look for a job after I graduate.

10 〜ながら: While doing 〜 [Accompanying activity]

The suffix ながら follows a verb in the stem form as in 食べながら, creating an adverbial phrase that expresses the activity that takes place simultaneously with the activity expressed by the main verb. For example, the sentence 食べながらテレビを見ます means that *one does eating and watching TV at the same time.*

Although which activity is emphasized depends on the context, the activity expressed by the main verb is normally the major activity and the activity expressed in the ながら phrase is the additional one that serves as the extra information. For example, sentence (a) is mainly about the speaker's brother's eating and the ながら phrase describes how he eats. By contrast, sentence (b) is mainly about his TV-watching and the ながら phrase describes how he watches TV.

(a) 兄はテレビを見ながら、 食べます。
My older brother eats while watching TV.

(b) 兄は食べながら、テレビを見ます。
My older brother watches TV while eating.

– Writing –

ⓐ ぎょうにんべん

イ	ぎょうにんべん *road, walking*
	Example: 行く *to go*, 後ろ *behind*, 往復 *round trip*, 待つ *to wait*

– Kanji List –

食事・出かける・地図・〜時・新聞・
卒業する・入学する・前・後・後ろ・
午前・午後・主人・お酒・ご飯

食 た-べる・ショク to eat	ノ 人 人 今 今 今 食 食 食 [9]
	Example: 食べる to eat, 食事 meal
事 こと・ごと・ジ affair, fact, engagement	一 一 一 一 写 写 写 事 [8]
	Example: 食事 meal, 仕事 job
出 で-る・だ-す・シュツ・シュツ to come, go out	丨 屮 虫 出 出 [5]
	Example: 出る to come out, to attend, 出かける to go out, 出す to take out, to submit
地 チ・ジ ground, land	一 十 土 圵 坳 地 [6]
	Example: 土地 land, 地下 basement, 地下鉄 subway
図 ズ・ト diagram, devise	丨 冂 冂 叉 図 図 図 [7]
	Example: 地図 map, 図書館 library
時 とき・ジ time, hour	丨 冂 月 日 日 旷 旷 旷 時 時 [10]
	Example: 4時 four o'clock, 時 time
新 あたら-しい・シン new	一 十 立 立 北 [5]
	Example: 新しい new, 新聞 newspaper

聞 き-く・き-こえる・ブン to hear, to listen	丨 冂 冂 冂 門 門 門 門 門 門 門 間 間 聞 [14]
	Example: 聞く to listen, 新聞 newspaper
卒 ソツ graduate	丶 亠 产 坛 夽 衣 夽 卒 [8]
	Example: 卒業する to graduate
業 わざ・ギョウ job, business	丶 丷 丷 丱 丱 严 严 严 严 堂 堂 業 業 [13]
	Example: 卒業する to graduate
入 はい-る・い-れる・ニュウ enter, put in	ノ 入 [2]
	Example: 入学する to enter a school, 入る to enter, 入れる to put in
学 まな-ぶ・ガク・ガッ study	丶 丷 丷 丷 严 学 学 学 [8]
	Example: 学生 student, 学校 school, 入学する to enter a school
前 まえ・ゼン before, front, previous	丶 丷 广 广 广 首 首 前 前 [9]
	Example: 三ヶ月前 three months before, 〜の前 before 〜
後 あと・のち・うし-ろ・ゴ・コウ after, later, back, behind	ノ ク 彳 彳 丬 伃 伃 後 後 [9]
	Example: 〜の後 after 〜, 〜の後ろ behind 〜
午 ゴ noon	ノ 广 仁 午 [4]
	Example: 午前 a.m., 午後 p.m.

主 おも-な・ ぬし・シュ chief, main lord, owner	丶 ニ 十 キ 主 [5]	
	Example: 主人 <ruby>しゅじん</ruby> one's husband, ご主人 <ruby>しゅじん</ruby> someone else's husband	
人 ひと・ジン・ ニン man, person	ノ 人 [2]	
	Example: 日本人 <ruby>にほんじん</ruby> Japanese 主人 <ruby>しゅじん</ruby> one's husband	
酒 さけ・シュ rice wine, liquor	丶 丶 氵 氵 汀 沂 沂 沔 酒 酒[10]	
	Example: お酒 <ruby>さけ</ruby> Japanese rice wine	
飯 めし・ハン cooked rice, meal, food	ノ 𠂊 𠂢 今 今 今 食 食 食 飣 飯 飯 [12]	
	Example: ご飯 <ruby>はん</ruby> cooked rice, meal	

– Review –

Q1. *Choose the appropriate option in the parentheses.*

1. シャワーを (あびます・あらいます)。

2. (きっぷ・きぶん) を買って、電車に乗りました。

3. (しごと・しょくじ) をして、お金をもらいました。

Q2. *Write the pronunciation of the following kanji phrases, and state what is common among the members of each set.*

1. 前・後

2. 前・後ろ・上・下・右・左

3. せん門・聞く・新聞・質問

4. 質問・近い・新しい

Q3. *Choose the appropriate option in the parentheses.*

1. 新聞を (読む・読んだ) 時、めがねをかけます。

2. 朝 (おきる・おきた) 時、シャワーをあびます。

3. おきゃくさんが (来る・来た) 時、そうじします。

4. 日本に行く時、(JFK・とうきょう) でティーシャツを買います。(JFK: John F. Kennedy airport at New York)

5. 日本に行った時、(JFK・とうきょう) でティーシャツを買います。

Q4. *Connect the two sentences using* 前に *or* 後に *, and make one sentence.*

1. 朝ご飯を食べます。それから、新聞を読みます。

2. 宿題をします。それから、テレビを見ます。

3. 手を洗います。それから、ご飯を食べます。

Q5. *Fill in the blanks, and state what the sentences mean.*

1. 私は _____ ながら勉強します。

2. 父は _____ ながら歩きます。

3. 兄は _____ ながらシャワーをあびます。

4. 弟は _____ ながらテレビを見ます。

Q6. *Fill in the blanks appropriately.*

1. さしみを _____。それとも、すしを _____。

2. さしみを _____。それか、すしを _____。

Tips and Additional Knowledge: Fortune Dolls

だるま is a traditional fortune doll that signifies "never give up". The bottom part is heavier than the top part, and even if it is pushed over, it springs right up again. It is red except its face, and its eyes are not painted when sold. When you make a wish, you put one eye on him. And as your wish comes true, you put on the other eye to congratulate your achievement.

まねきねこ (fortune cat) is a seated cat doll whose front paw is raised to invite people or money. It signifies "business prosperity and family happiness". Many stores and restaurants place it on the counter or at the cash register, wishing to draw a thousand customers or a fortune of money. When the cat's right paw is raised, they attract people, and when the left paw is raised, they attract money.

だるま　　　　まねきねこ

CHAPTER NINETEEN
Adding Implications

そのかばんは持ちやすいですか　Difficult or Easy

Notes Relating to This Lesson	
Grammar and Usage	
1 Transitive and intransitive verbs 74	2 Auxiliaries ....74 3 ～にくい・～やすい 76

📖 Basic Vocabulary and Kanji

おも￢い	重い・重くない	*adj. heavy*
いれる	*e-ru* 入れる・入れない・入れ・入れて	*v. to put* (かばんに本を入れる *to put a book in the bag*) 1
うご￢く	*k-u* 動く・動かない・動き・動いて	*v. to move*
も￢つ	*t-u* 持つ・持たない・持ち・持って	*v. to hold or carry by hand* (かばんを持つ *to carry a bag*)
もっている	持っている	*to have, to possess* (車を持っている *to have a car*)
～やすい	～やすい・～やすいです	*aux. to be easy to ~* (食べやすい *to be easy to eat*) 2 3
～にくい	～にくい・～にくいです	*aux. to be difficult to ~* (食べにくい *to be difficult to eat*) 2 3

Newly introduced kanji:

重い・入れる・動く・持つ・
物 (things)・動物 (animals)・食べ物 (food)

重	一 一 一 一 一 一 車 車 重
動	一 一 一 一 一 一 車 車 重 動 動
持	一 十 扌 扌 扌 扩 护 拝 持 持
物	丿 ソ 十 牛 牛 牜 物 物

💿 🗨 Dialog

Kaori Morita notices that Mary Carter is carrying a nice bag.

森田　　：あっ、そのかばんはいいですね。

カーター：そうですか。

森田　　：持ちやすいですか。

カーター：いいえ。重くて、持ちにくいです。でも、物は入れやすいです。大きいじしょも入ります。

森田　　：ああ、そうですか。どこで買ったんですか。

カーター：姉からもらいました。姉はたくさんかばんを持っているんです。

Guess and Try 1

Consider what the following sentences mean and state the difference between 入れる and 入る. Do you know any other pairs like 入れる and 入る? 1

1. かばんにじしょを入れます。
2. かばんにじしょが入ります。

Guess and Try 2

What do the following sentences mean? 2 3

1. 今日のくつは、はきやすいですか。それとも、はきにくいですか。
2. 先生は話しやすいです。
3. 今日のようふくは動きやすいです。

Guess and Try 3

Ask your partner whether kanji characters are easy to memorize. 2 3

🗣 Drill 1: Formation

食べる ➡ 食べやすいです

1. 読む   ➡

2. 歩く   ➡

3. 動く   ➡

4. 持つ   ➡

5. 入れる   ➡

6. 覚える   ➡

7. 探す   ➡

8. 習う   ➡

9. 作る   ➡

🗣 Drill 2: Mini Conversation

読みやすいですか ➡ いいえ、読みにくいです

1. 見やすいですか

2. 動きやすいですか

3. わかりやすいですか

4. 話しやすいですか

🏳 Task 1: Pair Work

Compare the following.

1. すし・さしみ

2. 大きい車・小さい車

3. 漢字・ひらがな

4. ？？？ (Your choice!)

For example:

A : すしと、さしみではどちらの方が食べやすいと思いますか。

B : すしの方が食べやすいと思います。手で食べられますから。

🏳 Task 2: Pair Work

Using the dialog as a model, question your partner about the items he / she has today (for example, pen, dictionary, jacket, shoes, bag and book).

📖 Short Reading

私は英語の辞書を二つ持っています。一つは大きい英和辞典です。いつも家で使っています。大きいので、持ちにくいです。でも、例文がたくさんあって、わかりやすいです。もう一つは、スキャン型電子辞書です。とても小さいので、ポケットに入れられます。単語をスキャンするだけで、意味がわかります。発音も聞けます。とても便利です。

(例文 *example sentence,* スキャン型電子辞書 *scan-type electronic dictionary,* 意味 *meaning*)

✏ Writing

Write about your dictionaries.

ぎょうざを食べすぎました Overdoing Something

<table>
<tr><td colspan="2">Notes Relating to This Lesson</td></tr>
<tr><td>Grammar and Usage</td><td>Culture</td></tr>
<tr><td>2 Auxiliaries ....74</td><td>Ⓐ ぎょうざ........ 78</td></tr>
<tr><td>4 ～すぎる ....76</td><td>Writing</td></tr>
<tr><td>5 ～ずつ ....76</td><td>ⓐ いとへん........ 78</td></tr>
</table>

📖 Basic Vocabulary and Kanji

ぎょうざ	餃子	n. (Chinese-style) dumpling Ⓐ
くるし⌐い	苦しい・苦しくない	adj. distressful, uncomfortable
はじめる	*e-ru* 始める・始めない・始め・始めて	v. to start
つづける	*e-ru* 続ける・続けない・続け・続けて	v. to continue
～はじめる	*e-ru* ～始める・～始めない・～始め・～始めて	aux. to start ~ing (食べ始める to start eating) 2
～おわる	*r-u* ～終わる・～終わらない・～終わり・～終わって	aux. to finish ~ing (食べ終わる to finish eating) 2
～つづける	*e-ru* ～続ける・～続けない・～続け・～続けて	aux. to continue ~ing (食べ続ける to continue eating) 2
～すぎる	*i-ru* ～過ぎる・～過ぎない・～過ぎ・～過ぎて	aux. to overdo ~ing (食べ過ぎる to eat too much) 2 4
～こ	～個	c. a counter for medium-sized inanimate objects
～ずつ		prt. each, at a time, by (2つずつ食べる eat two pieces at a time) 5

Newly introduced kanji:
苦しい・始める・終わる (to finish) ⓐ・
～個・竹下 (surname)

苦	一十廾芒芒苦苦苦
始	く女女 始始始始始
終	纟纟纟纟幺糸糸紵紵終終終
個	ノイ们们们個個個個
竹	ノ⺅竹竹竹竹

💿🗣 Dialog

Makoto Takeshita is eating ぎょうざ with his Chinese friend, Su-Yuan Han.

竹下 ： ああ、苦しい。ちょっと食べすぎました。

ハン ： いくつ食べたんですか。

竹下 ： 10個ぐらい。

ハン ： 少ないですよ。ぼくはいつも30個ぐらい食べますよ。

竹下 ： ちょっと多すぎますよ。日本人はたいてい7個ずつ食べるんですよ。

ハン ： そうですか。少ないですね。

Guess and Try 1
Circle the ones that are not read as you would predict.

いっこ (1個)　　　ななこ (7個)
にこ (2個)　　　はちこ／はっこ (8個)
さんこ (3個)　　きゅうこ (9個)
よんこ (4個)　　じゅっこ (10個)
ごこ (5個)　　　なんこ (何個)
ろっこ (6個)

Guess and Try 2

What is the difference between the following two sentences? ⑤

1. 子供たちがキャンディーを 10 個ずつ買いました。
2. 子供たちがキャンディーを 10 個買いました。

Guess and Try 3

Add すぎます to the underlined parts in the following sentences appropriately and state what the sentences mean. ② ④

1. ワインを飲みました。あたまが痛いです。
2. 日本の会社員はいそがしいです。家族と遊ぶ時間がとても少ないです。
3. ここは静かです。ちょっとさびしいです。
4. このアパートはいいです。

Guess and Try 4

What do the following sentences mean? ②

1. てがみを書き始めました。
2. てがみを書き終わりました。
3. 日本語を勉強しつづけます。

🗣 Drill: Formation

父・働きます —→ 父は働きすぎます

1. 弟・遊びます
2. 妹・テレビを見ます
3. アメリカの車・大きいです
4. 山田先生のしけん・難しいです
5. 田中先生のしけん・かんたんです
6. 兄・あたまがいいです

🏳 Task 1: Pair Work

Describe the following situations.

A

B

C

🏳 Task 2: Pair Work

Is there any activity which you think you had overly indulged in in the past? Talk about it with your partner.

For example:

A : 昨日コンピューターゲームをしすぎました。

B : ああ、よくないですね。(いいですよ。)

🏳 Task 3: Group Work

Evaluate Japan in terms of the following.

1. ホテル (hotels)　2. 食べもの (food)
3. こうつう (transportation)

For example:

A : 日本のホテルはどうですか。

B : ちょっと高すぎます。東京では一泊 2万円ぐらいです。(一泊 a night's lodging)

C : そうですか。ニューヨークと同じぐらいですよ。

D : 安いホテルもありますよ。

Degree Adverbs	
あまり (〜ない) not very ~	まあまあ〜 more or less ~
とても〜 very ~	ちょっと〜 a little bit ~
ぜんぜん (〜ない) not ~at all	

📖 Short Reading

　アメリカ人はよく日本人は働きすぎると言います。日本の会社員はたいてい定時には帰りません。有給休暇はありますが、あまりとりません。週末もよく仕事をします。ですから、あまり家族と遊ぶことができません。

(定時 fixed time; regular hours, 有給休暇 paid holiday)

✎ Writing

Compare the Japanese workers and those in your country.

お金を使ってしまいました It's Done!

Notes Relating to This Lesson	
Grammar and Usage	
6 ～しまう.........76	7 ～ほうがいい 77

 Basic Vocabulary and Kanji

こわ⌐す	*s-u* 壊す・壊さない・壊し・壊して	*v. to break* (カメラを壊す *to break a camera*)
こわれ⌐る	*e-ru* 壊れる・壊れない・壊れ・壊れて	*v. to break* (車が壊れた *The car broke down.*)
ま⌐つ	*t-u* 待つ・待たない・待ち・待って	*v. to wait* (ガールフレンドを待つ *to wait for one's girlfriend*)
わすれる	*e-ru* 忘れる・忘れない・忘れ・忘れて	*v. to forget* (宿題を忘れる *to forget one's homework*)
くせになる	癖になる	*to become a habit*
～しまう	*w-u* ～しまう・～しまわない・～しまい・～しまって	*aux. to complete ~ing* (食べてしまう *to complete eating something*) 6
～ほうがいい	～方がいい	*It is better to ~.* (ねた方がいい *to be better to sleep*) 7

Newly introduced kanji:

待つ・忘れる

待	⌐ 彳 彳 彳 彳 待 待 待 待
忘	⌐ 亠 亡 亡 忘 忘 忘

 Dialog

Kyungtaek Park is asking Makoto Takeshita to loan him some money.

パーク：すみません。ちょっと 1 万円かして下さいませんか。

竹下　：どうしたんですか。昨日、2 万円かしましたよね。

パーク：あの 2 万円はパチンコで<u>使ってしまいました</u>。

竹下　：パークさん、ギャンブルはやめた方がいいですよ。くせになるから、しない方がいいですよ。

Guess and Try 1

How does the speaker feel about the underlined part in the above dialog? 6

Guess and Try 2

しまう expresses the speaker's regrettable or happy feelings toward the completed event, or it just emphasizes that something is completed. State what しまう does in the following sentences. 6

1. 先生のコンピューターをこわしてしまいました。
2. 日本語を忘れてしまいました。
3. もう、ひらがなとカタカナを覚えてしまいました。
4. 行きましょう。
   — ちょっと、待って下さい。このコーヒーを飲んでしまいます。

Guess and Try 3

Fill in the blanks. 7

1. 薬を _____ 方がいいですよ。

   It is better to take medicine.

2. 薬を _____ 方がいいですよ。

   It is better not to take medicine.

Drill: Formation

食べました ➡ 食べてしまいました

1. 本をかしました

2. とけいをこわしました

3. 電話ばんごうを忘れました

4. きっぷをなくしました

5. ひらがなとカタカナを覚えました

6. 父とけんかをしました

Task: Group Work/Role Play

Pretend that you did the following. Talk about them and get some advice from your partner. Take turns.

1. 日本語のしけんで 0点 をとってしまった

2. 車のかぎをなくしてしまった

3. ガールフレンド (ボーイフレンド) とけんか
   をしてしまった

4. ともだちのコンピューターをこわしてし
   まった

5. ??? (Your choice!)

For example:

A ： 日本語のしけんで 0 点をとってしまった
     んです。

B ： それはよくありませんね。勉強しまし
     たか。

A ： いいえ、あまり勉強しませんでした 。

B ： ああ、そうですか。この次はよく勉強し
     た方がいいですよ。(この次 *next time*)

Short Reading

　私は中学生の時、東京から富山に引っ越しました。富山はよく雪が降ります。富山の中学校では冬はスキーをします。そして、一年に一回スキー場に行きます。私はスキーをしたことがありませんでした。スキーはとても難しくて、こわかったです。でも、スキー場に行って、スキーをしなくてはなりませんでした。日本のスキー場は人がたくさんいて、とても混んでいます。私はスキー場で滑りはじめました。でも、止まることができませんでした。それで、人にぶつかってしまいました。だれも怪我をしませんでしたが、ぶつかった人のストックが曲がってしまって、弁償しなくてはなりませんでした。

(引っ越す *to move to*, スキー場 *skiing area*, 〜なくてはならない *to have to do* 〜, こわい *scary; frightening*, 滑る *to slide; to ski*, 止まる *to stop*, 〜にぶつかる *v. to collide with* 〜, 怪我 *injury*, ストック *ski poles*, 曲がる *to bend*, 弁償する *to compensate*)

Writing

Write about some of your regrettable incidents.

ホテルをよやくしておきます　Get Ready!

Notes Relating to This Lesson	
Grammar and Usage	
8 ～おく.........77	

 Basic Vocabulary and Kanji

ひ˥しょ	秘書	n. secretary
ごみ˥	ゴミ・ごみ	n. trash, garbage
ぎゅうにゅう	牛乳	n. milk
たいふ˥う	台風	n. typhoon
よやくする	irr. 予約する	v. to make a reservation, to make an appointment (ホテルを予約する to make a reservation at a hotel)
すてる	e-ru 捨てる・捨てない・捨て・捨てて	v. to throw away (ゴミを捨てる to throw away the garbage)
しま˥う	w-u しまう・しまわない・しまい・しまって	v. to store, to put away (ようふくをしまう to store the clothes)
ため˥る	e-ru 貯める・貯めない・貯め・貯めて	v. to save up, to accumulate (お金を貯める to save money)
はら˥う	w-u 払う・払わない・払い・払って	v. to pay (授業料を払う to pay for the tuition)
～おく	k-u ～おく・～おかない・～おき・～おいて	aux. to do ~ in advance (本を読んでおく to read a book in advance) 8

Newly introduced kanji:

映画 (えいが) (movie)

映	丨 冂 月 日 日 旷 肌 映 映
画	一 フ 丆 币 雨 雨 画 画

 **Dialog 1**

A secretary is talking to the president of the company about his business trip.

ひしょ：社長（しゃちょう）。月曜日（げつようび）はホンコンですね。

社長　：ええ。

ひしょ：ホテルは水曜（すいよう）日（び）まで<u>よやくしておきました</u>。

社長　：ああ、ありがとう。

Guess and Try 1

What does the underlined part in the above dialog mean? 8

 **Dialog 2**

Makoto Takeshita and Ben Lee have just finished eating at a restaurant and they are about to leave.

竹下（たけした）：じゃあ、行きましょうか。

リー　：ええ。(Looking for his wallet.) あっ、さいふがない。

竹下　：忘（わす）れたんですか。

リー　：ええ。たぶんうちにあると思（おも）います。

竹下　：いいですよ。ぼくがはらっておきます。

リー　：すみません。

Guess and Try 2

Why did Mr. Takeshita say はらっておきます rather than はらいます in Dialog 2? 8

Guess and Try 3

Rephrase some parts in the following sentences using おく. 8

1. 映画がはじまりますよ。

　—じゃあ、ポップコーンを作りますよ。

2. 来年けっこんします。ですから、お金をためます。

3. 今晩たいふうが来ます。ですから、食べものを買います。

4. もう四月ですから、このコートはしまいます。

　—ええ、しまった方がいいですね。

5. このぎゅうにゅうはもう古いですから、すてますね。

　—ああ、どうも。

6. 私の電話ばんごうは 632-7400 です。

　—ああ、どうも。メモします。

🗣 Drill: Formation

書く　→　書いておきます

1. はらう
2. 社長に話す
3. ホテルをよやくする
4. ぎゅうにゅうを買う
5. ごみをすてる
6. ようふくをしまう
7. お金をためる
8. たん語を勉強する

🚩 Task 1: Classroom Discussion

Discuss what must be done before the following events.

1. 日本に行く
2. うちでパーティーをする
3. たいふうが来る

For example:

A　：日本に行く前に何をしておきますか。

B　：パスポートをとっておきます。それから、小さいじしょを買っておきます。それから、…

🚩 Task 2: Classroom Activity

Working in small groups, list 5 things you have to do as a preparation for some event. Each group takes turn to present the list and let other groups guess the event they are preparing for.

📖 Short Reading

　来年私は卒業します。卒業して、銀行に就職するつもりです。就職する前に、海外旅行をしておきたいと思います。まだ、ヨーロッパには行ったことがありませんから、ヨーロッパに行きたいと思います。今、アルバイトをして、お金をためています。それから、卒業する前に運転免許をとっておきたいと思います。

(就職する *to get a job,* 海外 *abroad; overseas,* ヨーロッパ *Europe,* 運転免許をとる *to get a driving license*)

✏ Writing

Write what you want to do before you graduate.

かびんがおいてあります Interior Decoration

Notes Relating to This Lesson	
Grammar and Usage	**Culture**
1 Transitive and intransitive verbs . . . . 74 9 ～ある 77	B うきよえ 78

Basic Vocabulary and Kanji

けんきゅ˥うしつ	研究室	*n. university faculty's office, laboratory*
え˥	絵	*n. picture, painting, drawing, illustration*
かびん	花瓶	*n. vase*
にんぎょう	人形	*n. doll*
かべ	壁	*n. wall*
ゆか	床	*n. floor*
てんじょう	天井	*n. ceiling*
おく	*k*-**u** 置く・置かない・置き・置いて	*v. to put*
はる	*r*-**u** 貼る・貼らない・貼り・貼って	*v. to post, to paste* (かべにポスターを貼る *to put up a poster on the wall*)
あける	*e*-**ru** 開ける・開けない・開け・開けて	*v. to open* (ドアを開ける *to open the door*)
しめ˥る	*e*-**ru** 閉める・閉めない・閉め・閉めて	*v. to close* (ドアを閉める *to close the door*)
つけ˥る	*e*-**ru** つける・つけない・つけ・つけて	*v. to turn on* (テレビをつける *to turn on the TV*)
けす	*s*-**u** 消す・消さない・消し・消して	*v. to turn off* (テレビを消す *to turn off the TV*)
～ある	*r*-**u** ～ある・～ない・～あり・～あって	*aux. to have been ~ed* (ドアが開けてある *The door is left opened.*)

Newly introduced kanji:

絵(え)・開(あ)ける・閉(し)める

絵	⺊ 乡 幺 糸 糸 糸 糹 紒 紒 絵 絵 絵
開	丨 ⺁ 𠃍 戸 門 門 門 門 門 閂 開 開
閉	丨 ⺁ 𠃍 戸 門 門 門 門 門 閂 閉

Dialog

Mary Carter and Yoko Yamada try to pay a visit to Professor Brown in his office at the university.

カーター　：ブラウン先生(せんせい)のけんきゅうしつはここですね。

山田　：ええ、そうだと思(おも)います。

カーター　：ドアが開けてありますよ。

山田　：でも、先生はいらっしゃいませんね。

カーター　：ちょっと見て下(くだ)さい。あそこにいけばなのかきがおいてありますよ。

山田　：ええ。ブラウン先生は今(いま)いけばなを習(なら)っているんですよ。

(花器(かき) *flower bowl*)

Guess and Try

Explain the difference between the following two sentences. 9

1. ラジオがあります。

2. ラジオがつけてあります。

Note: When the verb is an intransitive verb, いる is used instead of ある, even if the item is inanimate. For example, つける is a transitive verb (父がラジオをつけた *My father turned on the radio.*) and つく is an intransitive verb (ラジオがついた *The radio was turned on.*) and the former is used with ある, as in ラジオがつけてあります, but the latter is used with いる, as in ラジオがついています。 1 9

Drill: Formation

ようふく・かける → ようふくがかけてあります

1. かびん・おく
2. でんき・つける
3. まど・開ける
4. ドア・閉める
5. 絵・かける
6. カレンダー・はる

Task 1

Describe the room.

まどが _____

ようふくが _____

カメラが _____

スーツケースが _____

犬（いぬ）が _____

Task 2

Describe your classroom.

Task 3

State the location of the calendar and clock in your room. For example:

カレンダーはベッドのよこのかべにはってあります。

Task 4: Pair Work

Describe how things are arranged in your living room. Are there any paintings or ornaments?

Living Room	
ソファー *sofa*	テーブル *table*
ピアノ *piano*	ステレオ *stereo*
テレビ *TV*	暖炉（だんろ） *fireplace*
棚（たな） *shelf*	いす *chair*
花瓶（かびん） *vase*	花（はな） *flower*
人形（にんぎょう） *doll*	絵（え） *painting /drawing*
写真（しゃしん） *photograph*	トロフィー *trophy*
電気（でんき） *lamp / light / electricity*	

Short Reading

うちの居間（いま）には東洋（とうよう）の飾（かざ）り物（もの）がたくさんあります。中国（ちゅうごく）の花瓶（かびん）が５つ置いてあります。日本の浮世絵（うきよえ）が２つ掛けてあります。日本人形（にんぎょう）もガラスのケースに入（い）れて、棚（たな）の上に置いてあります。

(居間（いま） *living room,* 東洋（とうよう） *the Orient; the East,* 飾（かざ）り物（もの） *ornament, decoration,* 浮世絵（うきよえ） *ukiyo-e (a kind of colored woodblock print)* ❷, ガラスのケース *glass case,* 棚（たな） *shelf*)

Writing

Describe your living room.

– Grammar and Usage –

1　Transitive and intransitive verbs

Transitive verbs are the verbs that take a direct object and intransitive verbs are those that do not. For example, the transitive verb "to raise" takes a direct object, as in *He raises the flag*, but the intransitive verb "to rise" does not take a direct object, as in *The flag rises*. Although they both express the situation where something goes up, the item that goes up is the direct object of the verb *to raise*, but it is the subject of the verb *to rise*. Japanese has many such transitive / intransitive pairs and the item that undergoes the action is marked by the particle を if the verb is a transitive verb, but by が if the verb is an intransitive verb.

Transitive Verbs	
	Examples
あげる to raise	父が旗をあげた。 *My father raised the flag.*
入れる to put, to insert	かばんにじしょを入れた。 *(I) put the dictionary in the bag.*
こわす to break	弟がカメラをこわした。 *My brother broke the camera.*
つける to turn on	妹がテレビをつけた。 *My sister turned on the TV.*
消す to turn off	兄がテレビを消した。 *My brother turned off the TV.*
開ける to open	母がドアを開けた。 *My mother opened the door.*
閉める to close	母がまどを閉めた。 *My mother closed the window.*
始める to begin	3月に仕事を始める。 *(I) will start my job in March.*

Intransitive Verbs	
	Examples
あがる to rise	ほら。旗があがったよ。 *Look! The flag has risen.*
入る to enter, to go into	部屋に入った。 *(I) went into the room.*
こわれる to break	風船がこわれた。 *The balloon broke.*
つく to turn on	テレビがついた。 *The TV turned on (by itself).*
消える to be turned off	停電でテレビが消えた。 *Because of the blackout, the TV turned off (by itself.)*
開く to open	自動ドアが開いた。 *The automatic door opened.*
閉まる to close	風でドアが閉まった。 *The door closed because of the wind.*
始まる to begin,	早く！クラスが始まったよ。 *Hurry! The class has started.*

2　Auxiliaries

Japanese has many auxiliaries (auxiliary verbs and auxiliary adjectives) that directly follow regular verbs and adjectives. Some follow a verb or an adjective in the stem form, creating a complex predicate, while others follow a verb in the te-form, expressing the background information, implications and the speaker's attitude. The following table lists some auxiliaries.

Examples of Auxiliaries That Follow a Verb or an Adjective in the Stem Form
V^{Stem} + おわる　*To finish doing ...*
Example: 1. この本は読みおわりました。 　　　　　　　*I finished reading this book.* 　　　　　2. すぐ食べおわります。 　　　　　　　*(I) will finish eating soon.*

Examples of Auxiliaries That Follow a Verb or an Adjective in the Stem Form
V^{Stem} + だす *To get started doing ...* Example: 勉強しだしました。 べんきょう *(He) started to study.*
V^{Stem} + すぎる *To do ... too much* Adj^{Stem} + すぎる *To be too ...* Example: 1. 飲みすぎた。 の *(I) drank too much.* 2. このシャツは大きすぎます。 おお *This shirt is too big*
V^{Stem} + にくい *To be hard to ...* Example: 魚は食べにくい。 さかな た *Fish is hard to eat.*
V^{Stem} + はじめる *to start ...* Example: 1. 本を読みはじめました。 ほん よ *(I) started reading a book.* 2. 雨がふりはじめました。 あめ *It started raining.*
V^{Stem} + まくる *To do ... eagerly* Example: マンガを読みまくりました。 よ *I kept reading comic books.*
V^{Stem} + やすい *To be easy to ...* Example: サンドィッチは食べやすい。 *Sandwiches are easy to eat.*
V^{Stem} + つづける *To continue doing ...* Example: 日本語を勉強しつづけてください。 ご べんきょう *Please continue studying Japanese.*

V^{Stem} : a verb in the stem form
Adj^{Stem} : an adjective in the stem form

Examples of Auxiliaries that Follow a Verb in the Te-form
V^{Te} + ある *To have been done ...* Example: すしが作ってあります。 つく *Sushi has been made.*

Examples of Auxiliaries that Follow a Verb in the Te-form
V^{Te} + あげる *To do ... for someone* Example: 手紙を翻訳してあげます。 てがみ ほんやく *I will translate the letter (for you).*
V^{Te} + おく *To do ... in advance for future convenience* Example: ビールを買っておきます。 か *I'll buy beer in advance.*
V^{Te} + いく *To go on ...* Example: これからはコンピューターが安くなっていきますよ。 *From now on, computers will get cheaper (and continue to be that way).*
V^{Te} + いる *To be doing ... , to do ... regularly, to have done ...* Example: 1. 今、ねています。 いま *(He) is sleeping now.* 2. 毎日、パンを食べています。 まいにち た *I eat bread every day.* 3. 私は結婚しています。 けっこん *I am married.*
V^{Te} + くる *To come to ... , to begin to ...* Example: 1. 今までいろいろなことをしてきました。 いま *Up to now I have been doing various things.* 2. なっとうが好きになってきました。 す *Now I have begun to like fermented soybeans.*
V^{Te} + くれる *To do ... for me* Example: 手紙を翻訳してくれませんか。 てがみ ほんやく *Could you translate the letter for me?*
V^{Te} + しまう *To complete doing ...* Example: カメラをこわしてしまいました。 *I broke the camera (and I regret it).*
V^{Te} + ほしい *To want someone to do ...* Example: ここに来てほしいです。 き *I want (him) to come here.*

Examples of Auxiliaries that Follow a Verb in the Te-form
V^{Te} + みる *To try doing ... , to do ... and see how it is*   Example: 1. なっとうを食べてみました。   *I tried eating fermented soybeans.*   2. これを買ってみます。   *I will buy this and see how it is.*
V^{Te} + もらう *To have someone do ... for me*   Example: 手紙を翻訳してもらいました。   *I had (someone) translated the letter.*

V^{Te} : a verb in the te-form

3 　〜にくい・〜やすい: To be difficult / easy to do 〜 [Toughness]

The auxiliary adjectives 〜にくい and 〜やすい follow a verb in the stem form, and express that the relevant action is difficult and easy, respectively. For example, 食べにくい means *to be difficult to eat* and 食べやすい means *to be easy to eat*.

(a)　このコンピューターは使いやすいです。
This computer is easy to use.

(b)　このペンは書きにくいです。
This pen is difficult to write with.

(c)　この漢字は書きにくいです。
This kanji character is difficult to write.

4 　〜すぎる: To do 〜 too much, to be too 〜 [Extremity]

The auxiliary verb 〜すぎる follows a verb or an adjective in the stem form and expresses that the extent of the relevant action or property is too great and undesirable.

(a)　ぎょうざを食べすぎました。
I ate too many dumplings.

(b)　このかばんは大きすぎます。
This bag is too big.

(c)　兄はまじめすぎます。
My brother is too serious.

The adjective いい (good) is irregular and it becomes よすぎる after being followed by this auxiliary.

(d)　兄は頭がよすぎます。
My brother is too smart.

5 　〜ずつ: Each / at a time [Distributive marker]

The suffix 〜ずつ follows a quantity phrase such as 二人, 二つ and 三枚, and shows that the item associated to the quantity phrase is equally distributed over the items expressed by some phrase in the sentence. For example, 学生が部屋を一つ使いました is most likely interpreted as *the students shared one room*. If we add ずつ, as in 学生が部屋を一つずつ使いました, it means *the students used one room each*.

(a)　毎日、漢字を三つずつ覚えます。
(I) memorize three kanji characters each day.

(b)　学生にかみを二枚ずつあげました。
(I) gave the students two sheets of paper each.

(c)　クラスに先生が二人ずついらっしゃいます。
There are two teachers in each class.

(d)　一人ずつ会います。
(I) will see one person at a time.

6 　〜しまう: To complete 〜ing [Completion]

The auxiliary verb しまう follows a verb in the te-form. Depending on the context, it expresses the speaker's happy feelings, as in (a) and (b), or his / her regrettable feeling, as in (c) and (e), or just emphasizes the completion of some action, as in (f) and (g):

(a)　もう宿題をしてしまいました。
I have already finished my homework (and I am happy about it).

(b)　借金を返してしまいました。
I have paid off my debt (and I am happy about it).

(c)　さいふをおとしてしまいました。
I lost my wallet (and I regret it).

(d)　姉とけんかをしてしまいました。
I had a fight with my sister (and I regret it).

(e) 先生のコンピューターをこわしてしまいました。
I broke my teacher's computer (and I regret it).

(f) 古いかぐをすててしまいました。
I threw away my old furniture.

(g) 朝ご飯を食べてしまいます。
I will finish eating my breakfast.

7 〜ほうがいい: It is better (not) to 〜 [Recommending]

To recommend someone to do something, use the verb in the past tense and add 方がいい after it. Past tense is used even though it is not about the past at all.

(a) 食べた方がいいです。
It is better to eat.

(b) ねた方がいいですよ。
It is better to sleep.

To recommend someone **not** to do something, use the plain present negative form:

(c) 食べない方がいいです。
It is better not to eat.

(d) ねない方がいいです。
It is better not to sleep.

8 〜おく: To do 〜 in advance for future convenience [Preparation]

The auxiliary verb おく follows a verb in the te-form and expresses that the action denoted by the verb is done for future convenience. The nature of the future convenience varies depending on the context: it may be to prepare for some upcoming event as in (a), to reduce one's future job as in (b), to save someone else's job as in (c), or to prevent any possible problems that may arise in the future as in (d).

(a) リムジンをよやくしておきました。
I reserved a limousine (since you will have to go to the airport).

(b) 今、宿題をしておきます。
I will do my homework now, (so that I do not have to do it later).

(c) 私がはらっておきます。
I will pay (now, so that you do not have to pay / we do not get into trouble).

(d) ゴミをすてておきます。
I will throw away the garbage (now, so that you do not have to do it later / so that it doesn't get smelly).

9 〜ある: To have been 〜ed [The state of things]

The verb ある means *to exist*. For example, ドアがあります means *There is a door*. If we add a transitive verb in the te-form before the verb ある, the sentence expresses how something exists. For example, ドアが開けてあります literally means that a door exists after being opened, which actually means *The door has been opened* or *The door is open.*

(a) メモが書いてあります。
A memo has been written (and it is there).

(b) 部屋がそうじしてあります。
The room has been cleaned.

The item that exists may be marked by the particle を rather than が. When marked by を, the emphasis is not on the presence of the item, but on what has been done to it.

(c) ドアを開けてあります。
(I) left the door opened. / (I) have opened the door.

(d) お金をためてあります。
(I) have saved money.

When the verb is an intransitive verb, ある must be replaced by いる, regardless of whether the item is animate or inanimate.

(e) ドアが開いています。
The door has opened. / The door is open.

– Culture –

❶ ぎょうざ: Chinese-style dumplings

ぎょうざ are Chinese-style dumplings, which have become very popular in Japan. Unlike authentic Chinese dumplings, ぎょうざ in Japan are often very spicy, containing garlic, ginger and chives. They are usually pan-fried and are served with a spicy sauce. One serving usually consists of five to seven dumplings.

❷ うきよえ: Ukiyo-e

浮世絵 are colored woodblock prints that became popular in the Edo era.

歌麿 (1753–1806) is one of the most famous artists who specialized in depicting female subjects. 写楽, by contrast, was best known for portraits of Kabuki actors. 北斎 (1760–1849) is famous for landscape subjects.

– Writing –

Ⓐ いとへん

糸	いとへん *thread, tie* Example: 終わる *to end*, 結婚 *marriage*, 絵 *drawing*, ～級 *level ~*, 高級 *high class*

– Kanji List –

重い・入れる・動く・持つ・物・動物・食べ物・苦しい・始める・終わる・～個・竹下・待つ・忘れる・映画・絵・開ける・閉める

重 おも-い・ジュウ *heavy, important*	一 ニ 午 午 盲 盲 重 重 重　　[9]
	Example: 重い *heavy*
入 はい-る・い-れる・ニュウ *enter, put in*	ノ 入　　[2]
	Example: 入る *to enter*, 入れる *to put in*
動 うご-く・ドウ *move*	一 ニ 午 午 盲 盲 重 重 重 動 動　　[11]
	Example: 動く *to move*
持 も-つ・ジ *hold*	一 十 扌 扌 扩 扩 拦 持 持　　[9]
	Example: 持つ *to hold*
物 もの・ブツ・モツ *thing*	ノ ニ 牛 牛 牜 牞 物 物　　[8]
	Example: 物 *thing*, 動物 *animal*, 食べ物 *food*, 飲み物 *beverage*
食 た-べる・ショク *eat*	ノ 人 人 今 今 食 食 食 食　　[9]
	Example: 食べ物 *food*, 食べる *to eat*, 食事 *meal*, *dining*
苦 くる-しい・にが-い・ク *painful, bitter*	一 十 サ 世 节 苦 苦 苦　　[8]
	Example: 苦しい *painful*, 苦手だ *not good at*
始 はじ-める・はじ-まる・シ *begin, start*	く 女 女 如 如 始 始 始　　[8]
	Example: 始まる *to begin*, 始める *to begin*
終 お-わる・お-える・シュウ *end*	く 幺 幺 幺 弁 糸 糸 終 終 終 終　　[11]
	Example: 終わる *to end*

個 コ individual	ノ イ 们 们 佃 佃 佃 個 個 個 [10]
	Example: 3 個 *three pieces of medium-sized inanimate items*
竹 たけ・チク bamboo	ノ ／ ケ ヤ ケ 竹 [6]
	Example: 竹下 *Mr./Ms. Takeshita (surname)*
下 した・さ-がる・くだ-・る・カ・ゲ under, down	一 丁 下 [3]
	Example: 下 *under,* 竹下 *Mr./Ms. Takeshita (surname)*
待 ま-つ・タイ wait	ノ ク 彳 行 彳 社 往 待 待 [9]
	Example: 待つ *to wait*
忘 わす-れる・ボウ forget	' 亠 亡 亡 亡 忘 忘 [7]
	Example: 忘れる *to forget*
映 うつ-る・うつ-す・エイ reflect	丨 冂 日 日 日' 日日 映 映 映 [9]
	Example: 映画 *movie,* 映画かん *movie theater*
画 ガ・カク picture	一 丆 币 币 甬 西 画 画 [8]
	Example: 映画 *movie*
絵 え・カイ picture	' 纟 纟 纟 纟 糸 糹 紒 絵 絵 絵 絵 [12]
	Example: 絵 *picture*
開 あ-く・ひら-く・あ-ける・カイ open	丨 冂 冂 冂 冂 門 門 門 門 閂 開 開 [12]
	Example: 開く *to open,* 開ける *to open*

| 閉
し-まる・し-める・と-じる・ヘイ
close | 丨 冂 冂 冂 冂 門 門 門 門 閂 閉 閉 [11] |
| | Example: 閉まる *to close,* 閉める *to close* |

– Review –

Q1. *Fill in the blanks and complete the sentences.*

1. _____ を忘れました。

2. _____ をしまいます。

3. 古い _____ をすてました。

4. _____ をためました。

Q2. *Write the readings of the following kanji phrases and state what is common among the members of each set.*

1. 動く   働く
2. 開く   開ける   聞く   時間
3. 映画   明るい   暗い
4. 絵   会う   会社   社会学

Q3. *Fill in the blanks with some of the items in the box. You will have to conjugate them appropriately.*

1. ああ、苦しい。ちょっと、食べ_____。

2. このペンはいいですね。とても書き_____。

3. レポートはもう書き_____。5時間かかりました。

4. 私のコンピューターは古いですから、とても使い_____。

5. 去年日本語を勉強し_____。

6. 見て下さい。あそこに絵がかけて _____

_____ よ。きれいですね。

7. ホテルはもうよやくして_____。

8. 先生のコンピューターをこわして _____

_____。

- ある・- おく・- おわる・- しまう・- すぎる・
- にくい・- はじめる・- やすい

Q4. *Explain the difference between the two sentences in each pair.*

1. A. まどを開けました。
   B. まどを開けておきました。

2. A. まどを開けました。
   B. まどが開けてあります。

3. A. 早_{はや}くねて下さい。
   B. 早くねた方がいいですよ。

4. A. 子供_{こども}たちが 1 万円_{まんえん}ずつもらいました。
   B. 子供たちが 1 万円もらいました。

Tips and Additional Knowledge: The New Prefix, ちょう

The interesting prefix, 超 (ちょう), was invented by a young Japanese in the 1990's. It means *super* as in *supernatural* or *extremely*, and is normally added before an adjective.

(a) 超 (ちょう) きれい *extremely beautiful*
(b) 超おもしろい *extremely funny / interesting*
(c) 超きたない *extremely dirty*
(d) 超まじめ *extremely serious*

You can use this prefix only with close friends in an informal situation, for example, このマンガは 超 (ちょう) おもしろい *This comic book is super funny*. Do not use it in a polite / neutral context!

CHAPTER TWENTY
Giving and Receiving

私がつれていってあげますよ Giving and Helping

Notes Relating to This Lesson	
Grammar and Usage	
[1] To give 90	[4] ～ちゃん 91
[2] つれる 91	[5] ～に 92
[3] Auxiliaries that mean to give or receive 91	

📖 Basic Vocabulary and Kanji

か¯し・おか¯し	菓子・お菓子	*n. sweets, confectionery*
はな¯・おはな	花・お花	*n. flower*
あげる	*e-ru* あげる・あげない・あげ・上げて	*v. to give* [1]
さしあげ¯る	*e-ru* 差しあ上る・差し上げない・差上げ・差し上げて	*v. to (modestly) give* [1]
やる	*r-u* やる・やらない・やり・やって	*v. to give something to one's subordinate* [1]
つれる	*e-ru* 連れる・連れない・連れ・連れて	*v. to take (someone) with* [2]
～あげる	*e-ru* ～あげる・～あげない・～あげ・～あげて	*aux. to do something for someone* (本を読んであげる *to read a book (for someone))* [3]
～さしあげる	*e-ru* ～差し上げる・～差し上げない・～差し上げ・～差し上げて	*aux. to (modestly) do something for someone* [3]
～やる	*r-u* ～やる・～やらない・～やり・～やって	*aux. to do something for one's subordinate* [3]
～ちゃん	～ちゃん	*the respectful title for young children* (よう子ちゃん) [4]

Newly introduced kanji:

花・友達 (friend)・よう子

花	一 ナ サ サ 艾 花 花
友	一 ナ 方 友
達	一 十 土 キ キ 去 去 壹 幸 幸 達 達

💿 💬 Dialog 1

Yoshio Tanaka sees John Smith holding two boxes of sweets.

田中　：そのおかしはだれにあげるんですか。

スミス：友達にあげます。

田中　：じゃあ、そのおかしはだれにあげるんですか。

スミス：からての先生にさしあげます。

Guess and Try 1

Fill in the blank with an appropriate particle. [5]

私はスミスさん ＿＿＿＿ おかしをあげました。

Guess and Try 2

Choose the appropriate option(s) in the parentheses. [1]

1. 私は社長におかしを（あげました・さしあげました）。
2. 私はとなりの人におかしを（あげました・さしあげました）。
3. 私は父におかしを（あげました・さしあげました）。
4. 私はよう子ちゃんにおかしを（あげました・さしあげました）。
5. 私はよう子ちゃんのお母さんにおかしを（あげました・さしあげました）。
6. 父は社長におかしを（あげました・さしあげました）。
7. 犬におかしを（あげました・さしあげました・やりました）。

💿 💬 Dialog 2

John Smith appears to have some problem and Yoshio Tanaka is asking him what happened.

田中 ： どうしたんですか。

スミス ： パークさんのうちに行きたいんですが、ちょっと車がこわれてしまって。

田中 ： じゃあ、<u>ぼくの車でつれて行ってあげますよ</u>。

Guess and Try 3

Choose the appropriate option in the parentheses and state what the sentence means. ☐1

1. 犬を (つれて行きます・もって行きます)。
2. 花を (つれて行きます・もって行きます)。
3. スミスさんは私のうちにワインを (もって行きました・もって来ました)。

Guess and Try 4

Does the verb あげる in the underlined part in the dialog mean *to give*? ☐3

Guess and Try 5

Fill in the blanks. ☐3

1. よう子ちゃんにクッキーを _____ 。
   I will make some cookies for yoko.
2. 先生にもクッキーを _____ 。
   I will make some for our teacher, too.

🗣 Drill 1: Formation

弟 ⟶ 弟にあげます
先生 ⟶ 先生にさしあげます

1. 父
2. 社長
3. 友達
4. 友達のお母さん
5. よう子ちゃん
6. 田中くん

🗣 Drill 2: Formation

教える ⟶ 教えてあげます

1. 遊ぶ
2. 宿題をする
3. レストランにつれて行く
4. 車を買う

🗣 Drill 3: Formation

クッキーを作る ⟶ クッキーを作ってさしあげます

1. 電話ばんごうを書く
2. 花をもって行く
3. アパートを探す

📖 Task 1: Pair Work

Pretend that you will be staying with your Japanese friend's family for 3 months this summer. Tell your partner what gift you would bring for the following people.

1. 友達 (male)
2. 友達のお父さん
3. 友達のお母さん
4. 友達の妹さん

For example:

A ： 日本の友達には何をあげますか。
B ： 日本の友達にはＴシャツをあげます。

📖 Task 2: Pair Work

Suppose that a Japanese student is going to your country for a two-week visit for the very first time and you have agreed to show him around. Tell your partner what you would do for him. For example: ブロードウエーショーを見せてあげます。それから、…

📖 Task 3: Pair Work

Ask your partner whether he / she has any younger siblings, and if so, ask what he / she used to do for them. For example:

A ： Ｂさんは弟さんか妹さんがいますか。
B ： はい。妹が一人います。
A ： いいですね。小さい時に、どんなことをしてあげましたか。
B ： いっしょにゲームをしてあげました。それから、ごはんを作ってあげました。

📖 Short Reading

　昨日は敬老の日でした。私は祖母にネックレスを買ってあげました。姉は祖母にブラウスを買ってあげました。弟はお金がないので、何も買ってあげませんでしたが、祖母の肩をもんであげました。

(敬老の日 *Respect-for-the-Aged Day*, 肩 *shoulder*, もむ *to massage*)

✏️ Writing

Write about what you and your siblings usually do, or used to do, on your grandfather's or grandmother's birthday.

兄がくれました Being Given and Being Helped

Notes Relating to This Lesson

Grammar and Usage

1 To give 90	7 〜し 92
3 Auxiliaries that mean	
to give or receive 91	**Culture**
6 〜に 92	Ⓐ Congratulating gift . . 94

Basic Vocabulary and Kanji

おいわい	お祝い	n. celebration Ⓐ
てつだ￪う	*w-u* 手伝う・手伝わない・手伝い・手伝って	*v.* to assist, to help (宿題を手伝う *to assist (someone's) homework*)
くれる	*e-ru* くれる・くれない・くれ・くれて	*v. to give* 1
くださ￪る	*r-u* 〜下さる・〜下さらない・〜下さり・〜下さって	*v. to (kindly) give* 1
〜くれる	*e-ru* 〜くれる・〜くれない・〜くれ・〜くれて	*aux. to do something for me (us)* 3
〜くださる	*r-u* 〜くださる・〜くださらない・〜くださり・〜くださって	*aux. to (kindly) do something for me (us)* 3

Newly introduced kanji:

時計 (watch / clock) ・ 泣く (to cry)

計	` ＾ ＝ ≡ ≡ 言 言 言 計
泣	` ＝ シ シ 汁 汁 汁 泣

 **Dialog 1**

Yoshio Tanaka sees John Smith holding two neckties.

田中 ： そのネクタイはいいですね。

スミス： ええ、入学のおいわいに兄がくれたんです。

田中 ： そのネクタイもですか。

スミス： いいえ、これはからての先生が下さったんです。

Guess and Try 1

Choose the appropriate option in the parentheses. 1

1. 私は山田さんにおかしを (あげました・くれました)。
2. 山田さんは私におかしを (あげました・くれました)。
3. 山田さんは母におかしを (あげました・くれました)。
4. 山田さんは田中さんにおかしを (あげました・くれました)。
5. 父は母におかしを (あげました・くれました)。

Guess and Try 2

Choose the appropriate option in the parentheses. 1

1. 社長は私にチョコレートを (くれました・くださいました)。
2. 川口さんは私にチョコレートを (くれました・くださいました)。
3. よう子ちゃんは私にチョコレートを (くれました・くださいました)。
4. 父は私にチョコレートを (くれました・くださいました)。

Guess and Try 3

Fill in the blank.

たんじょうびのプレゼント ＿＿＿＿＿ 父が時計をくれました。 6

Ⓐ 🔊💬 **Dialog 2**

Mary Carter sees that a birthday cake has been placed on the table for her.

カーター ： あっ、大きいケーキ。だれが作ってくれたんですか。

山田 ： 私です。

カーター ： (Mary starts to cry.) 本当に山田さんはやさしいですね。いつも、日

本語を教えてくれるし、宿題も
てつだってくれるし。

山田 ： ちょっと、泣かないで下さいよ。

Guess and Try 4

Fill in the blanks. ③

1. その時計はいいですね。
— この時計は父が買って ＿＿＿＿＿＿＿。

2. このクッキーはおいしいですね。
— ええ。よう子さんのお母さんが作って
＿＿＿＿＿＿＿。

Guess and Try 5

Fill in the blanks and state what the sentence means.
⑦

パークさんは、あたまが ＿＿＿＿＿ し、スポーツ
が ＿＿＿＿＿＿ し、やさしいし、よく働きます。

🗣 Drill 1: Formation

兄 ➝ 兄がくれました
先生 ➝ 先生が下さいました

1. 父   2. 社長
3. 田中くん   4. 田中くんのお母さん
5. となりの方   6. よう子ちゃん

🗣 Drill 2: Formation

教える ➝ 教えてくれました

1. 話す   2. 遊ぶ
3. 見せる   4. おかしをもって来る
5. アパートを探す   6. ごはんを作る

🗣 Drill 3: Formation

教える ➝ 教えて下さいました

1. てがみを読む   2. 電話をかす
3. 話をきく   4. すしを作る
5. レストランにつれて行く

📲 Task 1: Group Work

Make a three-member group. Each of you takes an
item (for example, pen or pencil) and gives it to
another member in the same group so that every
member receives an item from someone. One of you
then announces what and to whom every member

has given. Return the item to the owner, and repeat
the activity with another member making the
announcement.

For example:

A ： B さんは C さんにえんぴつをあげました。
C さんは私にボールペンをくれました。私
は B さんにぼうしをあげました。

📲 Task 2: Group Work

Perform the above task, but pretend that one of you
is a teacher.

📲 Task 3: Pair Work

Talk about the people who are / were very nice to
you, stating what they do / did for you. You can talk
about your family members, roommates or friends.

For example:

A ： 私のルームメートはとてもやさしいです。
B ： ああ、そうですか。
A ： よく、ごはんをつくってくれます。
B ： 本当ですか。(いいですね。)

📲 Task 4: Pair Work

Write a thank you card for someone who is nice to
you in Japanese.

> お母さん
>   いつもおいしいものを作ってく
> れて、本当にありがとう。
>   ピーター

📖 Short Reading

　私の母はとても優しいです。小さい時、私は
食べ物の好き嫌いがありました。父や兄と同じ
ものを食べることができませんでした。それで、
母はいつも私に特別なものを作ってくれまし
た。父はよく甘やかしすぎだと言っていました。
でも、今は何でも食べられます。

(好き嫌い *likes and dislikes,* 特別な *special,*
甘やかす *to indulge; to spoil,* 何でも *anything*)

✏️ Writing

Write about someone who is / was very nice to you,
describing what he / she does / did for you.

おせいぼをいただきました　Gifts and Presents

Notes Relating to This Lesson	
Grammar and Usage	**Culture**
3 Auxiliaries that mean to give or receive... 91	B Seasonal gifts in Japan 94
8 To receive 92	
9 〜みる 92	

📖 Basic Vocabulary and Kanji

しんせき	親戚	*n. relative*
おじ・おじさん	叔父 / 伯父・叔父さん / 伯父さん	*n. uncle*
おば・おばさん	叔母 / 伯母・叔母さん / 伯母さん	*n. aunt*
おせいぼ	お歳暮	*n. year-end present* B
いただく	*k-u* 頂く・頂かない・頂き・頂いて	*v. to (modestly) receive* 8
なお¹す	*s-u* 直す・直さない・直し・直して	*v. to repair, to fix, to correct*
おくる	*r-u* 送る・送らない・送り・送って	*v. to send*
たの¹む	*m-u* 頼む・頼まない・頼み・頼んで	*v. to ask, to request* (兄に頼む *to ask my brother (to do something))*
〜もらう	*w-u* 〜もらう・〜もらわない・〜もらい・〜もらって	*aux. to have someone do ~* 3
〜いただく	*k-u* 〜頂く・〜頂かない・〜頂き・〜頂いて	*aux. to (modestly) have someone do ~* 3
〜みる	*i-ru* 〜みる・〜みない・〜み・〜みて	*aux. to try ~ing* 9

Newly introduced kanji:

<ruby>送<rt>おく</rt></ruby>る・<ruby>祖父<rt>そ ふ</rt></ruby> (grandfather)・<ruby>祖母<rt>そ ぼ</rt></ruby> (grandmother)

祖	` ラ ネ ネ 礻 祀 祀 袓 祖
送	` ⸯ ⸰ 关 关 关 送 送

🔊 💬 Dialog 1

Yoko Yamada is offering some cookies to Yoshio Tanaka.

田中　：　このクッキーはおいしいですね。

山田　：　ああ、それですか。それは、おじからもらったんです。

田中　：　これもですか。

山田　：　いいえ、それは、となりの<ruby>方<rt>かた</rt></ruby>から、おせいぼにいただいたんです。

Guess and Try 1

Choose the appropriate option in the parentheses. 8

1. これは祖父から (もらいました・いただきました)。

2. これは先生から (もらいました・いただきました)。

Guess and Try 2

Choose the appropriate option(s) in the parentheses. 10

私は祖母 (から・に) お<ruby>金<rt>かね</rt></ruby>をもらいました。

🔊 💬 Dialog 2

Jason Chen is telling Yoshio Tanaka that his bicycle broke down.

チェン：<ruby>昨日<rt>きのう</rt></ruby>じてん<ruby>車<rt>しゃ</rt></ruby>がこわれてしまったんです。

田中　：ああ、そうですか。この<ruby>間<rt>あいだ</rt></ruby>、私のもこわれて、兄になおしてもらいました。

チェン：ぼくのも、なおしてもらえませんか。

田中　：じゃあ、兄にたのんでみます。

Guess and Try 3

Fill in the blanks. ③

1. この宿題は難しいので、兄に教えて

＿＿＿＿＿＿＿＿＿＿＿ます。

2. この宿題は難しいので、先生に教えて

＿＿＿＿＿＿＿＿＿＿＿ます。

Guess and Try 4

Choose the appropriate option in the parentheses. ⑩

私は母 (に・から) 本を読んでもらいました。

Guess and Try 5

What does the underlined part in Dialog 2 mean? ⑨

🗣 Drill 1: Formation

兄 ⟶ 兄にもらいました

先生 ⟶ 先生にいただきました

1. 祖父　　　　　　2. 祖母
3. おじ　　　　　　4. おば
5. 社長　　　　　　6. 友達のおばさん
7. しんせきの人

🗣 Drill 2: Formation

漢字を教える ⟶ 漢字を教えてもらいました

1. てつだう　　　　2. 遊ぶ
3. うちに来る　　　4. 車をなおす
5. にんぎょうを買う

🗣 Drill 3: Formation

漢字を教える ⟶ 漢字を教えていただきました

1. てがみを送る　　　　2. 本をかす
3. おかしをもって来る　4. 話をきく

🏳 Task 1: Classroom Discussion

Discuss the custom of gift-giving in your country. Do you send gifts on Valentine's day, Christmas, Mother's day, Father's day, New Year's Day, etc.? If so, what do you send and to whom?

🏳 Task 2: Survey

Ask three of your classmates whether they received anything for their birthday this year.

For example:

A : 誕生日に何かもらいましたか。

B : はい、おじにコンピューターをもらいました。それから…

私	
さん	
さん	
さん	

📖 Short Reading

　日本人はよく夏と年末に贈り物をします。夏の贈り物はお中元と言います。年末の贈り物はお歳暮と言います。親戚や上司やお世話になった人に贈ります。デパートで買って、デパートの包装紙で包んでもらって、デパートで送ってもらいます。人気がある商品は石鹸や、お茶や、お菓子や、海苔などです。海苔や、お茶は軽いので、送料が安くて便利です。

(年末 the end of the year, 贈り物 present, 上司 one's superior (officer), 〜にお世話になる to be under the care of 〜, 贈る to give (a present), 包装紙 wrapping paper, 包む to wrap, 人気 popularity, 商品 merchandise, 石鹸 soap, 海苔 seaweed, 〜など etc, 軽い light-weight, 送料 postage)

✏ Writing

Write about the custom of gift-giving in your country.

すいせんじょう Study Abroad

Notes Relating to This Lesson			
Grammar and Usage			
11	～ので 93	13	Asking a favor
12	～のに 93		politely 94

📖 Basic Vocabulary and Kanji

すいせん じょう	推薦状	*n. recommendation letter*
しめきり	締め切り	*n. deadline*
ようし	用紙	*n. form, sheet*
じゅ⌐う しょ	住所	*n. address*
おねがい	お願い	*n. favor*
はじめ	始め・初め	*n. beginning*
おわり	終わり	*n. ending*
りゅうがく	留学	*n. study abroad*
ちょくせ つ	直接	*adv. directly*
～か	～課	*~ section, ~ division, Lesson ~*
～ので		*con. because ~ (日本人なので、日本語が話せます He can speak Japanese because he is Japanese.)* 11
～のに		*con. although ~ (日本人なのに、日本語が話せません Although he is Japanese, he cannot speak Japanese.)* 12

Newly introduced kanji:

住所 (じゅうしょ)

所	一 ㄱ ㄹ ㅋ 戸 戸 所 所 所
(てんわ)	

🔊 💬 Dialog

Paul Walker, a student in an American college, is asking his Japanese teacher to write a letter of recommendation for him.

ウォーカー ： 先生、じつは日本にりゅう学（がく）したいんですが。

先生 ： ああ、いいですね。

ウォーカー ： それで、一つ（ひと）おねがいがあるんです。

先生 ： はい。何でしょうか。

ウォーカー ： すいせんじょうを書いていただきたいんですが。

先生 ： ああ、いいですよ。

ウォーカー ： ああ、どうもありがとうございます。これが、ようしです。

先生 ： はい。

ウォーカー ： しめきりが来月のはじめ（らいげつ）なので、来週（らいしゅう）までにおねがいしたいんですが。

先生 ： はい。どこに送り（おく）ましょうか。

ウォーカー ： ちょくせつ、この大学のりゅう学生かに送っていただきたいんですが。

先生 ： はい。わかりました。

ウォーカー ： 住所はここに書いてあります。

先生 ： はい。じゃあ、ここに送っておきます。

ウォーカー ： おいそがしいところ、すみませんが、よろしくおねがいします。

Guess and Try 1

What do the following sentences mean? 13

1. 明日（あした）うちに来ていただきたいんですが。そして、母に会って（あ）いただきたいんですが。
2. 電話（でんわ）ばんごうを教えて（おし）いただけませんか。
3. すいせんじょうを書いていただけないでしょうか。

4. ここでタバコをすわないでいただきたいんで
   すが。

5. ここでタバコをすわないで下さい。

Guess and Try 2

What do the following sentences mean? ⑪ ⑫

1. よく勉強したので、100点をとりました。

2. よく勉強したのに、0点をとりました。

Guess and Try 3

Connect the two sentences in each set using ので or
のに. ⑪ ⑫

1. 安かったです。　たくさんの人が買いました。
2. 便利です。　たくさんの人が使います。
3. 便利です。　だれも使いません。
4. 日本人です。　すしがきらいです。

🗣 Drill 1: Formation

教えて ➝ 教えていただきたいんですが

1. 作って　　　　2. 話して
3. 読んで　　　　4. 見せて
5. しずかにして　6. きれいにして

🗣 Drill 2: Formation

うちに来て下さい ➝ うちに来ていただきた
いんですが

1. 名前を書いて下さい
2. 父に会って下さい
3. すいせんじょうを書いて下さい
4. 電話ばんごうを教えて下さい
5. カラオケをやめて下さい

🗂 Task: Skit

Using the dialog as a model, create a skit where a
student asks his / her teacher to write a letter of recommendation for him / her. Use the appropriate
intonation and gesture.

Study Abroad

留学 *study abroad*

留学生課 *international student office*

成績証明書 *transcript*

推薦状 *recommendation letter*

奨学金 *scholarship*

申請用紙 *application form*

旅費 *traveling expenses*

生活費 *living expenses*　授業料 *tuition*

ビザ *visa*　　　　　　パスポート *passport*

📖 Short Reading

　私は高校生の時、日本に一年留学した。
ホームステイをした。日本が本当に大好きだっ
た。食べ物も、ホストファミリーも、先生も、
友達も、大好きだった。ホストファミリーは
本当に親切だった。日本の先生には色々な
ことを教えていただいたり、助けていただい
たりした。友達にはよく一緒に遊んでもらっ
た。アメリカに帰る時はとても悲しかった。
昨日日本のホストファミリーに日本語で手紙
を書いた。自分で書いて、後で日本語の先生
に直していただいた。また、日本に留学したい。

　　　　　　　　ジョアナ・サルキン　大学生

(色々なこと *various things,* 助ける *to help; to
assist,* 〜たり、…たりする *do ~ and ..., for
example,* 悲しい *sad,* 自分 *oneself,* 後で *later*)

✏️ Writing

Write about your plans and ideas of studying
abroad.

– Grammar and Usage –

1 To give (あげる / くれる / さしあげる / くださる / やる)

あげる / くれる

The verbs あげる and くれる both mean *to give*. The choice between the two depends on how close the speaker is with the giver and recipient. The relative distance from the speaker is shown in the figure.

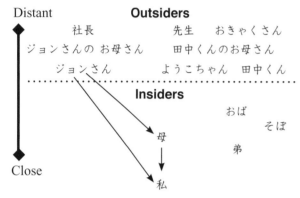

The verb くれる is used only when the recipient is the speaker's insider and the recipient is closer to the speaker than the giver. In all other contexts, あげる is used.

For example, in the following sentences, the recipients are the speaker's "insiders" (the speaker or the speaker's family members), which is graphically shown by the fact that the arrowheads in the figure are all in the insiders section. Furthermore, the recipients are closer to the speaker than the giver, which is shown by the fact that the arrows in the figure are all pointing downward.

(a) ジョンさんが私にチョコレートをくれました。

John gave me chocolate.

(b) ジョンさんが私の母にチョコレートをくれました。

John gave my mother chocolate.

(c) 母が私にチョコレートをくれました。

My mother gave me chocolate.

Sentence (d) is ungrammatical because the recipient is less close to the speaker than the giver although the recipient is the speaker's insider. Once くれました is replaced by あげました, as in (e), the sentence becomes grammatical.

(d) 私が母にチョコレートをくれました。
(✗)   (Ungrammatical)

(e) 私が母にチョコレートをあげました。

When the giving event takes place among the speaker's insiders, excluding the speaker himself, either あげる or くれる can be used. If くれる is used, it shows that the speaker is closer to the receiver than the giver. For example, unlike (f), (g) shows that the speaker feels closer to his brother than to his mother:

(f) 母が弟にチョコレートをあげました。
My mother gave my brother chocolate.

(g) 母が弟にチョコレートをくれました。
My mother gave my brother chocolate.

When the giving event takes place among outsiders, あげる is generally used.

(h) ジョンさんがマリーさんにチョコレートをあげました。
John gave Mary chocolate.

(i) ジョンさんがジョンさんのお母さんにチョコレートをあげました。
John gave his mother chocolate.

In the same context, くれる may be used if the recipient is someone to whom the speaker feels very close. For example, if the speaker feels very close to Mary, as if she were his own younger sister, he would use sentence (j) instead of sentence (h):

(j) ジョンさんがマリーさんにチョコレートをくれました。
John gave Mary chocolate.

さしあげる / くださる

The verb あげる *to give* must be replaced by さしあげる *to modestly give* when the receiver is socially superior to, and / or distant from the giver:

(k) 私は先生にチョコレートをさしあげました。

I gave the teacher chocolate.

(l) 父は社長にチョコレートをさしあげました。
My father gave the (company) president chocolate.

The verb くれる *to give* must be replaced by くださる *to kindly give* when the giver is socially superior to, and / or distant from the receiver.

(m) 先生は私にチョコレートをくださいました。

The teacher gave me chocolate.

(n) 社長は父にチョコレートをくださいました。

The (company) president gave my father chocolate.

Remember to use さしあげる or くださる when you feel like giving or receiving the item very respectfully, using two hands and slightly bowing, for example.

Note that the verb くださる conjugates as a **u**-verb whose root ends in the consonant **r**, but its –ます form is くださいます, not くださります.

やる

The verb あげる *to give* can be optionally replaced by やる *to give* when the receiver is socially lower than the giver. For example, when giving something to your pet, you may use やる instead of あげる.

私は犬_{いぬ}にステーキをやりました。

I gave a steak to my dog.

2 　つれる: To take or bring someone

When saying "to take or bring some person or some animal to somewhere", combine the verb つれる in the te-form and either 行_いく or 来_くる, depending on the location, as in つれて行く and つれて来る:

(a) 山田_{やまだ}さんは私のうちに 妹_{いもうと} さんをつれて来_きました。

Ms. Yamada brought her sister to my house.

(b) 山田さんはとしょかんに妹さんをつれて行_いきました。

Ms. Yamada took her sister to the library.

(c) こうえんに犬_{いぬ}をつれて行きます。

I will bring my dog to the park.

For inanimate items such as 花_{はな} and ワイン, use the verb もつ instead of つれる:

(d) 花をもって行きます。

I will bring flowers.

(e) ワインをもって来ました。

(He) brought wine.

3 Auxiliaries that mean "to give" or "to receive" (～あげる / ～くれる / ～もらう)

When one does something for someone else, you can add the verb あげる, くれる or もらう after the verb in the te-form. This clarifies who is offering help and who is receiving it. For example, sentence (a) literally means that *I read a book and I gave the service of reading to my brother*, which actually means that *I read a book to my brother.*

(a) 私は 弟_{おとうと} に 本_{ほん} を読_よんであげました。

I read a book to my brother.

(b) 兄は私に本を読んでくれました。

My brother read a book to me.

(c) 私は兄に本を読んでもらいました。

I had my brother read a book to me. /
My brother read a book to me.

Depending on the social status and the distance of the relevant parties, さしあげる、くださる、いただく or やる can be used.

(d) 私はとなりのおばあさんに本を読んでさしあげました。

I read a book to the old lady next door.

(e) 先生は私に本を読んでくださいました。

The teacher read a book to me.

(f) 私は先生に本を読んでいただきました。

The teacher read a book to me.

(g) 私は犬_{いぬ}にセーターを作_{つく}ってやりました。

I made a sweater for my dog.

4 　～ちゃん [Respectful title for young children]

Beside ～さん, there are several respectful titles that follow a person's name. ～ちゃん is the respectful title that can be used for both boys and girls. Young boys and young girls are commonly addressed by their first names followed by ～ちゃん, as in 健_{けん}ちゃん and よう子_こちゃん. In an extremely informal and very friendly context, some people use ～ちゃん for addressing adults, especially for their childhood friends.

5 〜に: To [Target (recipient)]

The particle 〜に can mark the recipient in a giving event.

(a) 私は兄に本をあげました。
I gave a book to my brother.

(b) 兄は私にコンピューターをくれました。
My brother gave me a computer.

(c) 犬にステーキをやりました。
I gave a steak to the dog.

6 〜に: For [Target (occasion)]

The particle に can specify the purpose or the occasion of an event.

(a) たんじょうびのプレゼントに時計をあげました。
I gave a watch (to him) for his birthday present.

(b) 入学のおいわいに父が時計をくれました。
My father gave me a watch as a congratulation gift for my admission to the school.

(c) 朝ごはんにみそしるを作りました。
I made miso soup for breakfast.

7 〜し: [Emphatic conjunction]

For listing actions and properties emphatically, use verbs and adjectives in the plain form and add し after each of them. The last verb or adjective may be in the regular sentence-final form.

(a) 宿題はしたし、明日のクイズの準備もしたし、もうねてもいいですね。
I not only have done my homework, but also have prepared for tomorrow's quiz, so I can go to bed now, right?

(b) 山田さんはきれいだし、頭もいい。
Ms. Yamada is pretty, and what's more she is smart.

(c) お金はないし、借金はあるし、困りました。
I don't have money and I am in debt, so I am in trouble.

8 To receive (もらう / いただく)

The verb もらう means *to receive*. Interestingly, the source of receiving is marked either by the particle 〜から or 〜に. The receiver (the subject of もらう) must be closer to the speaker than to the giver.

(a) 私は父にコンピューターをもらいました。
I received a computer from my father.

(b) 私は父からコンピューターをもらいました。
I received a computer from my father.

When the speaker or the speaker's insider receives something from his / her superior, もらう must be replaced by いただく.

(c) 私は先生からじしょをいただきました。
I received a dictionary from my teacher.

(d) 弟は先生からじしょをいただきました。
My younger brother received a dictionary from his teacher.

9 〜みる: To try 〜 ing [Trial]

The auxiliary verb みる follows a verb in the te-form, and shows that the action is done just as a trial.

(a) なっとうを食べてみました。
I tried fermented soybeans.

(b) 兄にたのんでみます。
I'll try asking my brother.

10 〜に: From [Target (source)]

The particle 〜に marks the source of the event when used with certain verbs such as もらう *to receive*, いただく *to receive*, きく *to hear* and かりる *to borrow*.

(a) 私は父にお金をもらいました。
I received some money from my father.

(b) 私は先生に本をいただきました。
I received a book from the teacher.

(c) 私は兄にその話をききました。
I heard about that story from my brother.

(d) 私は母にお金をかりました。
I borrowed some money from my mother.

The particle に can be replaced by the particle から in all of the above sentences. However, when the verbs もらう and いただく are used as auxiliary verbs, the particle に may not be replaced by から in most cases.

(e) 私は兄に本を読んでもらいました。
I had my brother read a book for me.

(f) 私は兄から本を読んでもらいました。
(✖)   (Ungrammatical)

11 ～ので: Because ～
[Reasons and causes]

The clause connective ～ので connects two sentences that are in a cause-and-effect relationship. The predicate that precedes ～ので is usually in the plain form.

(a) よく勉強したので、100点をとりました。
I studied very hard and so, I got 100 points.

(b) 高かったので、買いませんでした。
(It) was expensive and so, I did not buy (it).

Sentences (a) and (b) are equivalent to sentences (c) and (d):

(c) よく勉強しましたから、100点をとりました。

(d) 高かったですから、買いませんでした。

Although ～ので and ～から can be interchangeably used most of the time, the cause-and-effect relationship expressed by ～ので sounds more concrete, valid, or self-evident than the one expressed by ～から.

The sound だ at the end of the copula and na-type adjective changes into な when it precedes ～ので.

(e) 便利なので、たくさんの人が使いました。
It is convenient; therefore, many people used it.

(f) 兄はこの大学の学生なので、としょかんが使えます。
My brother is a student of this university; therefore, he can use the library.

12 ～のに: Although ～
[Conflict and contradiction]

The clause connective ～のに relates two facts that are contradicting or in conflict. The verbs and adjectives that precede ～のに are usually in the plain form.

(a) 兄は明日テストがあるのに、今晩パーティーに行きます。
Although my brother has a test tomorrow, he is going to the party tonight.

(b) 兄は明日テストがあるのに、今晩仕事をしなくてはいけません。
Although my brother has a test tomorrow, he has to work tonight.

(c) 私は明日テストがあるのに、今晩仕事をしなくてはいけないんです。
Although I have a test tomorrow, I have to work tonight.

The above sentences can be rephrased using the clause connective ～が:

(d) 兄は明日テストがありますが、今晩パーティーに行きます。

(e) 兄は明日テストがありますが、今晩仕事をしなくてはいけません。

(f) 私は明日テストがありますが、今晩し仕事をしなくてはいけません。

～のに cannot be used as widely as ～が can. First, ～が can be used for the speaker's controllable act, intention, suggestion or request, but ～のに cannot.

(g) 私は明日テストがありますが、今晩パーティーに行きます。
Although I have a test tomorrow, I am going to the party tonight.

(h) 私は明日テストがあるのに、今晩パーティーに行きます。   (✖)
(Ungrammatical)

(i) あまりおいしくありませんが、食べて下さい。
It is not very delicious, but please eat.

(j) あまりおいしくないのに、食べて下さい。
(✖)   (Ungrammatical)

Second, ～が can relate two situations that are in contrast, but ～のに cannot.

(k) 日本人は魚が好きですが、アメリカ人は好きじゃありません。
The Japanese like fish, but Americans do not.

(l) 日本人は魚が好きなのに、アメリカ人は
好きじゃありません。（✗）
(Ungrammatical)

だ at the end of the na-type adjective and copula changes into な when it precedes 〜のに.

(m) 便利<u>な</u>のに、だれも使いません。

It is convenient, but no one uses it.

(n) 兄はこの大学の学生<u>な</u>のに、としょかんが使えません。

My brother is a student of this university, but he cannot use the library.

13 Asking a favor politely (書いていただけないでしょうか, etc.)

For asking a favor of others very politely, phrases such as 〜いただく, 〜もらう, 〜くださる and 〜くれる are commonly used. The following phrases all mean, *Would you write a letter?*

(a) てがみを書いていただけないでしょうか。

(b) てがみを書いていただけませんか。

(c) てがみを書いていただきたいんですが。

(d) てがみを書いてもらえませんか。

(e) てがみを書いてくださいませんか。

(f) てがみを書いてくれませんか。

(g) てがみを書いてください。

It is usually considered to be more polite if the sentence contains a honorific form and a negative question form.

– Culture –

Ⓐ Congratulating gift (おいわい)

The Japanese typically send a gift of money to their family, relatives and friends on special occasions such as admission to a school, graduation, wedding and childbirth. For example, when one is admitted to a college, he / she may receive a gift of money, enclosed in a special envelope (like the one shown here), from each of his uncles, aunts and grandparents.

Ⓑ Seasonal gifts in Japan (おちゅうげん・おせいぼ)

There are two major gift-giving seasons in Japan: one is in summer and the other is at the end of the year. The summer gift is called お中元, and the end-of-year gift is called お歳暮. Popular お中元 and お歳暮 gifts are foods and beverages such as pasta, cheese, seaweed, dried shiitake mushrooms, cooking oil, canned foods, beer, sake, cookies and cake, and daily-life items such as soap and towels. They usually purchase the gifts at a well-known department store, have them wrapped with the store's wrapping paper, and then have them

sent directly to their relatives, superiors and friends by the store. So, the お歳暮 or お中元 corner of the department stores is very crowded with many people with address books, during these seasons.

– Kanji List –

花・友達・よう子・時計・泣く・送る・祖父・祖母・住所

花 はな・カ *flower*	一 ナ サ サ 艾 芋 花花 [7]
	Example: 花 *flower*, 花びん *vase*
友 とも・ユウ *friend*	一 ナ 方 友 [4]
	Example: 友達 *friend*
達 タツ・タチ・ダチ *attain, plural suffix*	一 十 土 キ 去 幸 幸 幸 幸 達達 [12]
	Example: 友達 *friend*

子 こ・シ child	⁊了子 [3]
	Example: 子供 *child*, よう子 *Yoko (a person's given name)*

時 とき・と・ジ time, hour	一冂日日日旷旷昨晴時時 [10]
	Example: 時計 *clock, watch*, 時 *time*, 時間 *time, hour*

計 はか-る・ケイ measure	`一⁀言言言言計 [9]
	Example: 時計 *clock, watch*

泣 な-く・キュウ weep, cry	`冫氵氵汁汁泣泣 [8]
	Example: 泣く *to cry, to weep*

送 おく-る・ソウ send	`⁀丷⁝关关送送 [9]
	Example: 送る *to send*

祖 ソ ancestor	`⁀ネネ礻礻礻初初 [9]
	Example: 祖父 *one's grandfather*, 祖母 *one's grandmother*

父 ちち・フ father	⁄ハグ父 [4]
	Example: 祖父 *one's grandfather*, 父 *one's father*

母 はは・ボ mother	乚𠃌𠃌母母 [5]
	Example: 祖母 *one's grandmother*, 母 *one's mother*

住 す-む・ジュウ dwell, inhabit	⁄イ仁仁仁住住 [7]
	Example: 住む *to live*, 住所 *address*

所 ところ・ショ・ジョ place, that which	一⁊⁊厂戸戸所所 [8]
	Example: 所 *place*, 住所 *address*

– Review –

Q1. *Choose the appropriate option in the parentheses.*

1. 大学に(卒業・入学・しゅうしょく)しました。
2. 社長におかしや、お花や、(しけん・お酒)をさしあげます。
3. おじさんや、おばさんや、(先生・おじいさん)をしんせきと言います。

Q2. *Write the readings of the following kanji phrases and state what is common among the members of each set.*

1. 花・薬・苦しい
2. 酒・泳ぐ・海・湖・泣く・漢字・洗う
3. 入学・大学・学校・学生・りゅう学・文学

Q3. *Look at each picture and describe what happened.*

1. 母 → 山田さんのお母さん　　2. 私 → 姉

3. 私 → 社長　　4. 社長 → 私

5. 母 ➡ 私　　6. メーガンさん ➡ 私

Q4. *Fill in the blanks.*

1. その時計（とけい）はいいですね。

 — ええ、入学（にゅうがく）のおいわいに父が＿＿＿＿＿
 んです。

2. そのペンはどうしたんですか。

 — 入学のおいわいにようこさんのお母さん
 が＿＿＿＿＿＿＿＿んです。

3. 昨日（きのう）は母のたんじょうびだったので、ネック
 レスを＿＿＿＿＿＿＿＿ました。

4. クリスマスに何かもらいましたか。

 — ええ、社長（しゃちょう）からチョコレートを
 ＿＿＿＿＿＿＿＿ました。

5. そのようふくはいいですね。

 — ああ、どうも。母が作って＿＿＿＿＿＿＿
 んです。

6. 明日（あした）、山田さんのたんじょうびですよ。何か
 しましょうか。

 — じゃあ、レストランにつれていって
 ＿＿＿＿＿ ＿＿＿＿＿＿ませんか。

7. 先生がすいせんじょうを書いて＿＿＿＿＿＿
 ました。

8. 先生にすいせんじょうを書いて
 ＿＿＿＿＿＿＿＿＿ました。

9. 先生にお花をもっていって＿＿＿＿＿＿ま
 しょう。

10. 妹（いもうと）を動物（どうぶつ）えんにつれていって＿＿＿＿＿
 ました。

Q5. *What would you say in Japanese in the following
 situations?*

1. You want to ask your teacher to write a letter of
 recommendation for you by next week.

2. Your neighbor is making a lot of noise at night
 and you couldn't sleep. You want to ask him to
 stop making noise.

3. Your car has broken down. You want to ask your
 friend to help fix it.

Q6. *Make a sentence by connecting the two sentences
 in each set, using* ので *or* のに.

1. 明日（あした）しけんがあります・勉強（べんきょう）します

2. 天気（てんき）がいいです・こうえんに行きます

3. 雨（あめ）がふっていました・兄はじてん車（しゃ）で大学
 に行きました

Tips and Additional Knowledge:
年末（ねんまつ）
The End of a Year

Like in many countries, the end of a year is a
big holiday season in Japan. Most Japanese
companies begin or have their 1- to 2-week
holidays on or around December 29th. On the
last business day of the year, employees will
usually clean the work place together. They
will then gather at a restaurant to have an end-
of-year party called 忘年会（ぼうねんかい）, and tell each
other 今年（ことし）もお世話（せわ）になりました *Thank
you for your help throughout this year*. When
they leave the party, they will say よいお年（とし）を
Best wishes for the coming year! to each other.

New Year's Eve is the most important family
time throughout the nation. Family members,
relatives, neighbors and friends will get
together to have a great feast, while watching a
national music show on TV. They often eat 年（とし）
越（こ）しそば *end-of-year buckwheat noodles*.

CHAPTER TWENTY-ONE
Describing Changes

肉を食べないようにしています **Effort for a Better Life**

Notes Relating to This Lesson	
Grammar and Usage	
1 ～ように 106	3 ～ないで 106
2 ～ようにする ... 106	

📖 Basic Vocabulary and Kanji

ど￢りょく	努力	n. effort
たま￢ご	卵・玉子	n. egg
けんこう	健康	n. health
かいだん	階段	n. stairs, stairway
じぶん	自分	n. self (自分で by oneself)
イーメ￢ール	(cf. E デ メール・電子メール)	n. electric mail
せつやくする	irr. 節約する	v. to save, to economize
うんどうする	irr. 運動する	v. to do exercise
はこぶ	b-u 運ぶ・運ばない・運び・運んで	v. to transport, to carry
こぼ￢す	s-u こぼす・こぼさない・こぼし・こぼして	v. to spill
できるだけ		adv. as much as one can
そして		con. and then, and (cf. それから)
しか￢し		con. but (cf. でも)

Newly introduced kanji:

自分・自転車 (bicycle) 運動する・運ぶ
<small>じ ぶん じ てんしゃ うんどう はこ</small>

自 ′ イ 冂 白 自 自

運 ′ ⼾ ⼾ ⼾ ⾔ ⾔ ⾔ 亘 軍 軍 運 運

🔊 💬 Dialog 1

John Smith is asking Yoko Yamada whether she does anything good for her health.

スミス：山田さんは何かけんこうにいいことを
<small>なに</small>
　　　　していますか。

山田　：①かぜをひかないように、毎日オレン
<small>まいにち</small>
　　　　ジジュースを飲んでいます。スミスさ
<small>の</small>
　　　　んは。

スミス：②ぼくは、肉や、チーズや、たまごを
<small>にく</small>
　　　　できるだけ食べないようにしていま
　　　　す。それから、③エレベーターを使わ
<small>つか</small>
　　　　ないで、かいだんを使うようにしてい
　　　　ます。

山田　：ああ、そうですか。

Guess and Try 1

What do the underlined sentence ① in the above dialog and the following sentences mean? 1

1. 先生、ちょっとわかりません。わかるよう
<small>い</small>
　 に言って下さい。

2. こぼさないように運んで下さいよ。

Guess and Try 2

What do the underlined sentence ② in the above dialog and the following sentences mean? 2

1. お金をせつやくするようにしています。そ
<small>かね</small>
　 して、使わない物は買わないようにしてい
<small>もの か</small>
　 ます。

2. 自分のことは自分でするようにしました。
　 しかし、りょうりはできませんでした。

Guess and Try 3

What do the underlined sentence ③ in the dialog and the following sentences mean? ③

1. 電話を使わないで、イーメールを使うようにしています。

2. 朝ごはんを食べないで、学校に行きました。

Guess and Try 4 (Optional)

State the difference between the following two sentences. ②

1. まどを開けるようにします。
2. まどが開くようにします。

🗣 Drill 1: Formation

食べる ⟶ できるだけ食べるようにしています

1. 運動する
2. かいだんを使う
3. 自転車に乗る
4. イーメールを使う
5. 自分で宿題をする
6. 安い物を買う
7. 電気をせつやくする

🗣 Drill 2: Formation

食べない ⟶ できるだけ食べないようにしています

1. 遊ばない
2. クラスを休まない
3. 薬をのまない
4. コンピューターゲームをしない

🏳 Task 1: Survey

Ask three of your classmates about the following. Use the dialog as a model.

1. 何かけんこうにいいことをしているか。
2. 何かお金のせつやくをしているか。(to save money)
3. 何か時間のせつやくをしているか。(to save time)

	私	さん	さん	さん
1				
2				
3				

🏳 Task 2: Role Play / Skit

A: Your employee has disappointed you many times. Complain to him / her.

B: Your boss complains about your working attitude. Apologize to him / her and tell him / her what effort you think you can make. For example, これからは (from now on) おくれないようにします.

📖 Short Reading

　私はコンピューターのプログラマーです。いつも座ってばかりいます。よく、首と肩が痛くなります。ときどき鍼や指圧をしてもらいます。私の事務所は5階ですが、エレベーターには乗らないようにしています。いつも階段を使うようにしています。車はできるだけ遠い所に駐車します。そして、できるだけ歩くようにしています。

(首 *neck*, 肩 *shoulder*, 鍼 *acupuncture*, 指圧 *shiatsu; acupressure*, 事務所 *office*, 駐車する *to park (a car)*)

✏ Writing

Write about your strategies for maintaining your health.

泳げるようになりました **Achievement and Progress**

Notes Relating to This Lesson	
Grammar and Usage	
4 ～ほしい........ 106	7 ～で.......... 107
5 ひと (人)...... 107	**Culture**
6 ～ようになる.... 107	A なっとう (納豆). 109

 Basic Vocabulary and Kanji

あ˥いさつ	挨拶	n. greeting (挨拶をする to greet)
も˥んく	文句	n. complaint (文句をいう to complain)
なっと˥う	納豆	n. fermented soybeans A
やっと		adv. finally (やっとおわりました It finally ended.)
さいきん	最近	adv. recently
～ほしい	～欲しい・～欲しくない	aux. to want someone to do ~ 4

Newly introduced kanji:

さいきん　と
最近・取る (to take)

最	一 冂 冃 冃 旦 昌 昌 昌 昌 昌 最 最
取	一 丁 ㄈ ㄈ 耳 耳 取 取

 Dialog

Ben Lee is asking Yoshio Tanaka when he learned to swim.

リー ：田中さんは何才ぐらいで泳げるようになりましたか。

田中 ：ぜったい、人に言わないで下さいよ。はずかしいんですが、まだ泳げないんです。

リー ：ああ、そうですか。

田中 ：リーさんは。

リー ：ぼくも泳げません。来週から、スイミングスクールに行くんです。

田中 ：本当に。

リー ：ガールフレンドが、ぼくに泳げるようになってほしいと言ったんです。

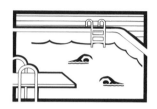

Guess and Try 1

What does 人 in the above dialog mean? 5

Guess and Try 2

What does the underlined part in the above dialog mean? 6 7

Guess and Try 3

What do the following sentences mean? 6

1. できるだけ、なっとうを食べるようにしました。
2. 最近、なっとうを食べるようになりました。
3. やっと、なっとうが食べられるようになりました。
4. 父は最近もんくを言わないようになりました。
5. 父は最近もんくを言わなくなりました。

Guess and Try 4

How do you say the following in Japanese? 4

1. I want a car.
2. I want to buy a car.
3. I want my brother to buy a car.

 Drill : Formation

およ
泳げる ⟶ 泳げるようになりました

1. 自転車に乗れる
2. クッキーが作れる

3. 日本語であいさつができる

4. なっとうが食べられる

5. 早くおきられる

6. 車が運転できる

7. クラスにおくれない

Task1: Pair Work

Ask your partner at what age he / she became able to do the following.

1. 泳ぐ

2. 自転車に乗る

3. りょうりができる

Task 2: Pair Work

Ask your partner about their progress in Japanese. Use the following scale.

1. カタカナが読める

2. 日本語であいさつができる

3. 日本語で道がきける

(道をきく to ask directions)

4. 映画やアニメの日本語がわかる

For example:

A : B さんはカタカナが読めるようになりましたか。

B : はい、よく読めるようになりました。(まだです。早く、読めるようになりたいです。)

A : ああ、そうですか。

Short Reading

私は「ノー」と言うのがとても苦手でした。友達が何か難しいことを頼んだ時は、いつも曖昧な返事をしていました。大学一年生の時、仲良しの友達と言語学のクラスを取っていました。その友達が私に宿題を見せてほしいと、頼みました。私は、断れなくて、宿題を見せてあげました。先生は、二人の宿題が似ていたので、二人とも叱りました。大好きな先生だったので、とても嫌でした。その時から、私はできるだけ「ノー」と言えるように練習しました。今は、「イエス」と「ノー」が簡単に言えるようになりました。

上田由紀子　19 歳

(曖昧 (な) *ambiguous; vague,* 返事 *reply,* 仲良し *close (relationship),* 断る *to refuse,* 似ている *to resemble,* 二人とも *both,* 叱る *to scold,* 嫌だ *unhappy*)

Writing

Write about some incident that made you change.

今日からここで働くことになりました **Decision**

Notes Relating to This Lesson

Grammar and Usage	Writing
8 ～ことにする vs. ～ことになる ... 108	ⓐ Writing postcards to say hello........ 110
Culture	
ⓑ Announcing a decision 109	

📖 Basic Vocabulary and Kanji

はくし か￘てい	博士課程	n. doctoral program
しゅうし か￘てい	修士課程	n. master's program
けいけん	経験	n. experience
みな￘さん	皆さん	n. everyone, all of you
いろいろ	色々	adv. for all sorts of things
いか￘が		q. how (the respectful form of どう)
も￘うす	s-u 申す・申さない・申し・申して	v. to (modestly) say (the humble form of 言う)

Newly introduced kanji:

申す (to say)・音楽 (music)・音 (sound)
数学 (mathematics)・
お願いする (to ask a favor)

申	丨 冂 冂 日 日 申
音	丶 亠 亠 立 立 音 音 音 音
数	丶 丷 丷 丬 半 米 米 娄 娄 娄 数 数
願	一 厂 厂 厂 严 原 原 原 原 原 原 原 願 願 願 願 願 願

Dialog 1

Yoko Yamada runs into her friend's brother and starts chatting with him.

山田 ： 数学のお勉強はいかがですか。はかせかていにいらっしゃるんですよね。

友達の兄 ： ええ、そうなんですが、数学の勉強をやめて、音楽を勉強することにしたんです。

山田 ： えっ、本当ですか。

友達の兄 ： ええ。それで、しゅうしかていから始めることになりました。

Guess and Try 1

What do the following two sentences mean? 8

1. 日本に行くことにしました。
2. 日本に行くことになりました。

Dialog 2

Makoto Takeshita is about to be introduced at his new workplace.

社長 ：今日から、うちで働いていただくことになった竹下さんです。

竹下 ：はじめまして。竹下真と申します。今日からこの会社で働くことになりました。コンピューターは大学で勉強しましたが、プログラムを作ったけいけんはとても少ないので、わからないことがたくさんあると思います。

みなさんにいろいろ教えていただきた
いと思っています。どうぞよろしくお
願いします。

Guess and Try 2

Why didn't Makoto say 今日からこの会社で働く
ことにしました? **B**

 **Drill 1: Formation**

音楽を勉強する ⟶ 音楽を勉強することにな
りました

1. 私がそうじをする
2. ここで働く
3. 来月けっこんする
4. はかせかていに入る
5. としょかんが使える
6. としょかんが使えない

Drill 2: Formation

大学院で勉強する ⟶ 大学院で勉強すること
にしました

1. お金をかりる
2. 父にてがみを書く
3. 会社をやめる
4. 新しい仕事を始める

Task: Classroom Activity

Introduction at a new workplace: Pretend that you
are going to start working at the Japanese company
of your dreams. Introduce yourself to your new col-
leagues, using Dialog 2 as a model.

Short Reading

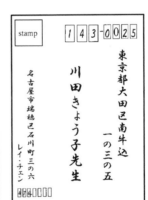

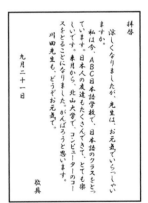

(拝啓 *opening phrase,* 涼しい *cool,* がんばろう
と思います *I'm thinking of trying my best.,* 敬具
closing phrase)

Writing

Write a postcard with news about yourself to your
teacher. ⓐ

ボタンをおすと、… Consequences

Notes Relating to This Lesson	
Grammar and Usage	**Writing**
⑨ 〜と、…する 108	とり 110
⑩ 〜くなる・〜になる . 109	
⑪ 〜と、…した 109	

📚 Basic Vocabulary and Kanji

ボタン		n. button
とり	鳥	n. bird
はこ	箱	n. box
ふうとう	封筒	n. envelope
おす	s-u 押す・押さない・押し・押して	v. to press
もどる	r-u 戻る・戻らない・戻り・戻って	v. to return
ちらかる	r-u 散らかる・散らからない・散らかり・散らかって	v. to become messy
びっくりする	irr. びっくりする	v. to be surprised
やっぱり		adv. expectedly (cf. やはり)

Newly introduced kanji:

鳥

鳥	′ ⺅ ⼾ ⼾ ⼾ ⾃ 鳥 鳥 鳥 鳥 鳥

💿 💬 Dialog 1

John Smith would like to buy a train ticket from a machine. He is consulting the man queuing next to him.

スミス ：このボタンは何ですか。

男の人 ：このボタンをおすと、230 円のきっ

ぷが出ます。

スミス ：えっ、お金を入れなくても、きっぷ
が出るんですか。

男の人 ：もちろん、お金を入れないと、出ま
せんよ。

スミス ：やっぱり。じゃあ、このボタンは何
ですか。

男の人 ：このボタン
をおすと、
お金がもど
ります。

Guess and Try 1

What do the following sentences mean? What do they have in common? ⑨

1. 3に2をたすと、5になります。
   （〜に…をたす *to add... to ~*）
2. 春になると、花がさきます。（さく *to bloom*）
3. この大学の学生だと、としょかんが使えます。
4. 薬をのまないと、よくなりません。⑩
5. 7時になると、父が帰ります。

Guess and Try 2

The following sentences are ungrammatical. Why? ⑨

1. 7時になると、私が帰ります。　　（✗）
   (Ungrammatical)
2. 7時になると、ねて下さい。　　（✗）
   (Ungrammatical)
3. 7時になると、行きましょう。　　（✗）
   (Ungrammatical)

🔴💬 Dialog 2

John Smith is telling Yoko Yamada about what had happened yesterday.

ジョン： 昨日パオロさんのアパートに行った
んですよ。

山田　： ああ、そうですか。

ジョン： ドアをノックすると、きれいな女の
人が出て来たんです。びっくりしま
した。

山田　： えっ、だれ。

ジョン： さあ。

Guess and Try 3

What do the following sentences mean? What do they have in common? ⑪

1. まどを開けると、鳥が入って来ました。

2. はこを開けると、大きいふうとうが入って
いました。

3. ちょっと、へんでしたが、食べてみると、お
いしかったです。

🗣 Drill 1: Formation

食べすぎる・おなかが痛くなります ⟶ 食べす
ぎると、おなかが痛くなります

1. お金がない・困ります

2. よく勉強する・100点が取れます

3. 左に曲がる・ぎんこうがあります

4. 日本語を習っておく・ビジネスにいいです

🗣 Drill 2: Formation

本屋に行く・マイクさんがいました ⟶ 本屋に
行くと、マイクさんがいました

1. うちに帰る・部屋がちらかっていました

2. はこを開ける・ようふくが入っていました

3. アパートに帰る・電気がついていました

4. 会ってみる・まあまあやさしい人でした

🚩 Task 1

Describe each of the following situations.

1.　　　　　2.　　　　　3.

🚩 Task 2

Make up a story that starts from picture 1.

1.　　　　　2. ?　　　　　3. ?

🚩 Task 3: Group Work

Make an unexpected story: Have each member of your group contribute a sentence one after another so that they can jointly make up an interesting story. Use 〜と、〜ました where necessary.

📖 Short Reading

　私は2年前に日本に行きました。空港に
友達が迎えに来てくれました。そして、その
友達のうちに行きました。玄関に入ると、彼
のお母さんが出て来ました。彼のお母さんは玄
関の床に膝を曲げて座る
と、頭を床の近くまで
下げて深くお辞儀をしま
した。私はとてもびっく

りしました。そして、ちょっと、困りました。
でも、私が日本にいる間、彼女は私に一番
親切にしてくださいました。

　　　　　　ジェフ・ブラウン　大学二年生

(空港 airport, 迎えに来る to pick up someone,
玄関 entrance; foyer, 膝 knee, 曲げる to bend, 下
げる to lower, 深く deeply, お辞儀をする to bow)

✏ Writing

Write about some surprising incident.

– Grammar and Usage –

1 ～ように: In a way that ～ [Desired manner, desired resulting state]

The dependent noun よう (lit. *appearance*) follows a verb in the plain present form and creates an adverbial phrase that expresses the desired manner or desired resulting state of the action, meaning *in a way that ~*.

(a) こわさないように運んで下さい。
Please carry (it) so you will not damage (it).

(b) ここから見えるようにおいて下さい。
Please place (it) so that (I) can see (it) from here.

(c) 母が言ったように作って下さい。
Please make (it) in a way that my mother said.

(d) 先生、ちょっとわかりません。わかるように言って下さいませんか。
Teacher, I do not understand. Can you say it in a way that I will understand?

(e) あっ、またコーヒーをこぼしたんですか。こぼさないように飲んで下さいよ。
Oh, you spilled your coffee again? Please drink it without spilling.

(f) また、10点ですか。
You got 10 points again?
— 今度は100点を取るようにどりょくします。
— I will make an effort to get 100 points next time.

(g) 車が買えるようにお金をためます。
(I) will save money so that (I) can buy a car.

2 ～ようにする: To try to ～ / to make a change so ～ [Making a change]

～ようにする follows a verb in the plain form and it means *to make some kind of change*. When the subject is the speaker, it expresses an effort-making.

(a) 野菜を食べるようにしました。
I tried to eat vegetables.

(b) たまごを食べないようにします。
I will try not to eat eggs.

(c) たまごを食べないようにしています。
I am trying not to eat eggs.

(d) 毎日窓を開けるようにします。
I try to open the window every day.

(e) 朝早く起きるようにしています。
I am trying to wake up early in the morning.

When the subject is not the speaker, it means *to make some arrangement to make a change*.

(f) 明日大工さんをよんで、この窓が開くようにします。
I'll ask a carpenter to come here tomorrow, and make it so this window will open.

(g) この窓は開かないようにしました。
I made it so this window will not open.

(h) どろぼうが入った時に、このアラームが鳴るようにしました。
I set this alarm to go off when a thief enters.

(i) 運転手が6時に来るようにします。
I'll make an arrangement so that a driver will come at 6 o'clock.

3 ～ないで: Without ～ing

The verb in the plain present negative form plus the particle で (～ないで) can mean *without doing something* or *not doing something*.

(a) 朝ごはんを食べないで、学校に行きました。
I went to school without eating breakfast.

(b) じしょを使わないで、宿題をしました。
I did my homework without using a dictionary.

(c) 電話を使わないで、イーメールを使うようにしています。
I try not to use a telephone, but an e-mail.

4 ～ほしい: To want someone to do ～

To want to do something is expressed by the suffix たい (see Chapter Eleven), as in (a), but *to want someone to do something* is expressed by the auxiliary ～ほしい, which follows a verb in the te-form, as in (b). In the latter, the person needed to do something is marked by the particle に, and the direct object must be marked by the particle を:

(a) 私は車が買いたいです。
I want to buy a car.

(b) 私は兄に車を買ってほしいです。
I want my brother to buy a car.

For expressing the speaker's desire for someone else not to do something, use the nai-form and で as in (c) or just negate ほしい as in (d).

(c) 私は兄にタバコをすわないでほしいです。
I want my brother not to smoke.

(d) 私は兄にタバコをすってほしくありません。
I don't want my brother to smoke.

5 ひと (人): Other people

人 literally means *person*, but it also means *other people* in some contexts. The word 人 is often used in statements about how to behave in society.

(a) 人に迷惑をかけないようにしてください。
Please try not to disturb others.

(b) 人のことを考えてください。
Please be considerate of others.

(c) 人の悪口を言ってはいけません。
You must not say bad things of others.

(d) 人のことは気にしない。
I do not worry about others.

Japanese has many proverbs that start with the word 人.

(e) 人は人、我は我
Others are others, and yourself is yourself. (Do what you believe right, regardless of what others do or say.)

(f) 人の噂も七十五日
Rumors last only 75 days.

(g) 人のふり見て我ふり直せ
Look at other people's behavior, and think about your own behavior.

(h) 人の口には戸は立てられぬ
We cannot put a door in other people's mouths. (People will talk.)

6 ～ようになる: To start ～ing / to become ～ [Getting a change]

～ようになる follows a verb in the plain form and it is used for expressing the situation where one sees some kind of change. For example, 私は早く起き

るようになりました means *I started to wake up early* or *I wake up early (now)*. Unlike ～ようにする, ～ようになる does not emphasize the speaker's conscious effort for making a change, but it just expresses what change has taken place, as you can see in the contrast between sentence (a) and sentence (b):

(a) 私は早く起きるようになりました。
I wake up early (now).

(b) 私は早く起きるようにしました。
I tried to wake up early.

～ようになる is often used with a potential form, to mean *to become able to do something*.

(c) 私は早く起きられるようになりました。
I became able to wake up early.

(d) やっと安心できるようになりました。
(Now,) we can feel at rest finally.

～ないように is often contracted to ～なく. For example, (e) can be rephrased as (f):

(e) 最近あまり文句を言わないようになりました。
(He) stopped complaining recently.

(f) 最近あまり文句を言わなくなりました。

7 ～で: At, in [Time]

The particle で specifies the time or age at which some period or state ends or changes. So, it is used with verbs such as おわる *to end*, やめる *to quit*, なくなる *to pass away* and なる *to become*.

(a) 5才で泳げるようになった。
I became able to swim at the age of five.

(b) 来週でこのセミナーは終わる。
This seminar ends next week.

(c) 結婚して、来年で20年になる。
Next year will be the 20th year since we got married.

(d) 祖父は89才で亡くなった。
My grandfather passed away at the age of 89.

(e) ジョンは16才で、医者になった。
John became a medical doctor at the age of 16.

8 ～ことにする vs. ～ことになる: I decided to ～ vs. it's been decided [Decision]

When a verb in the plain form is followed by ことにする or ことになる , it expresses decision making. For example, すきやきを食べることにしました means *(I / we) decided to eat sukiyaki* and すきやきを食べることになりました means *It was decided that (I / we) will eat sukiyaki*. The difference between ～ことにする and ～ことになる is that the former indicates a decision maker but the latter does not.

(a) 兄は日本に行くことにしました。
My brother has decided to go to Japan.

(b) 兄は日本に行くことになりました。
It has been decided that my brother will go to Japan.

(c) 試験を受けないことにしました。
(I) have decided not to take the exam.

(d) 試験を受けないことになりました。
It has been decided that (I) will not take the exam.

(e) ここで食べられることになりました。
It has been decided that we can eat here.

(f) ここで食べられないことになりました。
It has been decided that we cannot eat here.

9 ～と、…する: Whenever ～, ... happens [Automatic consequence]

Some events are automatically followed by other events due to the laws and rules in nature, mathematics, physics, society, household, etc. Such a situation can be expressed by ～と、…する. For example, 太陽が出ると、明るくなります means *when(ever) the sun comes out, it becomes bright*. As you can see, と is placed at the end of the subordinate clause, which expresses the initial event, and it is followed by the main clause, which expresses the consequence. Both clauses must be in the **present** tense, and the verbs and adjectives before the particle と must be in the plain form.

(a) 春になると、花がさきます。
When it is spring, flowers blossom. (A law in nature)

(b) 3に2をたすと、5になります。
If you add 3 to 2, we get 5. (A law in mathematics)

(c) 明るいと、寝られません。
When it is bright, I cannot sleep. (A fact that applies to someone)

(d) この大学の学生だと、図書館が使えます。
If you are a student of this college, you can use the library. (College regulation)

(e) 7時になると、父が帰ります。
When it is seven o'clock, my father comes home. (Routine)

This construction expresses an automatic consequence over which the speaker has no control, and it cannot be used for the speaker's controllable acts, suggestions, invitations, requests, or commands. Accordingly, the following sentences are all ungrammatical:

(f) 7時になると、私が帰ります。   (✗)
(Ungrammatical) Intended meaning: *When it is seven o'clock, I return home.*

(g) 暑くなると、アイスクリームを食べませんか。   (✗)
(Ungrammatical) Intended meaning: *When the weather becomes hot, why don't we eat ice cream?*

(h) 7時になると、行きましょう。   (✗)
(Ungrammatical) Intended meaning: *When it is seven o'clock, let's go (there).*

(i) 7時になると、ねてください。   (✗)
(Ungrammatical) Intended meaning: *When it is seven o'clock, please go to bed.*

10 ～くなる・～になる: To become ～

When an adverb such as 高く and きれいに is followed by the verb なる *to become*, it means to get (more of) the property expressed by the adverb. For example, 高くなる means *something becomes (more) expensive*, and きれいになる means *something becomes pretty (prettier)*.

(a) この辺の不動産は高くなりました。
The real estate properties around here became (more) expensive.

(b) 最近山田さんはきれいになりましたね。
Ms. Yamada became pretty (prettier) these days, didn't she?

(c) 薬をのまないと、よくなりません。
If you do not take medicine, you will not get better.

(d) 冬休みになると、キャンパスは寂しくなります。
When the winter vacation starts, the campus becomes a lonely place.

(e) 卒業した後は、就職は難しくなります。
Job-hunting becomes difficult after you have graduated.

For 〜くする・〜にする (to make something 〜), see Grammar and Usage note 9 in Chapter 10.

11 〜と、…した: When 〜, ... happened [Sporadic consequence]

Sometimes our attention is caught by what happened or what we found **after** doing something. Such situations can be expressed by 〜と、…した. For example, the following sentence states what the speaker found after opening the door:

(a) ドアを開けると、男の人が立っていました。
When I opened the door, a man was standing there.

In this construction, the first event (opening the door) is expressed in the subordinate clause followed by と, and the second event (finding a man standing) is expressed in the main clause. Importantly, only the main clause is in the past tense, and the subordinate clause is in the **present tense**, although both of them took place in the past. Note that the verbs and adjectives before と must be in the plain form.

(b) 窓を開けると、鳥が入って来ました。
When I opened the window, a bird came in.

(c) 箱を開けると、お金がたくさん入っていました。
When I opened the box, (I found) a lot of money in it.

(d) ちょっと、変でしたが、食べてみると、おいしかったです。
(It) was a little strange, but when I ate (it), (it) was delicious.

(e) 田中さんは話してみると、まあまあやさしい人でした。
When I talked to Mr. Tanaka, (I found that) he was more or less kind.

Since this construction expresses what happened or what the speaker found, the main clause cannot express any event that is controllable or expected for the speaker. For example, (f) is ungrammatical, while (g) is grammatical:

(f) ドアを開けると、犬を外に出しました。(✗)
(Ungrammatical) Intended meaning: When I opened the door, I let my dog out.

(g) ドアを開けて、犬を外に出しました。
I opened the door and let my dog out.

– Culture –

Ⓐ なっとう (納豆): Fermented soybeans

なっとう *fermented soybeans* are extremely healthy food that have high quality protein and good digestive enzymes. Unfortunately, most non-Japanese do not like it because of its strong flavor (smell) and gluey texture. なっとう is often served with soy sauce, mustard and / or chopped scallion.

Ⓑ Announcing a decision

When the Japanese make an announcement about their decisions, the phrase 〜ことになりました *It has been decided that* 〜 is used very commonly, and it is used more often than the phrase 〜ことにしました *(I) decided that* 〜.

There are two reasons why 〜ことになりました is preferred to 〜ことにしました. First, the Japanese are very shy about articulating their desires and wills. By using 〜ことになりました, they can avoid specifying the decision maker. Second, the Japanese generally respect teamwork more than individual work. Consequently, the decision made by a group is more respected than the decision made by an individual. By using 〜ことになりました,

they can give the impression that the decision is made not only by the speaker but also by all the people involved in it. Because of these reasons, they use 〜ことになりました very often for announcing a decision, even for their decisions concerning personal lives:

(a) 結婚することになりました。
   けっこん
   It has been decided that (I) will get married.

(b) ここで 働 くことになりました。
   はたら
   It has been decided that (I) will start working here.

(c) 私が 教 えることになりました。
   おし
   It has been decided that (I) will teach (it.)

– Writing –

ⓐ **Writing postcards to say hello**

You can write a postcard to your friends or teachers to say hello and let them know how you are doing. Start with the opening phrase, 拝 啓 and describe the weather or seasons and ask about the recipient's health, then, you can write about yourself, or whatever you would like to say. At the end, wish for the recipient's good health, indicate when you will get back to him / her, and / or ask the recipient to give your regards to his / her family or associates, followed by the closing phrase, 敬 具. The date is placed at the very end. At the end of the recipient's name, add a respectful title 様. You should replace 様 with 先 生 if the latter is appropriate.

Sender's name and address   Receiver's name and address

ⓑ とり

鳥	とり *bird* Example: 鶏 *chicken*, 鳩 *pigeon*, 鴨 *duck*, 鳴る *to sound*

– Kanji List –

自分・自転車・運動する・運ぶ・最近・取る・申す・音楽・音・数学・お願いする・鳥

自 (みずか-ら) ・ジ *self*	＇丨冂白白自　　　[6] Example: 自分 *self*, 自転車 *bicycle*
分 わ-かる・ ブン・フン *division, part, minute*	ノ 八分分　　　[4] Example: 自分 *self*, 5 分 *five minutes*
転 ころ-ぶ・ テン *roll, turn*	一厂厅厅自亘車軒軒転転　[11] Example: 運転する *to drive*, 自転車 *bicycle*
車 くるま・シャ *car*	一厂厅厅百亘車　　　[7] Example: 車 *car*, 自転車 *bicycle*
運 はこ-ぶ・ ウン *carry, fate*	一十サ艹艾花花　　　[7] Example: 運ぶ *to carry*, 運転する *to drive*, 運動 *exercise*
動 うご-く・ ドウ *move*	一二千斤斤自重重動動　[11] Example: 運動 *exercise*, 動く *to move*
最 もっと-も・ サイ *most*	一 口 日 旦 早 早 昌 昌 最 最　[12] Example: 最近 *recently*

近 ちか-い・ キン near, recent	´ イ イ 斤 斤 沂 近 近　　　[7]
	Example: 近い *near,* 近く *vicinity,* 最近 *recently*
取 と-る・シュ get, hold, acquire	ー Ｔ Ｆ Ｆ Ｅ 耳 取 取　　　[8]
	Example: 取る *to take,* 聞き取り *listening comprehension*
申 もう-す・ シン report, apply, excuse	ノ 口 冂 日 申　　　[5]
	Example: 申す *to say (humble),* 申請 *application*
音 おと・オン sound	´ 亠 六 立 产 音 音 音 音　　　[9]
	Example: 音楽 *music,* 音 *sound, noise*
楽 たの-しい・ ガク・ラク amuse, pleas- ant, music	´ イ 白 白 白 泊 泊 洎 迫 滐 楽 楽楽　　　[13]
	Example: 音楽 *music,* 楽しい *amusing,* 楽だ *easy*
数 かず・かぞ- える・スウ number, some, several	` ` ´ ¥ ¥ ¥ ¥ 娄 娄 娄 数 数数　　　[13]
	Example: 数学 *mathematics*
学 まな-ぶ・ ガク・ガッ study	` ` ` ´´ `´ ` 学 学 学 学　　　[8]
	Example: 学生 *student,* 大学 *university,* 文学 *literature*
願 ねが-う・ ガン pray, beg	ー 厂 厂 厅 斤 原 原 原 原 原 原 原 原 願 願 願 願 願 願　　　[19]
	Example: 願う *to pray,* お願いする *to request*
鳥 とり・ チョウ bird	´ イ 宀 戶 戶 阜 鳥 鳥 鳥 鳥 鳥　　　[11]
	Example: 鳥 *bird*

– Review –

Q1. *Write the readings of the following kanji phrases and state what is common among the members of each set.*

1. 最近・取る
2. 運ぶ・運転する・運動する
3. 音楽・立つ・暗い・新しい
4. 数学・教える・三枚

Q2. *Choose the appropriate option in the parentheses.*

1. できるだけ部屋をきれいにするように (なります・します)。
2. 兄は最近よくしゃべるように (なりました・しました)。
3. がんばって、おくれないように (なります・します)。

Q3. *Fill in the blanks using* 〜ようにする *or* 〜ようになる.

1. 肉ばかり食べてはいけませんよ。もっとやさいも ＿＿＿＿＿＿＿＿＿。
2. 田中さんの子供さんは今ニオです。最近 ＿＿＿＿＿＿＿＿＿。
3. たばこはけんこうによくありません。じゃあ、できるだけ ＿＿＿＿＿＿＿＿＿ ＿＿＿＿＿＿＿＿＿。
4. 大学のプールでよくれん習したので、上手に ＿＿＿＿＿＿＿＿＿。
5. 漢字をたくさん勉強したので、日本語の本が ＿＿＿＿＿＿＿＿＿。

Q4. *Fill in the blanks with* よう *or* こと.

1. よく CD をきいたので、日本語が上手に話せる ＿＿＿＿＿ になりました。
2. 今日からここで働く ＿＿＿＿＿ になりました。どうぞよろしくお願いします。
3. 前はお酒がきらいでしたが、最近はお酒が飲める ＿＿＿＿＿ になりました。

4. あの学生は最近よく勉 強 する＿＿＿＿＿
になりました。

5. 日本にりゅう学する＿＿＿＿になりました。

6. コレステロールが高いので、たまごを食べす
ぎない＿＿＿＿にします。

7. 来 年大学で日本語をとる＿＿＿にしました。

8. できるだけうちで日本語を勉強する
＿＿＿＿＿にします。

Q5. *Fill in the blanks.*

1. ＿＿＿＿＿＿と、100 点を取れますよ。
でも、＿＿＿＿＿と、0点ですよ。

2. 私はひこうきにのると、耳が＿＿＿＿＿
なります。

3. 買いものをしすぎると、＿＿＿＿＿。

Q6. *Pick a phrase from each of the boxes and make a
sensible sentence by connecting them appropriately.*

a. 使ってみた	ア．ケーキが入って いた
b. れいぞうこを 開けた	イ．不便だと思った
c. うちに帰った	ウ．友達が待って いた

Tips and Additional Knowledge: Puzzling English Loanwords

Japanese borrows many English words. Some
of these words puzzle native speakers of
English.

1. マンション (mansion)
   It refers to a modern condominium, not a
   giant luxurious house.

2. バイク (bike)
   It refers to a motorcycle, not a bicycle.

3. パンツ (pants)
   It means underwear and does not mean pants
   or trousers.

4. トレーニングパンツ (training pants)
   They are gym pants and are not for toilet
   training.

5. スマートだ (smart)
   It means skinny and does not mean intelli-
   gent.

6. サボる (to sabotage)
   It means to loaf on the job, or to cut classes.

7. カンニングをする (to do cunning)
   It means to cheat (on an exam).

8. アメリカン・コーヒー (American coffee)
   It refers to watery coffee or weak coffee.

CHAPTER TWENTY-TWO
Describing How Things and People Appear to Be

こわそうな人ですね **First Impressions**

Notes Relating to This Lesson	
Grammar and Usage	
① 〜そう（な）..... 120	② 〜しか（…ない）..120

Basic Vocabulary and Kanji

こわ˥い	怖い・怖くない	adj. scary, scared
つよ˥い	強い・強くない	adj. strong, powerful
よわ˥い	弱い・弱くない	adj. weak, not powerful
しんけ˥いしつ（な）	神経質だ・神経質じゃない	adj. too sensitive, nervous, temperamental
だめ˥（な）	駄目だ・駄目じゃない	adj. not good, hopeless
おち˥る	i-ru 落ちる・落ちない・落ち・落ちて	v. to fall
きがつよい	気が強い	strong-willed, hard-headed
きがよわい	気が弱い	coward, timid
そういえ˥ば	そう言えば	if you say so, it reminds me of that ~
〜そう（な）	〜そうだ・〜そうじゃない	to look like ~ ①
〜しか（…ない）		prt. only ②

Newly introduced kanji:

気が強い・気が弱い

 Dialog 1

Yoko Yamada and Mary Carter have just seen the new manager at the restaurant where they work.

山田 ：あっ、あの人が新しいマネージャーですよ。

カーター ：まあまあやさしそうな人ですね。

山田 ：そうですか。ちょっといじわるそうですよ。

カーター ：ええ、そういえば、ちょっと難しそうですね。

Guess and Try 1
State the difference between the following two phrases. ①

1. おもしろい人 　　　　2. おもしろそうな人

Guess and Try 2
Fill in the blanks. ①

おもしろい　　　→　おもしろそうな人です
　　　　　　　　　　おもしろそうです

こわい　　　　　→　1. _____ 人です
　　　　　　　　　　こわそうです

まじめ　　　　　→　まじめそうな人です
　　　　　　　　　　2. _____ そうです

まじめじゃない　→　まじめじゃなさそうな人です
　　　　　　　　　　3. _____ そうです

やさしくない　　→　やさしくなさそうな人です
　　　　　　　　　　4. _____ そうです

いい　　　　　　→　よさそうな人です
　　　　　　　　　　5. _____ そうです

Dialog 2

Ben Lee and John Smith are trying to buy a cheap used car.

リー ：これは古すぎますよ。

スミス ：ええ、ドアがおちそうです。それに、タイヤが三つしかありません。

リー ：それに、エンジンもこわれていそうですよ。

スミス ：これはだめですね。

Guess and Try 3

What do the underlined parts in Dialog 2 mean? ☐1

Guess and Try 4

Add しか to the underlined parts in the following sentences and make the necessary changes. ☐2

1. 学生が<u>三人</u>来ました。　2. <u>学生が</u>来ました。

3. パンダは<u>中国</u>にいます。

🗣 Drill: Formation

気が強いです　➡　気が強そうです

1. いじわるです	2. やさしいです
3. まじめです	4. あたまがいいです
5. しんけいしつです	6. おもしろいです
7. こわいです	8. 難しいです

👥 Task 1: Pair Work

Describe how the following people look.

1. 　2. 　3. 　4.

👥 Task 2: Classroom Discussion

Answer the following questions based on the illustrations in Task 1.

1. 一番しんけいしつそうな人はだれですか。
2. 一番いじわるそうな人はだれですか。
3. どの人と働きたいですか。

👥 Task 3: Pair Work

Ask your partner what he / she thought when he / she saw you for the first time.

For example:

A : はじめて私に会った時、どう思いましたか。

B : とてもきれいな人だと思いました。でも、ちょっとこわくて、いじわるそうな人だと思いました。

A : 今はどう思いますか。

B : 今はおもしろい人だと思っています。

Personality	
明るい *cheerful*	暗い *gloomy, depressed*
真面目 (な) *serious*	優しい *kind*
怖い *scary*	意地悪 (な) *mean*
頑固 (な) *stubborn*	静か (な) *quiet*
つまらない *boring*	厳しい *strict*
面白い *interesting, funny*	ひどい *terrible*
いい *good, nice*	繊細 (な) *sensitive*
ずうずうしい *impudent*	ずるい *sneaky*
気が弱い *weak-willed, timid*	気が強い *strong-willed, stubborn*
難しい *difficult*	気さく (な) *friendly and open-hearted*
神経質 (な) *too sensitive, nervous, temperamental*	

📖 Short Reading

私の親友はマイクさんです。私は二年前に日本語のクラスでマイクさんと知り合いました。初めて会ったときは、ちょっとこわそうな人だと思いました。でも、話してみると、とてもおもしろい人でした。少しずつ宿題をいっしょにするようになりました。最近は毎朝いっしょにテニスをします。私が困っている時はいつも助けてくれます。とても、いい友達です。

(親友 *best friend*, 知り合う *to get acquainted with ~*, 初めて *for the first time*, 少しずつ *little by little; gradually*, 毎朝 *every morning*, 助ける *to help*)

✏️ Writing

Write about one of your best friends, including your first impression of him / her.

天使のような人です **Simile**

📖 Basic Vocabulary and Kanji

て￣んし	天使	*n. angel*
おに￣	鬼	*n. ogre*
か￣みさま	神様	*n. god*
おひ￣めさま	お姫様	*n. princess*
おとな	大人	*n. adult*
あ￣かちゃん	赤ちゃん	*n. baby*
おや￣	親	*n. parent*
ちちおや	父親	*n. father*
ははおや	母親	*n. mother*
たすけ￣る	*e-ru* 助ける・助けない・助け・助けて	*v. to rescue, to help, to save*
まるで		*adv. just like, so to speak*
〜のよう（な）	〜のようだ・〜のようじゃない	*just like 〜* ③
〜みたい（な）	〜みたいだ・〜みたいじゃない	*just like 〜* ④
〜かた	〜方	*the way of 〜, the manner of 〜（食べ方 the way of eating）* ⑤

Newly introduced kanji:

天使・大人・親・父親・
ははおや しんせつ　　　　　　　　きって
母親・親切だ (thoughtful)・切手 (stamp)

親	＇ ＾ ゛ ゛ ゜ 立 辛 辛 亲 亲 亲
	亲 亲 亲 親
切	＇ 七 切 切

💿 🗨 Dialog

Yoko Yamada is talking to Mary Carter about Mr. Tanaka's sister.

山田　　：田中さんのお姉(ねえ)さんはとても親切で、まるで天使のような人なんです。

カーター：へえ。

山田　　：いつも困(こま)っている人をたすけてあげたり、病院(びょういん)でボランティアをしたり、子供(こども)に手話(しゅわ)を教(おし)えたりしているんですよ。（手話 *sign language*）

カーター：いい方(かた)ですね。

Guess and Try 1

Sentences 1 and 2 are sensible, but 3 and 4 are not. Guess why this is so. ③ ④

1. 私の母は男のような人です。　　（✔）
2. 私の母は男みたいな人です。　　（✔）
3. 私の母は女のような人です。　　（✘）
4. 私の母は女みたいな人です。　　（✘）

Guess and Try 2

What do the following sentences mean? ⑤

1. 日本の高校生(こうこうせい)はよく子供(こども)のような話(はな)し方(かた)をします。
2. こし (*lower back*) が痛(いた)いので、おじいさんのような歩(ある)き方をしています。

Guess and Try 3

What is the difference between the following two sentences? ⑥

1. 買_かいものをして、映画_{えいが}を見ました。
2. 買_かいものをしたり、映画_{えいが}を見たりしました。

Guess and Try 4

Fill in the blanks and state how to create the verbs in the たり form. ⑥

みる ⟶ みたり   かく ⟶ かいたり
する ⟶ 1. _____   かう ⟶ かったり
のむ ⟶ のんだり   とる ⟶ 2. _____
いく ⟶ 3. _____   あそぶ ⟶ 4. _____

🗣 Drill: Formation

Variation 1:
天使 ⟶ 天使のようです

Variation 2:
天使 ⟶ 天使みたいです

1. おに   2. おひめさま
3. かみさま   4. 子供_{こども}
5. 日本人   6. 父親_{ちちおや}
7. さむらい   8. マザー・テレサ
9. スーパーマン

🏳 Task 1

Describe your family members or friends, using の
ような人です, if you can.

For example:
私の母は _____ のような人です。父は
_____ のような人です。兄は···

🏳 Task 2

Pretend that your friend doesn't know the following
Japanese items, describe them using ～のようなも
のです. If you don't know some of them, ask someone who does. Make sure to include an item of your
choice.

1. おこのみやき
2. パチンコ
3. カプセル・ホテル Ⓐ

4. すきやき
5. とうふ
6. ？？？ (Your choice)

📖 Short Reading

　私の兄は 侍_{さむらい} のような人です。自分_{じぶん}の損得_{そんとく}
はあまり気_きにしないで、正_{ただ}しいと思_{おも}うことをし
ます。自分の利益_{りえき}のために自分の考_{かんが}えを変_かえ
たり、人に妥協_{だきょう}したりしません。ずるいこと
をする人や、お世辞_{せじ}ばかり言_いう人や、うそをつ
く人が嫌_{きら}いです。弱_{よわ}い人_{ひと}や困_{こま}っている人がい
ると、いつも助_{たす}けてあげます。

(損得_{そんとく} loss and gain, 気_きにする to care about,
正_{ただ}しい right; correct, 利益_{りえき} profit, ～のために
for ～, 考_{かんが}え opinion, 変_かえる to change, ～に妥
協_{きょう} する to compromise with (a person), ずるい
sneaky, お世辞_{せじ} flattering words, うそをつく to
tell lies)

No way, I don't lie!

✎ Writing

Describe one of your acquaintances, who has impressive characteristics.

男らしい人です Good Stereotypical Model of ...

Notes Relating to This Lesson

Grammar and Usage	Writing
7 ～らしい 122	ⓐ むしへん 123
8 ～がる 122	

 Basic Vocabulary and Kanji

むし	虫	n. bug, insect
ゆ⌐うき	勇気	n. courage
にんげん	人間	n. human being
がくしゃ	学者	n. scholar
だんせい	男性	n. man
じょせい	女性	n. woman
せきに⌐んかん	責任感	n. a sense of responsibility
つ⌐まり		adv. in short, put simply
～らしい	～らしい・～らしくない	to be a typical ~ (男らしい人 a manly man) 7
～がる	r-u ～がる・～がらない・～がり・～がって	to show the signs of ~ (兄はお金をほしがっている My brother wants money.) 8

Newly introduced kanji:

虫ⓐ・人間

虫	丶 冂 口 中 虫 虫

 **Dialog**

Kaori Morita is telling Mary Carter about her new boyfriend.

森田 ：私のボーイフレンドは本当に男らしい人なんです。

カーター ：つまり、どんな人。

森田 ：とてもゆうきがあって、強い人なんです。

カーター ：へえ。

森田 ：マリーさんのボーイフレンドは。

カーター ：私のボーイフレンドはあまり男らしくありません。虫はこわがるし、映画を見て泣くし。

Guess and Try 1

What do the following sentences mean? 7

1. 私のボーイフレンドはゆうきがあって、とても男らしい人です。
2. 山田先生はやさしいですが、きびしいです。それに、せきにんかんがあります。とても先生らしい先生です。
3. 田中先生はあまり先生らしくありません。
4. リーさんは今日ちょっとしずかですね。いつものリーさんらしくありませんね。

Guess and Try 2

Sentences 1 and 2 are appropriate, but sentence 3 is inappropriate. Guess why. 7

1. 私の母は女らしい人です。　　　　　(✓)
2. 私の母は男のような人です。　　　　(✓)
3. 私の母は男らしい人です。　　　　　(✗)

Guess and Try 3

Circle the appropriate option in the parentheses. Note that ～がる or ～がっています must be used for describing the third person's desire and feelings. 8

1. 私は車 (を・が) (ほしいです・ほしがっています)。
2. あなたは車 (を・が) (ほしいですか・ほしがっていますか)。

3. スミスさんは車 (を・が) (ほしいです・ほしがっています)。

4. 兄は車 (を・が) (買いたいです・買いたがっています)。

🗣 Drill 1: Formation

日本人 ⟶ 日本人らしいです

1. 父親　　　　　　　　2. 母親
3. がくしゃ　　　　　　4. 学生
5. アメリカ人　　　　　6. 人間

🗣 Drill 2: Formation

日本人 ⟶ 日本人らしくしてください

1. 父親　　　　　　　　2. 母親
3. 学生　　　　　　　　4. 女
5. 男　　　　　　　　　6. 社長

🏳 Task 1: Pair Work

Do you know any specific person or thing that has one of the following characteristics? If so, talk about him / her / it.

1. 子供らしくない子供
2. 大人らしくない大人
3. 犬らしくない犬
4. ねこらしくないねこ
5. 日本人らしくない日本人
6. _____?_____ 人らしくない _____?_____ 人 (your choice)

🏳 Task 2

Describe the typical traditional father (父親) in your country.

🏳 Task 3

Ask three of your classmates their favorite style of attire (服装).

For example:

A : どんな服装が好きですか。

B : 学生らしい服装が好きです。

(会社いんのような・動きやすい・男らしい・男のような・女らしい・女のような・まじめそうな・ロック・シンガーのような・おひめさまのような)

📖 Short Reading

典型的な日本女性はいつも優しくて、少し無口で、自分の考えはあまり主張しません。それから、自分の能力を隠して、家庭や職場の男性に従います。しかし、私の母は違います。国立研究所で、研究員をしています。自分の意見をはっきり言います。会議でよく外国に行きます。でも、僕と妹の面倒はよくみてくれました。

(典型的 (な) typical, 無口な not talkative, 考え opinion, 主張する to assert, 能力 ability, 隠す to hide, 家庭 home; household, 職場 one's job site, 従う to obey, 国立研究所 national laboratory, 研究員 researcher, 意見 opinion, はっきり clearly, 会議 conference, ～の面倒をみる to take care of ~)

✎ Writing

Write about the typical characteristics of the people in your country and talk about some people you know. Do they have typical characteristics or atypical characteristics? Or, write about some of the things discussed in Task 1 in this Lesson.

– Grammar and Usage –

1 ～そう (な): To look ～, ～-looking [Conjecture based on appearance]

The adjective formative ～そう (な) follows an adjective or a verb in the stem form. When it follows an adjective, it creates a new adjective that means ～-looking. It expresses the speaker's intuitive guess about the person or thing he / she is seeing. For example, おもしろそうな人 means *a person who looks interesting*.

(a) こわそうな人
   a scary-looking person / a person who looks scary

(b) 難しそうな本
   a book that looks difficult

(c) あの人はまじめそうな人ですね。
   That person is a serious-looking person, isn't he?

(d) あの人はまじめそうです。
   That person looks serious.

(e) あの人はやさしそうです。
   That person looks kind.

The adjective いい is irregular and it becomes よさそうな when followed by そう (な), as in よさそうな人 *a person who looks nice*.

For a negative adjective such as まじめじゃない and やさしくない, ～さそう (な) is added after dropping the final い, as in まじめじゃなさそう (な) and やさしくなさそう (な).

Since ～そう (な) expresses the speaker's conjecture, it cannot be used for a self-evident property such as color, size and shape. So, you cannot say 背が高そうな人 when you are actually seeing the person.

When ～そう (な) follows a verb in the stem form, it expresses the speaker's intuitive conjecture about what will happen or what has happened.

(f) あっ、ボタンがおちそうですよ。
   Oh, your button looks like it will fall off. / Oh, your button is about to fall off.

(g) 雨がやみそうですね。
   It looks like it's going to stop raining, doesn't it?

(h) 泣きそうになりましたが、泣きませんでした。
   I was about to cry, but I didn't.

(i) ドアがこわれそうです。
   It looks like the door will break. / The door is about to break.

(j) ドアがこわれていそうです。
   It looks like the door is broken. / The door looks broken.

2 ～しか (…ない): Only ～

The particle ～しか means *only*. It often follows quantity phrases, but it also follows noun phrases and their associated grammatical particles. In the latter, the particles が and を must be dropped, but other particles such as に, で, へ and と do not have to be dropped. The verb and adjective must be in the negative form when しか is used in the same sentence.

(a) 学生が三人しか来ませんでした。
   Only three students came.

(b) パンダは中国にしかいません。
   Pandas exist only in China.

(c) 学生しか来ませんでした。
   Only students came.

(d) 私は肉も魚も食べません。やさいしか食べません。
   I do not eat meat or fish. I only eat vegetables.

(e) このくつは 5,000 円です。でも、今 2,000 円しかないので、買えません。
   This pair of shoes is 5,000 yen. But I only have 2,000 yen now, so I cannot buy it.

(f) 私はレストランにはぜんぜん行きません。うちでしか食べません。
   I do not go to a restaurant at all. I eat only at home.

(g) 月曜日に大学に来ますか。
   Do you come to the university on Monday?
   — いいえ。私は火曜日にしか来ないんです。
   — *No. I come here only on Tuesdays.*

3 ～のよう (な): Just like ～ [Simile]

The dependent noun よう literally means *appearance*, and when it occurs in the construction ～のよう (な), following a noun, it creates an adjective that describes things and people in terms of similarities and resemblances. For example, 天使のような人 means *a person who is just like an angel*.

(a) 先生はかみさまのような人です。
The teacher is a person who is like God.

(b) 私の父はまるで子供のようです。母がいないと、何もできません。
My father is just like a child. If my mother is not there, he cannot do anything.

～のよう (な) cannot be used if what is being described is actually what is denoted by the noun before ～のよう (な). So, (c) is appropriate, but (d) is not:

(c) 私の母は男のような人です。
My mother is a person who is just like a man.

(d) 私の母は女のような人です。 (✘)
My mother is a person who is just like a woman.
(Inappropriate)

4 ～みたい (な): Just like ～ [Simile]

The adjective formative ～みたい (な) follows a noun and forms an adjective that means *just like ~*. For example, 天使みたいな人 means *a person who is just like an angel*. ～みたい (な) and ～のよう (な) are often interchangeably used, but the former is more colloquial than the latter. Like ～のよう (な), ～みたい (な) cannot be used if what is being described is actually what is denoted by the noun before ～みたい (な). So, (a) is appropriate, but (b) is not:

(a) 私の母は男みたいな人です。
My mother is a person who is just like a man.

(b) 私の母は女みたいな人です。 (✘)
My mother is a person who is just like a woman.
(Inappropriate)

5 ～かた: The method / way of ～ ing [Method / manner]

When the dependent noun 方 follows a verb in the stem form, it means *the method of ~ing* or *the way of ~ing*.

(a) 父の話し方はちょっとこわいです。
The way my father talks is a little scary.

(b) すしの食べ方を教えてください。
Please teach me how to eat sushi.

(c) ピザの作り方をしっています。
I know how to make pizza.

(d) 漢字の読み方を覚えてください。
Please memorize the pronunciation of kanji characters.

6 ～たり: Do ～, etc. [Partial list of activities]

You can list multiple activities you do or did randomly as examples in one sentence by using the verbs in the ～たり form. The verb する is placed at the very end of the sentence, following the verbs in the ～たり form, and its tense represents the tense of all the verbs in the ～たり form.

(a) 昨日は、ピザを食べたり、コーヒーを飲んだり、テレビを見たりしました。
As for yesterday, I ate pizza, drank coffee, watched TV, (and so on).

(b) 明日は、ピザを食べたり、コーヒーを飲んだり、テレビを見たりします。
As for tomorrow, I will eat pizza, drink coffee, watch TV, (and so on).

As shown in the table, the ～たり forms can be created simply by adding り at the end of the plain past form of the verbs, although the たり form does not mean "past".

Dictionary Form	Past-tense Form	たり Form
たべる *to eat*	たべた	たべたり
みる *to watch*	みた	みたり
かく *to write*	かいた	かいたり
およぐ *to swim*	およいだ	およいだり

Dictionary Form	Past-tense Form	たり Form
あそぶ to play	あそんだ	あそんだり
よむ to read	よんだ	よんだり
しぬ to die	しんだ	しんだり
はなす to speak	はなした	はなしたり
かう to buy	かった	かったり
とる to take	とった	とったり
いく to go	いった	いったり
くる to come	きた	きたり
する to do	した	したり

Note that たり can apply to adjectives.

(c) ここは静かだったり、静かじゃなかったり します。

　　This place is sometimes quiet, sometimes not quiet, etc.

(d) 成績は良かったり、悪かったりします。

　　My grades are sometimes good, and sometimes bad.

(e) お客さんは日本人だったり、中国人だったりします。

　　My customers are sometimes Japanese, Chinese, etc.

7　～らしい: To be a typical ～ [The attribute of typicality]

The adjective formative ～らしい follows a noun and creates an adjective that means *like the ideal model of* or *stereotypical ~*. For example, 男らしい男の人 means *a manly man*.

(a) 私のボーイフレンドはとても男らしい人 です。
　　My boyfriend is a manly man.

(b) 山田先生は先生らしい先生です。
　　Professor Yamada is the ideal model of a teacher.

(c) 田中先生はあまり先生らしくありません。
　　Professor Tanaka is not a typical teacher.

(d) リーさんは今日ちょっとしずかですね。 いつものリーさんらしくありませんね。
　　Mr. Lee is a little quiet today. He is not like himself.

～らしい is usually used positively, for praising people and things, but it may be used sarcastically.

It is important that what is being described is actually what is denoted by the noun before らしい. So, (e) is appropriate, but (f) is not:

(e) 私の母は女らしい人です。
　　My mother is the ideal model of a woman. / My mother is very feminine.

(f) 私の母は男らしい人です。　　　　(✗)
　　My mother is the ideal model of a man.
　　(Inappropriate)

8　～がる: To show signs of ～ [The third person's feelings]

The verb formative ～がる follows an adjective in the stem form, and creates a verb phrase that means *to show signs of ~*. The use of ～がる is required for describing the psychological / physiological perception of the third person with some adjectives such as ほしい *want*, ～たい *want to do*, うれしい *happy*, いや（な）*dislike*, 面倒（な）*troublesome*, こわい *scared*, 寂しい *lonesome*, うらやましい *envious*, おもしろい *amusing*, 苦しい *painful*, 寒い *cold* and 痛い *painful*. The rational behind this is the belief that one cannot see someone else's feelings, but can only see the signs of them.

(a) 私は車がほしいです。スミスさんも車 をほしがっています。
　　I want a car. Mr Smith wants a car, too.

(b) 私は車が買いたいです。スミスさんも車 を買いたがっています。
　　I want to buy a car. Mr. Smith wants to buy a car, too.

(c) 私はうれしいです。田中さんもうれし
がっています。
I am happy. Mr. Tanaka is happy, too.

(d) 私は犬がこわいです。兄も犬をこわがり
ます。
*I am afraid of dogs. My brother is also afraid
of dogs.*

(e) スミスさんは練習を嫌がっています。
Mr. Smith doesn't like to practice.

As you can see in the above examples, the particle
が turns into を once 〜がる is attached to the
adjective. In addition, 〜がる must be in the progressive form (〜がっている) when describing the
temporary mental state of the third person.

– Culture –

Ⓐ カプセル・ホテル: **Capsule hotel**

There are interesting business hotels called カプセ
ル・ホテル (capsule hotel) or カプセル・イン
(capsule inn) in major business cities in Japan. Each
room is only as spacious as a single bed, and one
can barely stand up in it. It has a TV and radio, and
there is a sauna that is shared by guests. These hotels
can be thought of as bee-hives. The room rate is
very economical and the rooms are mostly used by
male company workers, who tend to work late and
often miss the last train of the day.

– Writing –

ⓐ むしへん

虫	むしへん *insect*
	Example: 蚊 *mosquito*, 虹 *rainbow*, 蝦 *shrimp*, 蛇 *snake*

– Kanji List –

気が強い・気が弱い・天使・大人・親・
父親・母親・親切だ・切手・虫・人間

気 キ spirit, mind, air, atmosphere	ノ 一 二 气 气 気 気 [6]
	Example: 元気だ *healthy*, 病気 *sickness*, 天気 *weather*
強 つよ-い・キョ ウ force, strong	¬ ¬ ヲ 弓 弘 弘 弘 弘 強 強 強 [11]
	Example: 強い *strong*, 勉強 *study*
弱 よわ-い・ よわ-る・ジャ ク weak	¬ ¬ 弓 弓 弓 弱 弱 弱 弱 弱 [10]
	Example: 弱い *weak*
天 あめ・あま・ テン weather, sky	一 二 チ 天 [4]
	Example: 天使 *angel*, 天気 *weather*
使 つか-う・シ use	ノ イ 仁 伫 伫 伊 使 使 [8]
	Example: 使う *to use*, 天使 *angel*
大 おお-きい・ ダイ・タイ big, great	一 ナ 大 [3]
	Example: 大人 *adult*, 大きい *big*, 大学 *university*
人 ひと・ニン・ ジン *person*	ノ 人 [2]
	Example: 日本人 *Japanese person*, 人間 *human being*, 女の人 *woman*
親 おや・した- しい・シン parent, kinship	` 一 十 ウ 立 卒 辛 辛 亲 新 新 新 新 新 親 [16]
	Example: 親 *parent*, 母親 *mother*, 親切だ *kind*

父 ちち・フ father	ノ ハ グ父 [4]
	Example: 父 one's own father, 父親 father
母 はは・ボ mother	ﾉ ㄎ 囚 母 母 [5]
	Example: 母 one's own mother, 母親 mother
切 き-る・きっ・ セツ cut	ｰ t 切切 [4]
	Example: 切手 stamp, 親切だ kind
手 て・シュ hand	′ ニ 三 手 [4]
	Example: 切手 stamp, 手 hand, 上手だ skillful, 下手だ unskillful
虫 むし・ チュウ insect, bug	′ ⼝ ⼝ 中 虫 虫 [6]
	Example: 虫 insect, bug
間 あいだ・ カン・ゲン between, interval	｜ ⻔ ⻔ ⻔ ⻔ ⻔ 門 門 門 門 間 間 [12]
	Example: 時間 time, 間 between, 人間 human being

– Review –

Q1. *Choose the appropriate option in the parentheses.*

1. 姉はまじめで、やさしくて、(いじわるな・いい) 人です。
2. ジョンはゆうきがあって、(強い・弱い) 人です。
3. あの人は天使のような人ですが、ときどき (かみさま・おに) のようにおこります。

Q2. *Write the readings of the following phrases, and state what is common among the members of each set.*

1. 強い・弱い・勉強
2. 天気・天使
3. この間・人間・時間
4. 母親・父親・両親・親・親切です
5. 切手・上手・下手・苦手

Q3. *Fill in the blanks and complete the sentences, then state what they mean.*

1. この映画は ＿＿＿＿＿＿ そうですね。見ましょう。
2. この映画は ＿＿＿＿＿＿ そうですね。見るのをやめましょう。
3. あれ。くもがたくさんありますよ。雨が ＿＿＿＿＿＿ そうですね。
4. ホワイト先生はとても ＿＿＿＿＿＿ らしい先生ですね。
5. この子供はまだ5オなのに、＿＿＿＿＿＿ のような話し方をするんですよ。
6. 山田さんは日本人なのに、＿＿＿＿＿＿ のように英語を話すんですよ。
7. まだ夏なのに、＿＿＿＿＿＿ のようにすずしいですね。
8. 私は車がほしいです。よう子さんも車 ＿＿＿＿＿＿。
9. 私は日本の牛肉が食べたいです。パークさんも日本の牛肉 ＿＿＿＿＿＿。
(牛肉 beef)

Q4. *Make a sentence using たり and all of the items in each set, with additional words and particles if necessary. Conjugate the verbs appropriately.*

1. (明日・せんたくをする・買い物をする・そうじをする)
2. (昨日・食べる・飲む・コーヒー・ピザ・見る・テレビ)
3. (来年・大学のクラスを取る・アルバイトをする・りょこうをする)

Q5. *Add the particle 〜しか to the underlined parts, and make the necessary changes.*

1. 私の部屋には<u>つくえ</u>があります。
2. 昨日は<u>パン</u>を食べました。(パン *bread*)
3. <u>うち</u>で食べます。
4. 私は友達が<u>二人</u>います。
5. レストランで<u>2,000円</u>はらいました。
6. <u>父</u>からお金をもらいました。

Q6. *State what the person or animal, in each of the following pictures, wants or wants to do in Japanese.*

1.

2.

3.

4.

Tips and Additional Knowledge: Describing a Human, using a Non-human Item

The Japanese often describe people using a non-human item as in the following examples. Are you one of them?

1. 放送局 *broadcasting station*
(Someone who likes to spread rumors)
Example: 隣の奥さんは放送局だから、気をつけてね。

The housewife next door is a broadcasting station, so be careful.

2. 百科事典 *encyclopedia*
(Someone who is very knowledgeable)
Example: 田中さんは百科事典だから、田中さんに聞きましょう。
Mr. Tanaka is an encyclopedia, so let's ask him.

3. ハイエナ *hyena*
(Someone who tries to take other people's profit and benefit)
Example: あの男はハイエナのような人間だ。

That guy is like a hyena.

4. 働き蜂 *worker bee*
(Someone who works very hard)
Example: お宅のご主人は働き蜂だね。
Your husband is like a worker bee, isn't he?

5. 蛍光灯 *fluorescent light*

(Someone who is slow in grasping an idea, finding implications, or understanding jokes. (A fluorescent light takes a little while to be lit))

Example: 兄は蛍光灯だから、この冗談はわからないでしょう。

My elder brother is a fluorescent light, so he wouldn't understand this joke, I guess.

6. 電信柱 *electric pole*

(Someone who doesn't do anything, but just stands aside to look on while others are busy doing something)

Example: 電信柱みたいに立っていないで、何かしてよ。

Don't just stand like an electric pole, but do something.

7. 瞬間湯沸器 *quick gas water heater*

(Someone who has a short temper)

Example: 父は瞬間湯沸器だから、本当に困る。

My father is a quick gas water heater, so we are in trouble.

8. 雑草 *weed*

(Someone who can survive anywhere, and can overcome all difficulties)

Example: 雑草のような人間になってください。

Become a person like a weed.

9. 金づち *hammer*

(Someone who cannot swim)

Example: 私は金づちだから、泳ぎません。

I am a hammer, so I won't swim.

CHAPTER TWENTY-THREE
Evaluating Facts

もう着いたはずです Circumstantial Judgment

<table>
<tr><td colspan="2">Notes Relating to This Lesson</td></tr>
<tr><td>Grammar and Usage</td><td>Writing</td></tr>
<tr><td>1 ～はずだ........134
2 ～ということは…とい
うことです.......134</td><td> こざとへん.......137</td></tr>
</table>

📖 Basic Vocabulary and Kanji

せいせき	成績	*n. grade, score, performance*
やくそく	約束	*n. personal appointment, promise*
やくそく	約束	(*cf.* 予約（よやく） *reservation / business appointment*)
ぶちょう	部長	*n. the head of a department, division, or club*
しかた	仕方	*n. method, way* (勉強の仕方 *the way of studying*)
ただし⌐い	正しい・正しくない	*adj. correct, precise* (正しいこたえ *correct answers*)
つ⌐く	*k-u* 着く・着かない・着き・着いて	*v. to arrive* (ニューヨークに着く *to arrive at New York*)
しっか⌐りする	*irr.* しっかりする	*v. to become reliable, strong, responsible*
た⌐しか	確か	*adv. if I remember correctly, I suppose*
～ぶ	～部	*~ division, ~ club*
～はずだ	～はずだ・～はずじゃない	*aux. I suppose that ~.* 1
～ということは…ということだ		*The fact that ~ means that ...* 2

Newly introduced kanji:

部長（ぶちょう）・～部（ぶ）・仕方（しかた）・
正（ただ）しい・悪（わる）い (bad)・着（つ）く・
東京（とうきょう） (Tokyo)・大阪（おおさか） (Osaka)

正	一 丁 下 正 正
悪	一 一 一 后 申 亜 亜 悪 悪 悪
京	、 一 宀 亠 古 亨 京 京
阪	了 了 阝 阝 阝 阪 阪

💿 🗨 Dialog

John Smith and Yoko Yamada are talking about their friend, Mary, who has left Tokyo for Osaka a few hours ago.

スミス： もう7時（じ）ですね。マリーさんはもう大阪に着いたでしょうか。

山田 ： 東京を何時（なんじ）に出（で）たんですか。

スミス： たしか3時15分（ふん）です。

山田 ： 3時15分に出たということは、大阪に6時ごろに着くということですね。

スミス： ああ、そうですか。じゃあ、もう着いたはずですね。

Guess and Try 1

What do the following sentences mean? 1

1. 今（いま）、会社（かいしゃ）で働（はたら）いているはずですから、ちょっと会社に電話（でんわ）してください。

2. マリーさんはしっかりしていますから、やくそくは忘（わす）れないはずですよ。

3. カメラがありませんよ。
　 —えっ。つくえの上（うえ）においたはずですが、へんですね。

Guess and Try 2

Rephrase the following sentences using ～はず. [1]

1. 山田さんが行きます。
2. ジョンさんは帰りました。
3. 今度のバスケットボール部の部長はスミスさんです。
4. 日本の地下てつは便利です。
5. この時計は正しいです。

Guess and Try 3

What do the following sentences mean? [2]

1. 田中くんがお父さんにてがみを書いているということは、お金がないということですね。
2. 勉強しているのにせいせきが悪いということは、勉強の仕方が悪いということです。

🗣 Drill 1: Formation

高い ➡ 高いはずです

1. 正しい
2. 悪い
3. まじめだ
4. 便利だ
5. 行く
6. 行っている
7. 着いた
8. 食べられる
9. 日本人だ
10. 宿題だ

🗣 Drill 2: Mini Conversation

日本の土地は高いですか ➡ 高いはずです

1. この時計は正しいですか
2. 来年の日本語の先生は日本人ですか
3. スミスさんは帰りましたか
4. ニューヨークの地下てつは便利ですか

🏳 Task 1: Pair Work

Answer the following questions using ～はずです, ～と思います, ～でしょう or ～です, and share your ideas with your partner.

1. 石油が高くなると、どうなりますか。(石油 petroleum oil, どうなりますか What will happen?)
2. 利息が高くなると、どうなりますか。(利息 bank interest)
3. 子供を産む人が少なくなると、どうなりますか。

🏳 Task 2: Role Play

A: You organized a big surprise party for your friend, Yukiko, to celebrate her 20th birthday.

B: You were asked to come to A's house for a surprise party for Yukiko, but she has not shown up yet. You have been waiting for two hours.

📖 Short Reading

　いつも時間をかけて勉強しているのに成績が悪いということは、勉強の仕方が悪いということです。用語や単語は見つめるだけでは覚えられません。隠して自分で書いてみるという練習を繰り返すと、覚えられるはずです。それから、自分が先生だと思って、友達に教えてみたり、テストの問題を作ってみたりするのもいいでしょう。問題が作れるということは、重要なポイントが分かっているということだからです。

(時間をかける to spend time, 用語 (technical) term, 見つめる to stare at; to gaze at, 隠す to hide; to cover, 繰り返す to repeat, 重要 (な) important)

✏ Writing

Write your opinions on how to study effectively.

もっと早く帰るべきです Strong Personal Opinions

 Basic Vocabulary and Kanji

おくさん	奥さん	n. someone else's wife 3
つま	妻	n. one's own wife 3
かない	家内	n. one's own wife 3
おっと	夫	n. one's own husband 3
かたづける	e-ru 片付ける・片付けない・片付け・片付けて	v. to put things in order, to tidy up (へやを片付ける to tidy up the room, おもちゃを片付ける to put toys in order)
めんどうをみる	面倒を見る	v. to take care of, or look after a person or an animal (こどもの面倒を見る to take care of the children)
ちゃんと		adv. tidily, properly, perfectly, correctly
とにかく		adv. anyway, in any case
もっと		adv. more, some more (もっと食べてください Please eat some more.)
～べきだ	～べきだ・～べきじゃない	aux. It should be the case that ~. (学生は勉強するべきだ Students should study.) 4
～なさい		Do ~ (かたづけなさい Tidy up!) 5

Newly introduced kanji:

奥<ruby>奥<rt>おく</rt></ruby>さん・<ruby>妻<rt>つま</rt></ruby>

<ruby>家内<rt>か ない</rt></ruby>・<ruby>家<rt>いえ</rt></ruby> (house)・<ruby>夫<rt>おっと</rt></ruby>

奥	′ ′ ′ 门 内 内 内 甬 甬 甬 奥 奥 奥
妻	一 ラ ヨ 彐 垂 妻 妻 妻
家	′ ′ 宀 宀 宀 宇 宇 家 家 家
内	l 冂 内 内	夫	一 二 チ 夫

 **Dialog**

A married couple are quarreling.

妻 : あなたはもっと<ruby>早<rt>はや</rt></ruby>くうちに<ruby>帰<rt>かえ</rt></ruby>るべきですよ。もっと<ruby>子供<rt>こども</rt></ruby>のめんどうを見てください。

夫 : わかった。わかった。もう<ruby>少<rt>すこ</rt></ruby>し早く帰ります。すみません。

妻 : それから、くつしたはゆかの<ruby>上<rt>うえ</rt></ruby>におかないで、ちゃんとかたづけて。

夫 : あーあ、うるさい先生みたい。

妻 : (With a firm tone) とにかく、早くそのくつしたをかたづけなさい。

夫 : ああ、こわい。

Guess and Try 1

Ask your Japanese friends how their parents address each other at home and how they refer to each other in front of other people. 3

Guess and Try 2

State the difference among the following sentences: 4 5 6

1. 食べてくださいませんか。
2. 食べてください。
3. 食べた<ruby>方<rt>ほう</rt></ruby>がいいですよ。

4. 食べるべきです。

5. 食べなさい。

6. 食べろ。 6

Note: For expressing what one should not do, the negative element usually appears after べき, as below:

食べるべきではありません。
One should not eat.

食べるべきじゃありません。
One should not eat.

Guess and Try 3

Observe the following patterns, and state how the plain command form is created. 6

1. 食べる → 食べろ
2. 見る → 見ろ
3. 飲む → 飲め
4. 書く → 書け
5. 買う → 買え
6. する → しろ
7. 来る → 来い

Drill 1: Formation

そうじをする → そうじをするべきです

1. 勉強する   2. 早くねる
3. もっと本を読む   4. クラスに出る
5. ビタミンCをとる 6. ちゃんとしまう
7. コーヒーをやめる

Drill 2: Formation

そうじをするべきです → そうじをしなさい

1. 子供のめんどうをみるべきです
2. ちゃんとかたづけるべきです
3. 部屋をそうじするべきです
4. まじめにするべきです
5. 新聞を読むべきです

Task 1: Pair Work / Skit

Pretend that you and your partner are a married couple, and act out an arguing scene. Use the dialog as a model.

Task 2

Complete the following sentences creatively, and then talk about them with your partner in Japanese. Use Short Reading (below) as an example.

1. ＿＿＿＿＿＿＿＿ はぜったいにするべきではないと思います。

   (For example: カンニング *cheating on examination*)

2. ＿＿＿＿＿＿＿＿ はもっとするべきだと思います。

   (For example: リサイクリング *recycling*)

Short Reading

飲酒運転はしてはいけないことになっています。日本の公務員は飲酒運転で捕まると、仕事を失うこともあります。しかし、実際はたくさんの人がしています。真夜中に高速道路を運転していると、ちょっとおかしい車がたくさんあります。たぶん飲酒運転の車だと思います。私は飲酒運転は絶対にするべきではないと思います。

(飲酒運転 *drunk-driving*, 公務員 *public service worker / official*, 捕まる *to get caught*, 失う *to lose; to be deprived of ~*, 実際 *reality*, 真夜中 *midnight*, 高速道路 *highway*, おかしい *strange; unusual; odd*)

Writing

Write about the things that you think we should do or we should not do.

好きかどうか考えます Choosing Your Major

Notes Relating to This Lesson	
Grammar and Usage	
7 ～うちに 136	9 ～によって 137
8 ～か（どうか）....136	

 Basic Vocabulary and Kanji

みんな		pron. everyone, everything
きめる	e-ru 決める・決めない・決め・決めて	vt. to decide (せんこうを決める to decide on one's major)
かんがえる	e-ru 考える・考えない・考え・考えて	vt. to consider, to think (山田さんのことを考える to think about Ms. Yamada)
まず		adv. first of all (まず朝ごはんを食べる to eat breakfast first)
～うちに		before ～, while ～ (子供がねているうちに while the children are sleeping) 7
～かどうか		whether or not ～ (いいかどうか考える to consider whether (it) is good or not) 8
～によって		depending on ～ (人によってちがう to differ depending on the person) 9

Newly introduced kanji:

決める・考える・違う (to differ)・
専攻 (academic major)・専門 (specialty)

決	丶 丶 氵 沪 沪 決 決
考	一 十 土 耂 耂 考
違	丿 ナ ヰ 中 去 当 音 音 音 章 違 違
専	一 厂 戸 戸 亩 由 吏 専 専
攻	一 丁 工 丌 攻 攻
門	丨 冂 冂 冃 阝 門 門 門

 **Dialog**

Paul Kenny is asking Yoko Yamada when Japanese college students decide their major.

ケニー ： 日本の大学生はみんな大学に入る前に専攻を決めるんですか。

山田 ： ええ。アメリカの学生は。

ケニー ： 人によって違います。たくさんの人は勉強してみて、好きかどうか考えて、決めますよ。

山田 ： へえ。そうですか。私は高校生のうちに決めた方がいいと思いますが。

Guess and Try 1

Is there anything common among the following sentences? 7

1. あかちゃんがねているうちに、新聞を読みます。
2. 明るいうちに、行きましょう。
3. けいさつが来ないうちに、にげましょう。
   （にげる to run away, to escape）

Guess and Try 2

Explain the difference between the following two sentences. 7

1. 山田さんがここにいるうちに、宿題をします。
2. 山田さんがここにいる間に、宿題をします。

Guess and Try 3

Fill in the blanks with one of the following items:
(日・人・ばしょ (place)) 8

1. カフェテリアのたべものは毎日同じですか。

　— いいえ、＿＿＿＿＿＿によって違います。

2. 日本は雪がふりますか。

　— いいえ、＿＿＿＿＿＿によって、違います。

3. アメリカ人はみんな背が高いんですか。

　— いいえ、＿＿＿＿＿＿によって、違います。

Guess and Try 4

Fill in the blanks with ～か or ～かどうか, and state what each sentence means. 9

1. 英語を話します＿＿＿＿＿＿。

2. 英語を話す＿＿＿＿＿＿わかりません。

3. 何語を話す＿＿＿＿＿＿わかりません。

Note: だ at the end of a na-type adjective and a copula is usually deleted before か or かどうか in the embedded sentences:

スミスさんはすしが好き (だ) かどうか しっていますか。
Do you know if Mr. Smith likes sushi?

これはいくら (だ) か教えてください。
Please let me know how much this one is.

🗣 Drill: Formation

日本語は難しいですか ⟶ 日本語は難しいかどうか しっていますか

だれが来ますか ⟶ だれが来るかしっていますか

1. テストはたくさんありますか

2. しゅうしょくにいいですか

3. 学生は何人いますか

4. 先生はどなたですか

5. 山田さんの専攻は何ですか

🏳 Task 1

Ask your partner what he / she thought about or will think about when deciding his / her major.

For example:

A ： Bさんは専攻を決めましたか。

B ： はい、数学に決めました。/ まだ決めて いません。

A ： 専攻を決める時、何を考えましたか。/ 専攻を決める時、何を考えますか。

B ： まず、おもしろいか (どうか) 考えました。/ まず、おもしろいか (どうか) 考えます。

🏳 Task 2

Ask your partner what questions he / she would ask when applying for a part-time job. Take turns.

For example:

A ： Bさんはアルバイトをするとき、どんなことをききますか。

B ： まず、給料はいくら (だ) かききます。それから、…

📖 Short Reading

　私の姉の専攻は人類学です。専攻を決める とき、姉はまず好きかどうか考えました。仕 事は探しにくいかもしれないと思いましたが、 一番興味があるものを専攻にしました。兄 は専攻を決める時、まず仕事が探しやすいかど うか考えました。そして、兄はコンピューター・ サイエンスを専攻にしました。私の友達のマ リーさんは将来、医者になりたいので、生 物学を専攻にしました。私はまだ専攻を決め ていません。アジア学に興味がありますが、コ ンピューター・サイエンスも将来役に立つと 思います。両方勉強するかもしれません。

(人類学 *anthropology,* 生物学 *biology,* アジア 学 *Asian studies,* 役に立つ *to become useful,* 両方 *both*)

✎ Writing

Write about how the people around you decided on their academic major.

– Grammar and Usage –

1 〜はずだ: I suppose that 〜 [Circumstantial conclusion]

はずだ follows a verb or an adjective in the pre-nominal form, and expresses the situation that is supposed to hold or to have held judging from the circumstantial facts related to time, place, regulations, actions, etc. For example, スミスさんはもうすぐ来るはずです means *I suppose that Mr. Smith will come soon*, and the speaker says so judging from what he / she knows about Mr. Smith's plan, the time of speech, and all the surrounding facts.

(a) スミスさんは来たはずです。
I suppose Mr. Smith came.

(b) 今朝速達で出しましたから、明日の朝着くはずです。
Since I mailed it out by express mail this morning, I suppose it will be delivered tomorrow morning.

(c) もう2時ですね。もう、日本に着いているはずですね。
It is already 2 o'clock. (He) is supposed to have arrived in Japan.

(d) 20年前は、家が安かったはずです。
I suppose that houses were cheap 20 years ago.

(e) あなたは学生ですから、入場料は100円のはずです。
Since you are a student, the admission fee for you is 100 yen, I suppose.

(f) 今、オフィスで働いているはずですから、ちょっとオフィスに電話してください。
As (he) is supposed to be working at the office now, please call (him) at his office.

(g) ここに時計をおいたはずなのに、ないんです。
I thought I had placed my watch here, but it is not here.

(h) このコンピューターは便利なはずです。
This computer is supposed to be convenient.

2 〜ということは…ということです: 〜 means ... [Implication]

"Sentence 1 ということは Sentence 2 ということです" means *Sentence 1 means Sentence 2*. It is used for specifying the interpretation or implication of some fact. The verbs and adjectives in Sentence 1 and Sentence 2 must be in the plain form.

(a) アメリカで生まれたということはアメリカ人だということですね。
The fact that you were born in the US implies that you are American.

(b) 田中くんがご両親に手紙を書いているということは、お金がないということですね。
Mr. Tanaka is writing a letter to his parents. That means he does not have any money.

(c) 部屋の電気がまだついているということは、だれかいるということです。
The fact that the light in the room is still on means that there is someone in the room.

(d) 日本のパスポートがあるということは、日本人だということです。
The fact that (he) has a Japanese passport means that he is a Japanese citizen.

(e) 勉強しているのにせいせきが悪いということは、勉強の仕方が悪いということです。
If your grades are bad even though you are studying, it means that your way of studying is bad.

3 Spouses

主人 *husband* and 家内 *wife* are the terms that are most commonly used when one is referring to his / her own spouse in front of others in a neutral or formal context. On the other hand, when one is referring to someone else's spouse, ご主人 *husband*, 旦那さん *husband*, and 奥さん *wife* are most commonly used. 夫 and 妻 are typically used for written documents such as a legal document and an application form, but may be used for referring to one's own spouse in front of others. Spouses often address each other by their first names or their first names plus some respectful title such as さん. Wives sometimes address their husbands as あなた, which literally means *you*.

4 　～べきだ: It should be the case that ～, you should ～ [Strong subjective opinion]

べきだ follows a verb in the plain present affirmative form and expresses the speaker's strong subjective opinion about what should be the case.

(a) 学生はもっと勉強するべきです。
Students should study more.

(b) 教師は学生に厳しくするべきです。
Teachers should be strict to students.

するべきだ is often contracted to すべきだ, as in 勉強すべきです and 厳しくすべきです. For expressing what should not be the case, the negative element usually appears after べき, as in (c) and (d).

(c) 食べるべきではありません。
One should not eat.

(d) 食べるべきじゃありません。
One should not eat.

And for expressing what should have been done, conjugate べきだ to the past tense as in (e) rather than conjugating the verb of the action:

(e) 食べるべきでした。
(I) should have eaten.

5 　～なさい: Do ～ [Polite command]

～なさい follows a verb in the stem form and expresses a polite command. It is appropriately used by teachers with students, or by parents with children, but is not necessarily appropriate in other contexts because it is a command.

(a) 早く食べなさい。
Eat quickly.

(b) しずかにしなさい。
Be quiet.

(c) 名前を書きなさい。
Write your name.

～なさい does not have a negative form. Negative polite command is expressed by ～のをやめなさい or ～てはいけません.

(d) 食べるのをやめなさい。
Stop eating.

(e) 食べてはいけません。
You must not eat.

6 　～ろ: Do ～ [Plain command]

The plain command is created by adding **ro** or **e** at the end of the verb in the root form (**ro** for **ru**-verbs and **e** for **u**-verbs), as in 食べろ (tabe-ro) *Eat!* and 飲め (nom-e) *Drink!*. The plain command forms of する and くる are しろ and こい, respectively. The negative counterpart is created by adding な at the end of a verb in the dictionary form, as in 食べるな *Don't eat!* and 飲むな *Don't drink!*.

Plain command forms sound extremely blunt and rough, except when they are used in an embedded sentence, as in ボタンをおせと説明書に書いてあります *It says to press the button on the instruction manual.*

Dictionary Form	Root Form	Plain Command Affirmative	Plain Command Negative
たべる *to eat* taberu	たべ tabe	たべろ tabe-ro	たべるな taberu-na
みる *to watch* miru	み mi	みろ mi-ro	みるな miru-na
かく *to write* kaku	かk kak	かけ kak-e	かくな kaku-na
およぐ *to swim* oyogu	およg oyog	およげ oyog-e	およぐな oyogu-na
あそぶ *to play* asobu	あそb asob	あそべ asob-e	あそぶな asobu-na
よむ *to read* yomu	よm yom	よめ yom-e	よむな yomu-na
しぬ *to die* shinu	しn shin	しね shin-e	しぬな shinu-na
まつ *to wait* matsu	まt mat	まて mat-e	まつな matsu-na
はなす *to speak* hanasu	はなs hanas	はなせ hanas-e	はなすな hanasu-na
つくる *to make* tsukuru	つくr tsukur	つくれ tsukur-e	つくるな tsukuru-na
かう *to buy* kau	かw kaw*	かえ ka-e	かうな kau-na
する *to do* suru	—	しろ shiro	するな suru-na
くる *to come* kuru	—	こい koi	くるな kuru-na

* The consonant **w** is deleted if followed by any sound other than the vowel **a**.

7 ～うちに: While / before ～
[The time adverbial that bears a threat]

～うちに forms a time adverbial clause that means *while ～* or *before ～*, and it specifies the time period during which the action denoted by the main verb takes place. Since うち is a noun, the verbs and adjectives that precede it must be in the pre-nominal form.

The important pragmatic implication ～うちに offers is that something bad will happen if the action is not performed during the specified period or before the specified event. For this reason, sentence (a) is appropriate, but sentence (b) is not: assuming that reading can be done more easily when a baby is asleep than when he / she is awake.

(a) あかちゃんがねているうちに、本を読みます。　　(✔)
   While the baby is sleeping, I will read a book.

(b) あかちゃんがおきているうちに、本を読みます。　　(✘)
   Intended meaning: *While the baby is awake, I will read a book.* (Inappropriate)

The following two sentences are grammatical, but (c) implies that Ms. Yamada's presence is beneficial or necessary for the speaker to finish his / her homework, whereas (d) does not have such an implication:

(c) 山田さんがここにいるうちに、宿題をします。

(d) 山田さんがここにいる間に、宿題をします。

The following are additional examples:

(e) 明るいうちに、行きましょう。
   Let's leave (here) while it is bright.

(f) 暗くならないうちに、帰りましょう。
   Let's go home before it gets dark.

(g) かぜが悪くならないうちに、薬をのんでください。
   Please take the medicine before your cold gets bad.

(h) しめきりが来ないうちに、もうしこみます。
   I will apply before the deadline.

(i) 大学生のうちに、りょこうをします。
   While I am a college student, I will go on a trip.

8 ～か (どうか): If ～, whether (or not) ～ [Embedded question]

Verbs like 知る *to know*, 分かる *to understand*, きく *to ask* and 教える *to teach / to let someone know* can take a question sentence as the content of what is known, understood, asked, or taught. Such a question is called an embedded question. An **embedded question** must be followed by the particle か, and the verbs and adjectives in it must be in the plain form, as in the following sentences:

(a) 私はスミスさんが何語を話すか知っています。
   I know what language Mr. Smith speaks.

(b) 田中さんはスミスさんが何語を話すか知っていますか。
   Does Mr. Tanaka know what language Mr. Smith speaks?

(c) 私はスミスさんが英語を話すか知っています。
   I know if Mr. Smith speaks English.

(d) 昨日パーティーにだれが来たか教えてください。
   Please let me know who came to the party yesterday.

だ at the end of a na-type adjective and a copula is usually deleted in embedded questions.

(e) スミスさんはすしが好き(だ)か知っていますか。
   Do you know if Mr. Smith likes sushi?

(f) これはいくら(だ)か教えてください。
   Please let me know how much this one is.

If the embedded question does not contain a question word such as だれ and いつ, ～か may optionally be followed by どうか as in the following examples:

(g) 田中さんが英語を話すか(どうか)知っていますか。
   Do you know whether (or not) Mr. Tanaka speaks English?

(h) スミスさんはアメリカ人 (だ) か (どうか)
しらべてください。

Please check whether (or not) Mr. Smith is an American.

(i) スミスさんが来るか (どうか) 教えてください。

Please let me know whether (or not) Mr. Smith is coming.

---

9 ~によって: **Depending on ~**
[Determinant factors]

The phrase 〜によって *depending on ~* specifies the criteria for variation or decision expressed by verbs such as 違う *to differ*, 決まる *to be decided*, 分ける *to divide* and かえる *to change*.

(a) カフェテリアのたべものは 毎日同じですか。

Is the food at the cafeteria the same every day?

— いいえ、日によって 違います。

— No, it is different, depending on the day.

(b) アメリカ人はみんな背が 高いんですか。

Are all Americans tall?

— 人によって、 違います。

— It depends on each person.

(c) 大学のコースはみんな 難しいですか。

Are all the college courses difficult?

— いいえ、コースによって 違います。

— No, it depends on the course.

(d) 成績はテストの点数によって 決まります。

The grade is decided depending on the test scores.

(e) 成績によってクラスを分けます。

We will divide the classes based on the grades.

(f) 成績によって 宿題をかえます。

We will change the homework depending on the grades.

– Writing –

ⓐ こざとへん

	こざとへん *hill, mound*
阝	Example: 大阪 *Osaka*, 〜階 *~th floor*, 陸 *land*, 太陽 *sun*

– Kanji List –

部長・〜部・仕方・正しい・悪い・着く・東京・大阪・奥さん・妻・家内・家・夫・決める・考える・違う・専攻・専門

部 ブ *department, part*	丶 一 ナ ㄄ 立 ㊄ 咅 咅 咅 部 部 [11]
	Example: テニス部 *tennis club*, 部長 *division head*
長 なが-い・チョウ *long, eldest, chief*	丨 ㇐ ㇒ ㇒ ㇗ 手 長 長 [8]
	Example: 長い *long*, 部長 *division head*, 社長 *company president*
仕 つか-える・シ *serve*	ノ イ 仁 什 仕 [5]
	Example: 仕方 *method*, 仕事 *job, work*
方 かた / がた・ホウ *direction, way, means*	丶 ㇒ 方 方 [4]
	Example: 仕方 *method*, あの方 *that person*, 〜の方 *~'s side*
正 ただ-しい・セイ・ショウ *correct, right*	一 丁 下 正 正 [5]
	Example: 正しい *correct*
悪 わる-い・アク *bad, ill*	一 ㇐ ㇐ 戸 亜 亜 亜 悪 悪 悪 [11]
	Example: 悪い *bad*

着 つ-く・き-る・チャク arrive, wear, reach	、ソ 艹 艹 芦 芦 差 差 着 着 着 着　[12]
	Example: 着る to wear, 着く to arrive
東 ひがし・トウ east	一 ｢ 戸 戸 百 車 東 東　[8]
	Example: 東 east, 東京 Tokyo
京 キョウ・ケイ capital	、 一 ｝ 亠 亩 亨 京 京　[8]
	Example: 東京 Tokyo, 京都 Kyoto
大 おお-きい・ダイ・タイ big, great	一 ナ 大　[3]
	Example: 大きい big, 大学 university
阪 さか・ハン slope	' ３ ß ß' ß' 阪 阪　[7]
	Example: 大阪 Osaka
奥 おく・オウ deep, inside, madam, interior	' ｢ 巾 冂 冂 冉 南 南 南 奥 奥 奥　[12]
	Example: 奥さん someone else's wife, madam
妻 つま・サイ wife	一 ヲ ョ 肀 肀 妻 妻 妻　[8]
	Example: 妻 one's wife
家 いえ・や・カ・ケ house	、 ｳ 宀 宀 宁 宇 宇 宇 家 家　[10]
	Example: 家 house, 家内 one's own wife
内 うち・ナイ inner, within, inside	｜ 冂 内 内　[4]
	Example: 家内 one's own wife
夫 おっと・フ・フウ husband	一 二 チ 夫　[4]
	Example: 夫 one's husband

決 き-める・き-まる・ケツ・ケッ determine	、 ｼ ｼ 沪 沪 決　[7]
	Example: 決める to decide
考 かんが-える・コウ consider	一 十 土 耂 耂 考　[6]
	Example: 考える to think
違 ちが-う・イ differ	' ｳ 虍 肀 吾 吾 告 査 查 韋 韋 違 違　[13]
	Example: 違う to differ
専 もっぱ-ら・セン exclusive, sole	一 ｢ 戸 戸 百 申 車 専 専　[9]
	Example: 専門 specialty, 専攻 academic major
攻 せ-める・コウ attack	一 ｢ 工 エ' 玏 攻 攻　[7]
	Example: 専攻 academic major
門 かど・モン gate	｜ ｢ ｢ ｢ ｢ ｢ 門 門 門　[8]
	Example: 専門 specialty

– Review –

Q1. *For each of the following words, pick the counterpart from the box.*

1. つま

2. おくさん

3. いい

4. おなじ

| a. ただしい |
| b. おっと |
| c. ちがう |
| d. わるい |
| e. ごしゅじん |

Q2. *Write the pronunciation of the kanji characters in the following sentences.*

1. 部長が大阪に着きました。
2. 家ではティーシャツを着ています。
3. せいせきが悪いです。
4. うちの家内です。
5. 人によって違います。

Q3. *Fill in the blanks with either* はず *or* べき.

1. あなたは学生ですから、もっと勉強する _____ です。

2. 昨日送りましたから、明日着く _____ です。

3. へんですね。ここにおいた _____ なのに、ありませんね。

4. 私はもっとがんばる _____ なんです。

5. 勉強した _____ なのに、せいせきがよくありませんでした。

6. 日本は今冬ですから、オーストラリアは今夏の _____ です。

Q4. *Fill in the blanks.*

1. 日本語のせいせきが悪いということは _____ ということです。

2. このクラスはしけんがないということは _____ ということです。

3. 日本に5年住んだということは _____ ということです。

4. 父はテレビがきらいです。ですから、_____ _____ うちに、テレビを見ます。

5. ピザはあつくないと、おいしくありません。ですから、_____ うちに、食べます。

6. あかちゃんが_____ うちに、新聞を読みます。

7. ブラウンさんは来ましたか。

   — さあ、_____ わかりません。

8. 夏休みにどこに行きますか。

   — _____ わかりません。

Q5. *Answer the following questions in Japanese.*

1. あなたの大学の先生はみんなやさしいですか。

2. あなたがとっているクラスはみんなしけんがありますか。

3. あなたは毎日3時間以上勉強しますか。
   (3時間以上 *three hours or more*)

Tips and Additional Knowledge: Female Speech Particle わ

わ is a female speech emphasis particle used at the end of a sentence following verbs and adjectives. It is often followed by the particle よ or ね. It is usually appropriately used only by women.

(a) 私が行くわよ。
   I'll go there.

(b) きれいだわ。
   It's beautiful.

(c) ちょっと高いわね。
   It's a little expensive, isn't it?

(d) あの人は日本人だわ。
   That person is Japanese.

CHAPTER TWENTY-FOUR
What Would You Do?

テニスをしよう Your Intention and Attempt

Notes Relating to This Lesson

Grammar and Usage	Writing
1 ～よう 148	ⓐ うまへん.........153
2 ～ようとおもう ..148	
3 ～ようとする 149	

📖 Basic Vocabulary and Kanji

せんぱい	先輩	n. one's senior
こうはい	後輩	n. one's junior
のうりょく	能力	n. ability
ざんねん（な）	残念だ・残念じゃない	adj. regrettable, disappointing
うける	e-ru 受ける・受けない・受け・受けて	v. to receive, to take (an exam)
にげる	e-ru 逃げる・逃げない・逃げ・逃げて	v. to escape
もうしこむ	m-u 申し込む・申し込まない・申し込み・申し込んで	v. to apply
かならず	必ず	adv. without fail, by all means
うそをつく	嘘をつく	to tell a lie
～きゅう	～級	level ~

Newly introduced kanji:

受ける・申しこむ・～級・試験 (exam / test) ⓐ

受	ァ ぐ ⼧ ⼧ ⼧ 受 受
級	く ⼇ ⼇ ⼇ ⼇ 糸 糸 約 級 級
試	、 ー ⼆ ⼆ ⾔ ⾔ ⾔ ⾔ 訂 訂 試 試
験	１ ⼕ ⼕ ⼕ ⼕ ⼕ 馬 馬 馬 馬 馬 駖 駖 駖 駖 験 験 験

💿💬 Dialog 1

A senior student is inviting a junior student to play tennis.

せんぱい　：明日ひま？

こうはい　：はい。

せんぱい　：じゃあ、いっしょにテニスを<u>しよう</u>。

こうはい　：ああ、いいですね。<u>しましょう</u>。

Guess and Try 1

What is the difference between the two underlined parts in the above dialog? 1

Guess and Try 2

Fill in the blanks and state how the volitional form (for example, 食べよう) is created. 1

食べる ⟶ 食べよう　　見る ⟶ 1.＿＿＿＿＿

読む ⟶ 読もう　　話す ⟶ 2.＿＿＿＿＿

買う ⟶ 3.＿＿＿＿＿　　遊ぶ ⟶ 4.＿＿＿＿＿

持つ ⟶ 5.＿＿＿＿＿　　作る ⟶ 6.＿＿＿＿＿

する ⟶ しよう　　来る ⟶ 来よう

💿💬 Dialog 2

A student of Japanese is talking to his teacher about a Japanese exam.

学生：去年日本語のうりょく試験を受けようと思って、申しこんだんです。

先生：ああ。

学生：でも、かいじょうで試験を受けようとした時、おなかが痛くなって受けられなかったんです。
（会場　meeting / event venue）

先生：それはざんねんでしたね。じゃあ、今年はがんばってください。

学生　：　はい。今年はかならず１級を受けます。

先生　：　だいじょうぶですか。３級の方がいいんじゃないですか。

```
┌─────────────────────────┐
│    にほんごのうりょくしけん    │
│   日本語　能力試験         │
│                         │
│  Japanese Language       │
│  Proficiency Exam        │
│                         │
│        4 級             │
└─────────────────────────┘
```

Guess and Try 3

What do the underlined parts in Dialog 2 mean? ② ③

Guess and Try 4

What do the following sentences mean? ① ② ③

1. 日本に行こう。
2. 私は日本に行こうと思いました。
3. 私は日本に行くと思いました。
4. 私は日本に行こうとしました。
5. 私はできるだけ日本に行くようにしました。

Drill 1: Conjugation

食べる → 食べよう

1. 探す
2. わらう
3. 泣く
4. 申しこむ
5. 受ける
6. にげる
7. 取る
8. 待つ
9. 決める
10. する

Drill 2: Formation

日本に行く → 日本に行こうと思います

1. 日本にりゅう学する
2. 今年卒業する
3. 父に話す
4. 社長にたのむ
5. ビジネスのクラスを取る
6. 学長にお願いする
7. 日本語のうりょく試験を受ける

Drill 3: Formation

日本に行く → 日本に行こうとしました

1. カンニングをする
2. お酒を飲む
3. うそをつく
4. 車をこわす

Task 1

State what the person is trying to do in each of the following situations using 〜としています。

1.　　　2.　　　3.　　　4.

Task 2: Pair Work

Ask your partner the following questions. Take turns, then share them in the class.

1. 今度の日曜日は何をするか。
2. 今度の夏休みは何をするか。
3. 来学期はどのコースを取るか。

Short Reading

前から、いつかダイビングをしてみたいと思っていました。海底の魚や珊瑚礁を自分の目で見てみたいと思っていました。今度の夏休みに沖縄に行ってダイビングのレッスンを受けようと考えています。友達の夏子さんといっしょにレッスンを受けようと思います。

(海底 the bottom of the sea, 珊瑚礁 coral reef, 沖縄 Okinawa (name of a place))

Writing

Write about something that you wanted to try for a long time.

もし―おく円もらったら If By Any Chance

Notes Relating to This Lesson	
Grammar and Usage	
4 Demonstratives for the items outside of the visual field 149	5 ～たら、…した...150 6 ～たら、…する...150

 ## Basic Vocabulary and Kanji

がくい	学位	n. academic degree
かねも￥ち	金持ち	n. rich person
わか￥い	若い・若くない	adj. young
しゅうしょくする	irr. 就職する	v. to find employment
も￥し		adv. if (by any chance)

Newly introduced kanji:

金持ち・若い図書館 (library)・
映画館 (movie theater)

若	一 十 サ ナ 芝 芋 若 若
館	ノ 𠆢 𠆢 𠆢 今 今 𣦵 飠 飠' 飠' 飠' 館 館 館 館 館

 ## Dialog 1

John Smith is talking to Yoko Yamada about their former classmate.

スミス : 昨日、図書館に行ったら、ポールさんがいたんですよ。

山田 : えっ、ポールさん？ その人は学生ですか。

スミス : 覚（おぼ）えていないんですか。社会学（しゃかいがく）をいっしょに取（と）っていた人ですよ。

山田 : ああ、あの人ですか。あのめがねをかけて、よくしゃべる人ですよね。

スミス : ええ、そうです。

Guess and Try 1

What is the difference between the two underlined parts in Dialog 1? Based on your guess, choose the appropriate option in the parentheses in the following sentences. 4

1. ポケモンをしっていますか。
   ― ええ。もちろん。（ それ・あれ ）はアメリカでも人気（にんき）がありますね。

2. ポケモンをしっていますか。
   ― いいえ。（ それ・あれ ）は何ですか。

Guess and Try 2

Fill in the blanks. Then, state how to create たら forms (for example, 食べたら). 5

食べる → 食べたら　　書く → 書いたら
泳ぐ → 1. _____　　取る → 2. _____
する → 3. _____　　若い → 4. _____
きれいだ → 5. _____
日本人だ → 6. _____

Guess and Try 3

Fill in the blank so that the following two sentences can be synonymous. 5

図書館に行ったら、ポールさんがいました ≡
図書館に _____、ポールさんがいました

Dialog 2

Ken Kawaguchi is telling Yoko Yamada his problem.

川口 : じつは大学をやめようと思っているんです。お金がないんです。

山田 : でも、来年は卒業（そつぎょう）ですよ。

川口 : ええ。

山田 : 卒業して、がくいをもらったら、しゅうしょくしやすいですよ。

川口 : そうですね。

山田 : ええ、そうですよ。もう少しがんばってくださいよ。

Guess and Try 4

What does the underlined part in Dialog 2 mean? 6

Guess and Try 5

What do the following sentences mean? 6

1. 7時になったら、明るくなります。
2. 7時になったら、映画が始まります。
3. 7時になったら、電話してください。
4. （もし）元気になったら、また働くつもりです。
5. （もし）高かったら、クレジットカードを使います。
6. （もし）私が鳥だったら、空 (sky) をとびます (fly)。

Drill 1: Conjugation

食べる ➡ 食べたら

1. 運ぶ
2. 着く
3. わかる
4. おちる
5. 来る
6. もらう
7. 卒業する
8. 入学する
9. しゅうしょくする
10. しっている

Drill 2: Conjugation

高い ➡ 高かったら
まじめだ ➡ まじめだったら

1. 安い
2. 若い
3. 親切だ
4. 元気だ
5. 弱い
6. 書きにくい
7. わかりやすい
8. 金持ちだ
9. こわそうだ
10. 元気になりたい

Drill 3: Formation

高い・買わないでください

　　➡ 高かったら、買わないでください

1. おもしろそうだ・見てみます

2. きらいだ・食べなくてもいいです
3. 日本人だ・日本語が話せるはずです
4. 金持ちだ・楽でしょう
5. 若い・学いを二つ取るかもしれません
6. わからない・電話をしてください

Task 1: Group Work

What would you do if you won one million dollars? Talk about it in your group, and then share it in the class.

For example:
A：もし 100 万ドルもらったら、どうしますか。
B：まず、車を買います。
C：どんな車ですか。
B：ポルシェです。
A：それから？
B：それから、…

Task 2: Role Play

A: Your father's company went bankrupt, and he cannot pay for your tuition fees. You are thinking of quitting college. （つぶれる *to become bankrupt*)

B: Your friend looks sad, and you wonder what happened. You are willing to give him / her some advice if he / she needs it.

Short Reading

　もし一億円もらったら、まずローンを返します。それから、大きい家と車を買います。それから、父と母と弟に 100 万円ずつあげます。そして、残りは銀行の定期預金に貯金します。

（一億円 *one hundred million yen*, ローン *loan; debt*, 100 万円 *one million yen*, 残り *leftover*, 定期預金 *CD; fixed deposit*, 貯金する *to deposit (money)*)

Writing

Write what you would do if you got one hundred million yen.

日本に行くなら、**JR** パスを買ってください **Traveling**

Notes Relating to This Lesson	
Grammar and Usage	**Culture**
7 〜なら 151	Ⓐ Some towns in Tokyo
8 〜てき（な）. 152	 152
	Ⓑ JR パス 153

📖 Basic Vocabulary and Kanji

な˺ごや	名古屋	*pn. Nagoya (name of a place)*
あきは˺ばら	秋葉原	*pn. Akihabara (name of a place)* Ⓐ
かんこう	観光	*n. sightseeing*
りょかん	旅館	*n. Japanese-style inn*
みせ˺・おみせ	店・お店	*n. store*
りょこうが˺いしゃ	旅行会社	*n. travel agency*
しんか˺ん˺せん	新幹線	*n. Shinkansen (bullet train in Japan)*
でんとう	伝統	*n. tradition*
こうきゅう（な）	高級だ・高級じゃない	*adj. high grade, high class, fancy*
〜なら		*if〜* 7
〜てき（な）	〜的だ・〜的じゃない	*typical 〜, like 〜 (日本的だ very Japanese)* 8

Newly introduced kanji:

名古屋 ・ 京都 (Kyoto) ・
店 ・ 高級 だ ・ 〜的

都	一 十 土 少 者 者 者 者゛者 都
店	丶 亠 广 广 广 店 店 店
的	丿 丁 白 白 白 的 的

💿 🗨 Dialog

An American student, Mike Baker, is going to visit Japan for the very first time. He is consulting Mariko Lord.

ベーカー ： 来月（らいげつ）日本に行こうと思っているんですよ。

ロード ： ああ、そうですか。①日本に行くなら、JR パスを買った方（ほう）がいいですよ。しんかんせんが安く乗（の）れますから。

ベーカー ： ああ、そうですか。ホテルはどんなところがいいですか。

ロード ： ②日本的なホテルなら、りょかんが一番（いちばん）いいですよ。ちょっと高いですが。

Guess and Try 1 (Open discussion)
Do you know any interesting towns in Tokyo? Do you know JR パス？ Ⓐ Ⓑ

Guess and Try 2
What do the underlined parts in the above dialog mean? 7

Guess and Try 3
Fill in the blanks and state how to form the なら form (for example, 食べるなら). 7

食べる ⟶ 食べるなら

行く ⟶ 行くなら

食べない ⟶ 1. _____

食べた ⟶ 2. _____

高い　　　　→　3. _____

便利だ　　　→　便利なら

日本人だ　　→　4. _____

日本人だった　→　5. _____

Guess and Try 4 (optional)

State what the following sentences mean, paying attention to the time of the events. ⑦

1. 日本に行くなら、京都に行ってください。
2. 日本に行くなら、ニューヨークのりょこう会社でJRパスを買ってください。

🗣 Drill 1: Formation

かんこう・京都

　　→　かんこうなら、京都がいいですよ

1. 日本的なホテル・りょかん
2. 安い店・あきはばら
3. 安いホテル・YMCA
4. 高級なレストラン・ぎんざ
5. でんとう的なたてもの・京都

🗣 Drill 2: Formation

日本に行く・JRパスを買った方がいいですよ

　　→　日本に行くなら、JRパスを買った方がいいですよ

1. 海に行く・ビーチチェアーを持って行った方がいいですよ
2. 外国に行く・パスポートを持って行かなくてはいけませんよ
3. フランスに行く・フランス語を少し勉強した方がいいですよ
4. 東京に行く・東京ディズニーランドを見た方がいいですよ

🏳 Task 1: Group Work

Pretend that you want to go to one of the following places next month, ask other members in your group for advice or recommendations.

1. ニューヨーク *New York*
2. ホンコン *Hong Kong*
3. ??? *(Your choice)*

For example:

A：ニューヨークはどこがおもしろいですか。

B：かんこうなら、エンパイアーステートビルや、セントラルパークがいいですよ。セントラルパークには動物園もあります。

A：ああ、そうですか。

C：それから、…

🏳 Task 2: Group Work

Discuss in your group what advice can be given to someone who has the following problems.

1. 日本に6ヶ月りゅう学するが、北海道に行った方がいいか東京に行った方がいいか分からない。
2. りょうこうをする時に、クレジットカードを持って行った方がいいかトラベラーズ・チェックを持って行った方がいいか分からない。

📖 Short Reading

日本にはいろいろおもしろいところがあります。日本の伝統的な建物を見るなら、京都がいいでしょう。民芸品を買いたいなら、浅草がいいでしょう。高校生や若い人のファッションが見たいなら、原宿がいいでしょう。高級なお店やギャラリーを見るなら、銀座がいいでしょう。安いカメラや、電気製品を買いたいなら、秋葉原がいいでしょう。

(民芸品 *folk craft goods*, 電気製品 *electric commodities*)

✎ Writing

Write about the good places to visit if someone is going to your country or your parent's country.

– Grammar and Usage –

1 ～よう: Let's ～ [Volitional form]

The volitional form of a verb can be created by adding **yō** or **ō** at the end of a verb in the root form: **yō** for a **ru**-verb and **ō** for an **u**-verb. That is, you drop **ru** from a **ru**-verb and add **yō**, or you drop **u** from an **u**-verb and add **ō**. The volitional forms of the two major irregular verbs する and くる are しよう and こよう, respectively. The examples are found in the following table:

Dictionary Form	Root Form	Volitional Form
たべる to eat	たべ tabe	たべよう tabe-yō
みる to watch	み mi	みよう mi-yō
かく to write	かk kak	かこう kak-ō
およぐ to swim	およg oyog	およごう oyog-ō
あそぶ to play	あそb asob	あそぼう asob-ō
よむ to read	よm yom	よもう yom-ō
しぬ to die	しn shin	しのう shin-ō
まつ to wait	まt mat	まとう mat-ō
はなす to speak	はなs hanas	はなそう hanas-ō
つくる to make	つくr tsukur	つくろう tsukur-ō
かう to buy	かw kaw*	かおう ka-ō
する to do	—	しよう shiyō
くる to come	—	こよう koyō

* The consonant **w** is deleted if followed by any sound other than the vowel **a**.

Volitional form is the plain counterpart of ～ましょう, which is discussed in Chapter Five Volume 1, and it means *Let's do* ~ when used at the end of a sentence.

(a) テニスをしよう。
    Let's play tennis.
(b) テニスをしましょう。
    Let's play tennis.

When used at the end of an embedded sentence, it shows one's intention or will. (See Grammar and Usage note 2 in this chapter.)

2 ～ようとおもう: To be thinking of ～ing [Volitional plan]

The verbs in the volitional form （～よう） can be used with a verb that expresses thinking such as 思う *to think* and 考える *to consider*, expressing one's intention or will. For example, 行こうと思います means *I'm thinking of going*. The use of volitional forms emphasizes one's conscious intention as you can see in the difference between (a) and (b): (a) expresses the speaker's willingness, but (b) merely expresses what the speaker thinks will happen to him / her regardless of his / her will.

(a) 私は行こうと思います。
    I'm thinking of going (there).
(b) 私は行くと思います。
    I think I will go (there).
(c) スペインは行ったことがないので、来月行こうと思います。
    I have never been to Spain, so I am thinking of going there next month.
(d) 前の試験は悪かったので、今度の試験はがんばろうと考えています。
    The previous exam was bad, so I am thinking of trying my best for the next one.
(e) あまり好きじゃありませんが、食べようと思います。
    I do not like (it) very much, but I am thinking of eating (it.)

For expressing the third person's intention and will, the main verbs, for example, 思う and 考える, must be in the progressive form, as in (f).

(f) 弟は日本にりゅう学しようと思っています。
My brother is thinking of studying abroad in Japan.

③ ～ようとする: To attempt to ～ [Momentum attempt]

When the verb する follows a verb in the volitional form, it expresses a momentum act of attempt, for example, なっとうを食べようとしました means that someone attempted or tried to eat fermented soybeans by bringing them to his / her mouth. Depending on the context, either the act of attempt, as in (a), or the time of the attempt, as in (b), is emphasized.

(a) なっとうを食べようとしましたが、くさくて食べられませんでした。
I tried to eat fermented soybeans, but they were smelly and I couldn't eat (them).

(b) 食べようとした時に、電話が来ました。
When I tried to eat, the phone rang.

To express a long-term conscious effort or continuous conscious effort, ～ようにする must be used, as in (c), and to express just an intention or will, ～ようと思う must be used, as in (d) to (e).

(c) 毎日なっとうを食べるようにしました。
I tried to eat fermented soybeans every day. (Long-term effort)

(d) 朝ご飯になっとうを食べようと思いました。
I thought of eating fermented soybeans for breakfast. (Intention or will)

(e) 夏休みにはできるだけ勉強しようと思います。
I would like to study Japanese as much as possible during the summer vacation. (Intention or will)

④ Demonstratives for the items outside of the visual field (あれ, etc.)

The pronouns あれ and それ can be used for referring to the items that are outside of the visual field of the speaker and listener.

When both the speaker and listener know the identity of the item, あれ is used:

(a) ピカチューをしっていますか。
Do you know Picachu?
— ええ。もちろん。あれはアメリカでも人気がありますね。
— *Yes. Of course. That is popular in the US, too.*

On the other hand, if only one of the parties knows it, それ is used.

(b) ピカチューをしっていますか。
Do you know Picachu?
— いいえ。それは何ですか。
— *No. What is that?*

(c) 昨日デジタル・カメラを買いました。でも、弟がそれをこわしてしまったんです。
Yesterday, I bought a digital camera, but my brother broke it.

The parallel distinction holds with あの and その, and あそこ and そこ.

(d) 昨日ブラウンさんに会いました。
I saw Mr. Brown yesterday.
— ああ、あの人は日本語のクラスを取っていましたね。
— *Oh! That person was taking a Japanese class, right?*

(e) 明日ブラウンさんに会います。
I will see Mr. Brown tomorrow.
— その人は先生ですか。学生ですか。
— *Is that person a teacher, or a student?*

(f) 明日ことぶきに行きます。
I will go to Kotobuki (restaurant) tomorrow.
— ああ、あそこはおいしいですね。
— *Oh, (the food) there is delicious, isn't it?*

(g) 明日ことぶきに行きます。
I will go to Kotobuki (restaurant) tomorrow.
— そこはおいしいですか。
— *Is (the food) there delicious?*

(h) 戦争中は大変でしたね。
It was very tough during the war, right?
— ええ、あの頃は食べ物がありませんでしたね。
— *Yes, we didn't have food during that period, did we?*

(i) 私は1970年にアメリカに来ました。
I came to the United States in 1970.
— その時はもう結婚していましたか。
— *At that time, were you already married?*

5 ～たら、… した: After / when ～, … [Sporadic consequence]

There are some cases where one's attention is caught by what happened **after** doing something. Such situations can be expressed by ～たら、… した as well as ～と、… した. For example, both sentences below state what happened after opening the window:

(a) まどをあけたら、鳥が入って来ました。
After / when I opened the window, a bird came in.

(b) まどをあけると、鳥が入って来ました。
After / when I opened the window, a bird came in.

The たら form is created by adding ら at the end of the plain past form of verbs and adjectives as shown in the following table:

	Dictionary Form	Plain Past Tense Form	たら Form
Verbs	食べる	食べた	食べたら
Copula	日本人だ	日本人だった	日本人だったら
Adjectives	便利だ	便利だった	便利だったら
	高い	高かった	高かったら

The たら-clause in this context can be replaced by a simple sentence and the connective word そうしたら, as in:

(c) まどをあけました。そうしたら、鳥が入って来ました。

I opened the window. Then a bird came in.

6 ～たら、… する: After / when / whenever / if ～, … [Conditioned consequence]

～たら、… する expresses the situation where the action / state expressed by the main clause in a sentence takes place after the action / state expressed by the たら -clause. Depending on the speaker's presupposition, it expresses a "generic condition", "temporal condition", "hypothetical condition" or "counterfactual condition". The use and examples of each case are as follows:

Conditions Expressed by たら:

A. [Generic Condition] After / whenever / when ~
It can happen, and whenever it happens, ...

The たら-clause can specify the generic condition, where the situation described in it is almost **always** followed by another situation due to generic facts, laws and rules in nature, mathematics, society and family.

For example:

(a) 朝になったら、明るくなります。
When the morning comes, it becomes bright.

(b) 薬をのんだら、よくなります。
After I take the medicine, I get better.

(c) 父はおこったら、どなります。
My father shouts whenever he gets mad.

B. [Temporal condition] After / when ~
It will happen for sure, and when it happens, ...

The たら-clause can specify the temporal condition, where the described situation is assumed to certainly take place, and the entire sentence expresses what happens **when** it takes place.

For example:

(d) うちに帰ったら、電話してください。
When you get home, please call me.

(e) この映画がおわったら、ねます。
When this movie ends, I will go to bed.

C. [Hypothetical condition] If ~
It may or may not happen, but if it happens, ...

The たら-clause can specify the hypothetical condition, where the described situation is just hypothetical, and may or may not take place, and the entire sentence expresses what happens **if** it takes place. It is often used with the adverb もし (if).

For example:

(f) （もし）元気になったら、また働くつもりです。
If I get better (Lit. become healthy), I will work again.

(g) （もし）高かったら、クレジットカードを使います。

If it is expensive, I will use the credit card.

(h) （もし）日本人だったら、電話ばんごうをきいてください。

If he is a Japanese, please ask for his telephone number.

D. [Counterfactual condition] If ~

It would never happen, but if it happens, ...

The たら-clause can specify the counterfactual condition, where the described situation is not only hypothetical but also very unrealistic, and the entire sentence expresses what would happen if, by any chance, that **unrealistic** situation comes true. It is usually accompanied by the adverb もし.

For example:

(i) （もし）私が鳥だったら、空をとびます。

If I were a bird, I would fly in the sky.

(j) （もし）死んだおばあさんが帰って来たら、いろいろ話しをするでしょう。

If my late grandmother came back (from the heaven), I would talk with her about many things.

Some sentences may be interpreted ambiguously depending on the context. For example, 山田さんが来たら、私は帰ります can be a temporal condition (*When Ms. Yamada comes, I will leave*) or a hypothetical condition (*If Ms. Yamada comes, I will leave*) depending on how sure the speaker is about Ms. Yamada's coming.

The たら-clause can be replaced by the と clause only if it expresses the generic or temporal condition and the main clause expresses a definite event rather than an open statement such as a suggestion or a request.

(k) 父はうちに帰ったら、すぐ着がえます。

My father immediately changes his clothes when he gets home.

(l) 父はうちに帰ると、すぐ着がえます。

My father immediately changes his clothes when he gets home.

(m) うちに帰ったら、電話してください。

When you get home, please call me.

(n) うちに帰ると、電話してください。（✗）

(Ungrammatical)

7　～なら: If ～ / if you are talking about ～ [Supposition]

Our opinions and ideas change depending on the context. The なら clause defines the context or supposition on which the statement in the main clause is based, meaning *if ~* or *if you are talking about ~*. なら follows verbs and adjectives in the plain form, except that だ that appears at the end of a copula and a na-adjective must be dropped, as summarized in the following table:

	Plain Form	なら Form
Verbs	食べる 食べた	食べるなら 食べたなら
Copula	日本人だ 日本人だった	日本人なら 日本人だったなら
Adjectives	便利だ 便利だった	便利なら 便利だったなら
	高い 高かった	高いなら 高かったなら

Unlike the たら-clause, the なら-clause does not emphasize or impose restrictions on the temporal order between two events. For example, the event expressed by the なら-clause (going to Japan) can take place before the event expressed by the main clause as in (a), or after it as in (b):

(a) 日本に行くなら、京都に行ってください。とても、きれいですよ。

If you are going to Japan, please go to Kyoto (after you get there). It's very beautiful.

(b) 日本に行くなら、ニューヨークで JR パスを買ってください。

If you are going to Japan, buy a Japan Rail Pass in New York (before going to Japan).

Accordingly, unlike the たら-clause, the なら-clause cannot express a sporadic consequence in the past, a temporal condition for the future, or a generic condition, which focuses on what event / state followed / follows what event.

(c) 図書館にいったら、ポールさんがいました。

When I went to the library, Paul was there. (Sporadic consequence)

(d) 図書館に行ったなら、ポールさんがいました。(✗)

(Ungrammatical) Intended meaning: as above.

(e) 映画が終わったら、宿題をします。

When the movie is over, I will do my homework. (Temporal condition)

(f) 映画が終わるなら、宿題をします。(✗)

(Ungrammatical) Intended meaning: as above.

The なら-clause tends to be used when the main clause expresses open statements such as suggestions, speculations, conjectures, requests and intentions:

(g) 安いカメラを買いたいなら、秋葉原がいいと思います。

If you want to buy a cheap camera, I think Akihabara would be (a) good (place to go).

(h) 観光なら、京都がいいと思います。

For sightseeing, I think Kyoto would be (a) good (place to go).

(i) 日本に行ったなら、日本のタクシーを見ましたね。

If you have visited Japan, you must have seen Japanese taxis, right?

(j) フランスの高校の学生だったなら、フランス語を話すはずですね。

If he used to go to a French high school, I suppose he speaks French.

(k) 前の試験が難しくなかったなら、今度の試験は難しくします。

If it is true that the previous exam was not difficult, I will make the next exam difficult.

(l) (もし) 私が鳥なら、空をとびます。

If I were a bird, I would fly in the sky.

(m) 安いなら、買います。安くないなら、買いません。

If it is cheap, I will buy it. If it is not cheap, I will not buy it.

8 ～てき (な) [Adjective formative]

The suffix ～的 (な) is attached to words of Chinese origin to create adjectives that mean *typical of ~*, *related to ~*, or *~ -like*.

(a) 経済 *economics* → 経済的 (な) *economical*

(b) 家庭 *home* → 家庭的 (な) *homey*

(c) 日本 *Japan* → 日本的 (な) *very Japanese*

(d) 伝統 *tradition* → 伝統的 (な) *traditional*

(e) 教育 *education* → 教育的 (な) *educational*

(f) 論理 *logic* → 論理的 (な) *logical*

(g) 批判 *criticism* → 批判的 (な) *critical*

(h) 科学 *science* → 科学的 (な) *scientific*

– Culture –

Ⓐ Some towns in Tokyo

東京 is the capital of Japan and also the largest city in Japan. It is the center of government, business, transportation and entertainment. You can get around 東京 by subways and taxis. The following are some towns you may want to visit in Tokyo.

• 秋葉原 is the world famous electric town in Tokyo. It is full of stores that sell cameras, cell phones, computers and electric commodities such as TVs, stereos, kitchen appliances, etc.

あきはばら (秋葉原)

- 浅草 was developed around 浅草観音 (Asakusa Kannon temple). Many shopping arcades with a friendly atmosphere are crowded with tourists. You can buy folk craft goods such as Japanese dolls, paintings, umbrellas, kimonos and figurines as well as Japanese tea and confections.

あさくさ (浅草)

- 銀座 is clustered with high-class boutiques, galleries, restaurants, bars and stores, and considered to be the most expensive place in Japan, and possibly in the world.

ぎんざ (銀座)

- 原宿 is a town where young people, especially teenagers, gather on weekends. They enjoy dancing, or just walking around wearing unusual costumes and make-up. You will be able to see performances and hear live music on the street.

はらじゅく (原宿)

Ⓑ JR パス: **Japan Rail Pass**

If you are traveling around in Japan, it is a good idea to purchase a JR Pass (Japan Rail Pass), which is offered by "Japan Railways". A Japan Rail Pass offers great value and convenience, and it is available only to non-Japanese sightseeing visitors with some exceptions and can be bought from outside of Japan. It gives its bearer almost unlimited travel on JR lines and affiliated buses and ferries.

– Writing –

ⓐ うまへん

うまへん *horse*	
馬	Example: 試験 *exam*, 駅 *railway station*, 駐車 *parking*

– Kanji List –

受ける・申しこむ・〜級・試験・金持ち・若い・図書館・映画館・名古屋・京都・店・高級だ・〜的

受 う－ける・う－かる・ジュ receive	ノ ハ ハ ハ ハ 受 受 受 [8]
	Example: 受ける *to take (an exam)*, 受験 *exam-taking*
申 もう－す・シン report, apply, excuse	丨 口 日 日 申 [5]
	Example: 申す *to say*, 申しこむ *to apply*
級 キュウ level	〈 乡 纟 纟 糸 糸 糸 紆 級 級 [9]
	Example: 二級 *second level*

試 こころ-みる・ため-す・シ try, test	`丶 亠 訁 言 言 訂 試 試 [13]` 試試
	Example: 試験 exam

験 ケン proof, examine	`１ Г Г Г Ｆ 馬 馬 馬 馬 馬' 駒 [18]` 駖駖駖駖験験
	Example: 試験 exam

金 かね・キン gold, metal, money	`ノ 人 人 今 全 全 余 金 [8]`
	Example: 金持ち rich person, 金曜日 Friday, お金 money

持 も-つ・ジ hold	`一 十 扌 扌 扩 扩 拌 持 持 [9]`
	Example: 金持ち rich person, 持つ to hold, 持って行く to bring

若 わか-い・ジャク young	`一 十 艹 艹 艾 芒 若 若 若 [8]`
	Example: 若い young

図 ズ・ト diagram, devise	`丨 冂 冂 冈 図 図 図 [7]`
	Example: 図書館 library, 地図 map

書 か-く・ショ write, book, document	`ㄱ ㅋ ヨ ヨ 聿 聿 書 書 書 書 [10]`
	Example: 書く to write, 図書館 library

館 カン large building, hall	`ノ 𠂉 𠂤 今 今 今 食 食 食' 食' 飵 飵 [16]` 飵飵館館
	Example: 大使館 embassy, 映画館 movie theatre, 図書館 library

映 うつ-る・うつ-す・エイ reflect	`丨 冂 日 日 日 旷 時 映 映 [9]`
	Example: 映画 movie, 映画館 movie theater

画 ガ・ガク picture	`一 厂 厈 而 而 面 面 画 画 [8]`
	Example: 映画 movie, 映画館 movie theatre

名 な・メイ・ミョウ name, famous, members	`ノ ク タ タ 名 名 [6]`
	Example: 名前 name, 名古屋 Nagoya

古 ふる-い・コ old	`一 十 十 屮 当 当 [6]`
	Example: 古い old, 名古屋 Nagoya

屋 や・オク roof, shop, house	`一 冖 尸 尸 尸 居 屈 屋 屋 [9]`
	Example: 部屋 room, 名古屋 Nagoya, 花屋 flower shop

京 キョウ・ケイ capital	`一 亠 亠 宁 古 宁 京 京 [8]`
	Example: 東京 Tokyo, 京都 Kyoto

都 みやこ・ト capital, big city, Tokyo	`一 十 土 夬 者 者 者 者' 者' 都 [11]`
	Example: 京都 Kyoto

店 みせ・テン shop	`丶 亠 广 广 庐 店 店 店 [8]`
	Example: 店 store, 店員 salesclerk, 書店 bookstore

高 たか-い・コウ high, expensive	`丶 亠 亠 古 古 宁 高 高 高 高 [10]`
	Example: 高級だ high grade, 高校 high school, 高い expensive

的 テキ target, suffix to make na-adjectives	`ノ 丨 自 自 白 白' 的 的 [8]`
	Example: 文化的だ cultural

– Review –

Q1. *Choose the appropriate option in the parentheses.*

1. 来週、試験を (取ります・受けます)。

2. 大学を (卒業・入学) して、がくいをもらいました。

3. 田中さんは (お金・金持ち) です。

4. せんぱいと、(こうこう・こうはい) が話していました。

Q2. *Write the readings of the following phrases and state what the members of each set have in common.*

1. 本屋・名古屋・肉屋・魚屋・部屋

2. 京都・東京

3. 図書館・映画館・ご飯・飲む

4. 試験・話す・英語・読む

Q3. *Fill in each blank using one of the items in the box.*

行く　　行こう　　行き　　行って

1. フロリダには友達がいるので、今度 _____ と思います。

2. 母は明日病院に _____ と思います。

3. _____ としましたが、車がこわれて行けませんでした。

4. 明日東京に _____ つもりです。

5. 日本に _____ たいです。

6. 新しいレストランに _____ みます。

Q4. *Choose the appropriate option(s) in the parentheses.*

1. すみません。(あれ・それ) はいくらですか。
— これは 500 円です。

2. 昨日プリクラに行きました。
— えっ、(あれ・それ) は何ですか。

3. 田中さんが新しい部長になりました。
— ああ、そうですか。でも、(あの・その) 人はちょっといじわるですよ。

4. コンピューターを (買ったら・買うなら)、私がいい店につれて行ってあげます。

5. よく勉強 (すると・したら)、100 点がとれますよ。

6. よく勉強 (すると・したら)、ゆっくり休んでください。

7. ナイフを (使うと・使ったら)、ちゃんとしまってください。

8. まっすぐ (行くと・行ったら)、大きいたてものが見えます。

Q5. *Fill in the blanks and complete the sentences.*

1. わかりませんでしたが、先生にきいたら、_____ した。

2. お酒を飲んだら、いつも _____ _____ 。

3. このテレビがおわったら、_____ _____ 。

4. もし明日ひまだったら、_____ _____ 。

5. もし私が金持ちだったら、_____ _____ 。

6. 日本語のじしょなら、_____ _____ 。

7. さむいなら、_____ _____ 。

8. 宿題が少ないクラスなら、_____ _____ 。

Tips and Additional Knowledge: Terms for Emergency

In case of emergency, call the police or fire department. The police emergency number is 110. If you need an ambulance or fire engine, call 119. You should know the words and phrases in the following table in case of emergency.

助けて！ *Help!*	泥棒 *thief*
事故 *accident*	火事 *fire*
病気 *sickness*	ガス漏れ *gas leak*
警察 *police*	消防署 *fire department*
救急車 *ambulance*	消防車 *fire engine*
救急病院 *emergency hospital*	

CHAPTER TWENTY-FIVE
Your Way of Thinking

あまいものなら何でも食べます　Food Craving

Notes Relating to This Lesson

Grammar and Usage

📖 Basic Vocabulary and Kanji

さと￢う	砂糖	n. sugar
しお￢	塩	n. salt
あまい	甘い・甘くない	adj. sweet
から￢い	辛い・辛くない	adj. (hot) spicy
しょっぱ￢い	しょっぱい・しょっぱくない	adj. salty
ふと￢る	r-u 太る・太らない・太り・太って	v. to gain weight
すっぱ￢い	酸っぱい	adj. sour
くさ￢る	r-u 腐る・腐らない・腐り・腐って	v. to get spoiled
にが￢い	苦い・苦くない	adj. bitter
やせる	e-ru 痩せる・痩せない・痩せ・痩せて	v. to lose weight
いっしょうけ￢んめい (に)	一生懸命 (に)	adv. hard
こんな～		this kind of ~, such ~ (cf. どんな～)
～でも		prt. even 1

Newly introduced kanji:

苦い・太る

太	一ナ大太

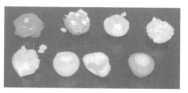

Japanese sweets (和菓子) A

💿 🗨 Dialog

Kyuntaeg Park is asking Yoko Yamada what kind of food her sister likes.

パク ： 山田さんの妹さんは、どんなものが好きですか。

山田 ： あまいものが好きです。①あまいものなら何でも食べます。②さとうでも食べるんですよ。

パク ： ええ？妹さんは太っていますか。

山田 ： いいえ。③何を食べても太らないんです。

パク ： へえ。いいですね。

Guess and Try 1

Do you know any Japanese sweets? A

Guess and Try 2

What do the underlined parts in the above dialog mean? 1 2 3 4

Guess and Try 3

Choose the appropriate option in the parentheses. 1

1. 兄は (難しい・かんたんな) 問題でもわかります。

2. 弟は (難しい・かんたんな) 問題でもわかりません。

Guess and Try 4

Fill in the blanks with question words such as どこ and だれ. If necessary, add a particle. 2

1. こんなかんたんな料理は _____ でも作れます。

2. ＿＿＿＿＿＿ でも行きます。＿＿＿＿＿＿ でもします。ですから、けっこんしてください。

3. えび (shrimp) じゃないなら、＿＿＿＿＿＿ でも食べます。

Guess and Try 5
What do the following sentences mean? ③ ④

1. いっしょうけんめい勉強しても、100点は取れませんでした。いくら勉強しても、100点は取れないんです。

2. 私の弟は父が話しても、聞きません。だれが話しても、聞きません。

🗣 Drill 1: Formation
さとう ⟶ さとうでも食べます

1. まずいもの　　　　2. とてもからいもの
3. くさったもの

🗣 Drill 2: Formation
魚・食べます ⟶ 魚なら何でも食べます

1. お酒・飲みます　　2. 食べもの・食べます
3. 安いもの・買います 4. マンガ・読みます

🗣 Drill 3: Mini Conversation
田中さんにきく ⟶

S 1: 田中さんにきいても、だめでした
S 2: じゃあ、だれにきいても、だめでしょう

1. この薬をのむ　　　　2. 2度たのむ
3. ネックレスを買ってあげる
4. たくさん勉強する

🗂 Task 1
The teacher pretends to be eating something. Based on his / her acting, state the kind of food your teacher is eating (for example, すっぱいもの, あついもの and 魚).

🗂 Task 2: Pair Work
Using the dialog as a model, ask your partner what kind of food he / she likes, then, ask about his / her family members' preferences.

🗂 Task 3: Group Work
Talk about any experiences and feelings of 魚介類 (seafood).

For example:
A : Bさんはぎょかいるいが好きですか。
B : はい。
A : この間ボストンで牡蠣 (oyster) を食べました。とてもおいしかったです。
B : Aさんは鰻を食べたことがありますか。
A : …

Seafood		
烏賊 *squid*	鰻 *eel*	海老 *shrimp / prawn*
貝 *shellfish*	牡蠣 *oyster*	蟹 *crab*
鯖 *mackerel*	蛸 *octopus*	鱈 *cod*
河豚 *blowfish*	鱒 *trout*	鮪 *tuna*

📖 Short Reading
　私の母は食べものなら、何でも食べます。外国の食べものもよく食べます。食べたことがないものでもよく食べます。パンやご飯などの炭水化物も大好きです。でも、ちょっと太りすぎているのでダイエットをしなくてはいけません。他の人が近くでおいしいものを食べていると、とても苦しくなります。私の父はやせています。そして、あまり食べることが好きではありません。世の中は公平なのでしょうか。それとも、不公平なのでしょうか。

(パン *bread,* 炭水化物 *carbohydrate,* 世の中 *world; society,* 公平 *fair,* 不公平 *unfair*)

✏ Writing
Write your opinion about food, including your experiences. Also write about your family members' preferences on food.

もっと早く始めればよかったのに **Regretting**

Notes Relating to This Lesson	
Grammar and Usage	
5 なかなか(〜ない) 167	7 〜れば 167
6 しかたがない 167	

 Basic Vocabulary and Kanji

じゅうたい	渋滞	*n. traffic jam*
くうこう	空港	*n. airport*
まちが⌐える	***e-ru*** 間違える・間違えない・間違え・間違えて	*v. to mix up, to make a mistake*
ギリギリになる		*to become close to the last minute*
なかなか(〜ない)		*adv. (not) easily ~* (なかなか漢字が覚えられない *(I) cannot memorize kanji easily.*) 5
しかたがない	仕方がない	*cannot be helped* 6

Newly introduced kanji:

空港（くうこう）・結婚（けっこん）(marriage)・間違える（まちが）

空	⼀ ⼧ ⼧ ⼧ 空 空 空 空
港	⼀ ⼀ ⼀ ⼀ ⼀ ⼀ ⼀ ⼀ 洪 洪 港 港
結	⼓ ⼓ ⼓ ⼓ ⽷ ⽷ ⽷ ⽷ 結 結 結 結
婚	⼄ ⼥ ⼥ ⼥ ⼥ 妌 妌 婚 婚 婚 婚

 **Dialog**

A student who did not finish his homework is talking to his / her teacher.

学生： 先生、宿題（しゅくだい）がまだ終（お）わっていないんです。

先生： いつ始（はじ）めたんですか。

学生： 今朝（けさ）です。

先生： この宿題は先週（せんしゅう）出（だ）したんですよ。もっと早（はや）く始（はじ）めれば、よかったんですよ。

学生： はい。でも、ギリギリにならないと、なかなか始められないんです。

先生： 本当（ほんとう）に仕方（しかた）がないですね。

Guess and Try 1
What does the underlined part in the above dialog mean? 7

Guess and Try 2
Fill in the blanks. 7

食べる → 食べれば
書く → 書けば
読む → 1. _____
買う → 2. _____
する → すれば
来る → 来（く）れば
高い → 高ければ
安い → 3. _____
食べない → 4. _____
いい → よければ

Guess and Try 3
Fill in the blanks creatively. 7

1. 車のじゅうたいにあったんですか。電車に_____ば、ちこくしなかったと思いますよ。
   (〜に遭（あ）う *to encounter ~*)

2. ジョージさんと結婚したんですか。マイクさんと結婚_____ば、よかったのに。

3. また、間違えたんですか。よく_____ば、間違えなかったでしょう。

4. 羽田空港に行ったんですか。成田空港に＿＿＿＿＿ば、もっと早く着いたはずです。

Guess and Try 4

Choose the appropriate option in the parentheses. ⑤

この漢字はなかなか (覚えられます・覚えられません)。

🗣 Drill: Formation

ほかの店も見る ⟶ ほかの店も見ればよかったのに

1. JR パスを買う
2. ホームステーをする
3. 前の日にする
4. 住所をチェックする
5. 私の言うことを聞く
6. よく 考えてから決める

🚩 Task 1: Role Play

A: Something bad had happened to you. Talk about it with your friend.

B: Your friend tells you about his / her regrettable incident. Ask questions, find out what caused it, and give him / her some comments on it.

🚩 Task 2: Pair Work

Reflect on your high school or teenage years, and tell your partner what you think you should have done or you shouldn't have done at that time.

For example:

A : 高校生の時、もっと 遊べばよかったと思います。

B : それから。

A : それから、あまり 母の言うことをきかなければよかったと思います。

B : どうしてですか。

📖 Short Reading

　小さい時、両 親は私に水泳を習った方がいいと言いました。でも、私は水の中に顔を入れるのがこわくて、習いませんでした。今は水泳を習えばよかったと思っています。私の友 達はほとんど泳げますが、私は今でも泳げません。今年の夏は 湖 の近くで友達と過ごしましたが、私だけが泳げませんでした。飛行機が海に落ちたら、私は助からないでしょう。でも、飛行機が本 当に海に落ちたら、泳げる人でもたぶん助からないでしょう。

(水泳 *swimming*, 過ごす *to spend (time)*, 助かる *to be saved*)

✏️ Writing

Write about what you think you should have done in your childhood.

火事があったそうです **Hearsay**

Notes Relating to This Lesson	
Grammar and Usage	
⑧ ～そうだ 168	⑨ ～で 169

📖 Basic Vocabulary and Kanji

か￢じ	火事	n. fire
じ￢こ	事故	n. accident
けが￢	怪我	n. injury (けがをする to get injured)
じしん	地震	n. earthquake
こうずい	洪水	n. flood
つなみ	津波	n. tsunami, big wave
どろぼう	泥棒	n. thief
へ￢いき￢んてん	平均点	n. average (score)
ちゅうかんし￢けん	中間試験	n. mid-term exam
きまつし￢けん	期末試験	n. final exam
うわさ	噂	n. rumor
にんき	人気	n. popularity (人気がある to be popular)
～によると		according to ~
～そうだ	～そうだ・～そうじゃない	aux. I heard that ~, they say that ~ ⑧

Newly introduced kanji:

火事・事故・平均点・中間試験・
期末試験・週末 (weekend)・人気

故	一 十 古 古 古 古 故 故
平	一 丆 亏 平 平
均	一 十 圡 圴 坮 均 均
末	一 二 キ 末 末

💿 🗨 Dialog

Yoko Yamada and John Smith are talking about yesterday's fire.

山田 ： 昨日の新聞によると、<u>さくら通りの病院で火事があったそうですよ。</u>

スミス ： ええ。しっています。ぼくの友達があの病院でかんごしをしているんです。

山田 ： ああ、そうですか。

スミス ： その友達によると、かんじゃさんが3人けがをしたそうです。

Guess and Try 1

What does the underlined part in the above dialog mean? ⑧

Guess and Try 2

State the difference between the two sentences in each set. ⑧

1. A. うわさによると、あの会社のコンピューターはよくこわれるそうです。
   B. このパソコンはこわれそうです。
2. A. このじしょは便利だそうです。
   B. このじしょは便利そうです。
3. A. 日本語の先生はやさしいそうです。
   B. 日本語の先生はやさしそうです。

Guess and Try 3

Fill in the blanks and state what form そうです (hearsay) follows. ⑧

帰る ⟶ 帰るそうです

帰った ⟶ 帰ったそうです

高い ⟶ 1.＿＿＿＿＿そうです

高かった ⟶ 2.＿＿＿＿＿そうです

便利だ ⟶ 3.＿＿＿＿＿そうです

日本人だ ⟶ 4.＿＿＿＿＿そうです

日本人だった ⟶ 5.＿＿＿＿＿そうです

Guess and Try 4

Fill in the blanks with appropriate particles. ⑨

1. 明日うち＿＿＿＿ パーティーがあります。
2. うち＿＿＿＿ パソコン があります。

🗣 Drill: Formation

日本でじしんがあった ➡ 日本でじしんがあっ
たそうです

1. 山田さんのうちにどろぼうが入った
2. 近くで事故があった
3. 台湾でこうずいがあった
4. スミスさんのお父さんはおいしゃさんだ
5. 日本のテレビドラマは人気がある
6. 中間試験の平均点は75点だった
7. スミスさんはからてを習っている
8. 田中さんは来月結婚する
9. 来月この大学に新しいカフェテリアができる

🏳 Task 1: Group Work

Write one or two interesting facts that you heard
about Japan, then share them in your group.

For example:

A ： 日本ではバレンタイン・デーに女の人が男
　　の人にチョコレートをあげるそうですよ。

B ： 本当ですか。／ ああ、私も聞きました。

1. ＿＿＿＿＿＿＿＿＿＿＿＿＿＿＿＿＿＿＿＿＿＿＿
2. ＿＿＿＿＿＿＿＿＿＿＿＿＿＿＿＿＿＿＿＿＿＿＿

🏳 Task 2: Group Work

Write one or two news items that you got to know
about recently, then share them in your group.

1. ＿＿＿＿＿＿＿＿＿＿＿＿＿＿＿＿＿＿＿＿＿＿＿
2. ＿＿＿＿＿＿＿＿＿＿＿＿＿＿＿＿＿＿＿＿＿＿＿

📖 Short Reading

秋田犬は日本の犬ですが、アメリカでもとて
も人気があります。大きくて、強いですが、
テディーベアに似ていて、優しい犬です。あ
の有名な忠犬ハチ公 (1923–1935) も秋田犬
でした。秋田犬を初めてアメリカに連れて来
たのはヘレン・ケラーだったそうです。ヘレン・
ケラーは秋田犬の子犬を 1937 年にペットとし
てアメリカに連れて来ました。戦後は沢山の
アメリカ兵が秋田犬をアメリカに連れて帰っ
たそうです。

ジェフ・ブラウン

(秋田犬 (あきたいぬ・あきたけん) *Akita (a
breed of dog)*, テディーベア *teddy bear*, 〜に似
る *to look like ~*, 忠犬ハチ公 *Loyal Dog
Hachi-Ko*, 初めて *for the first time*, 〜として *as
~*, 戦後 *after the war (WWII)*, アメリカ兵
American soldier)

✎ Writing

Write about some interesting story in history, society or culture.

何かあったようですね Conjecture

Notes Relating to This Lesson	
Grammar and Usage	
10 ～ようだ 169	
11 ～らしい 169	

Basic Vocabulary and Kanji

きゅうきゅ￢うしゃ	救急車	n. ambulance
あつま￢る	*r-u* 集まる・集まらない・集まり・集まって	v. to gather
ぶつかる	*r-u* ぶつかる・ぶつからない・ぶつかり・ぶつかって	v. to collide (車にぶつかる to crash into a car, 車とぶつかる to collide with a car)
しぬ	*n-u* 死ぬ・死なない・死に・死んで	v. to die
やきもちをやく		to be jealous
～ようだ	～ようだ・～ようじゃない 10	aux. it seems to be ~
～らしい	～らしい・～らしくない 11	aux. it seems to be ~

Newly introduced kanji:

集まる・死ぬ

集	ノ イ イ゛ 疒 什 什 佯 隹 隼 隼 集 集
死	一 ァ ゟ タ 歹 死

 Dialog

John Smith and Yoko Yamada see a crowd on the street from their car.

山田 ： あっ、あそこに人が集まっていますね。

スミス： ええ。①何かあったようですね。

山田 ： あっ、きゅうきゅうしゃが来ましたよ。

スミス： ええ。ちょっと、見て来ます。

(John goes into the crowd, observes what happened, and comes back to his car.)

スミス： ②タクシーとトラックがぶつかったらしいですよ。

Guess and Try 1

What do the underlined parts in the above dialog mean? 10 11

Guess and Try 2

The sentences with ～ようです and ～らしいです both express the speaker's conjecture and they can be used interchangeably most of the time, but there is some difference between the two. For example, ～ようです is appropriate in all of the following sentences, but ～らしいです is appropriate only in (3) and (4). Guess why. 10 11

1. へんな味 (taste) ですね。この牛乳は悪くなっている (らしい (✗)・よう (✔)) ですよ。

2. あっ、動きませんよ。死んでいる (らしい (✗)・よう (✔)) です。

3. このクラスは難しい (らしい (✔)・よう (✔)) です。

4. 日本のものは高い (らしい (✔)・よう (✔)) です。

Guess and Try 3

Complete the following. 10 11

1. 帰る　　帰 __る__ ようです

　　　　　帰 __る__ らしいです

2. 帰った　帰 _____ ようです

　　　　　帰 _____ らしいです

3. 高い　　　　高＿＿＿＿ようです
　　　　　　　高＿＿＿＿らしいです

4. 高かった　　高＿＿＿＿＿＿＿ようです
　　　　　　　高＿＿＿＿＿＿＿らしいです

5. 便利だ　　　便利＿＿＿＿ようです
　　　　　　　便利＿＿＿＿らしいです

6. 日本人だ　　日本人＿＿＿＿ようです
　　　　　　　日本人＿＿＿＿らしいです

7. 日本人だった
　　日本人＿＿＿＿＿＿＿＿ようです
　　日本人＿＿＿＿＿＿＿＿らしいです

Guess and Try 4
The following sentences are ambiguous. State the nature of the ambiguity. 10 11

1. あの人は日本人のようです。
2. あの人は日本人らしいです。

🗣 Drill 1: Mini Conversation
今度（こんど）の試験（しけん）は難（むずか）しいですか
　　→ ええ、難しいようです
1. だれかいますか　2. これはじしんですか
3. これはダイヤモンドですか
4. 田中さんはやきもちをやいていますか
5. 明日は雪がふりますか

🗣 Drill 2: Mini Conversation
今度の試験（しけん）は難しいですか → ええ、難しいらしいです
1. 昨日事故（じこ）がありましたか
2. 昨日山田さんは来ましたか
3. 明日山田さんは来ますか
4. 日本のけいざいはいいですか
5. 平均点（へいきんてん）は高かったですか
6. あの店（みせ）は安いですか

🚩 Task 1
Your teacher does some action without saying anything. Observe and guess what he / she is doing (for

example, 何（なに）か読（よ）んでいるようですね。), then it's your turn to do the action.

🚩 Task 2
Look at each of the following pictures, and guess what is going on, then share your opinion with others.

1 　2. 　3.

🚩 Task 3
Look at each picture and guess the kind of person it is showing.

1. 　2. 　3.

📖 Short Reading
　うちの隣（となり）には本田（ほんだ）さんの家族（かぞく）が住（す）んでいます。本田さんと奥（おく）さんと9才（さい）の子供（こども）さんが住んでいます。本田さんも奥（おく）さんも働（はたら）いているので、昼間（ひるま）はうちにいません。でも、週末（しゅうまつ）によく話（はな）します。もう一方（いっぽう）の隣（となり）には中年（ちゅうねん）の男性（だんせい）が一人で住んでいるようです。働いていないようで、いつも家（いえ）に一人でいるようです。まだ、話したことはありません。向（む）かいの家にはおじいさんとおばあさんが住んでいます。暇（ひま）なようで、いつも窓（まど）から外（そと）を見ています。

（昼間（ひるま） *daytime*, もう一方（いっぽう） *the other side*, 中年（ちゅうねん）の *middle-aged*, 向（む）かいの家（いえ） *the house across the (street)*）

✏️ Writing
Write about the people who live near your house, apartment, or dormitory room.

– Grammar and Usage –

1 〜でも: Even 〜 [The least expected item]

The pragmatic particle 〜でも follows a noun and shows that the speaker considers the item to be one of the least expected items for the given situation. For example, in the sentence くさったものでも食べます, くさったもの *a spoiled food* is one of the things that are least expected to be eaten. Note that particles が and を **must** not occur with 〜でも, and other particles such as に may occur with 〜でも.

(a) こんな簡単な問題は子供でもできます。
Even a child can solve such an easy problem.

(b) こんな難しい問題は大人でもできません。
Even an adult cannot solve such a difficult problem.

(c) マイクさんは漢字がとくいです。難しい漢字でもわかります。
Mike is good at Kanji. He even knows difficult kanji characters.

(d) ジョージさんは漢字が苦手です。かんたんな漢字でもわかりません。
George is not good at kanji. He doesn't even know easy kanji characters.

(e) あぶないところ(に)でも行きます。
He even goes to dangerous places.

2 なんでも・だれでも: Any 〜 [Free-choice items]

When particle 〜でも is combined with a question word, as in 何でも and だれでも, it means *any ~*. For example, 何でも食べます means *I will eat anything*, and だれでもできます means *Anyone can do it*.

(a) 私は魚が好きです。魚なら、何でも食べます。
I like fish. I will eat anything if it is fish.

(b) えびじゃないなら、何でも食べます。
If it's not shrimp, I eat anything.

(c) こんなかんたんな料理はだれでも作れます。
Anyone can make such an easy dish.

(d) クラスの人と話しますか。
Do you talk with your classmates?
— ええ、私はだれとでも話します。
— *Yes, I talk with anyone.*

(e) ATM はどこにありますか。
Where can I find an ATM machine?
— どこにでもあります。
— *You can find one anywhere.*

(f) 明日おじゃましてもいいですか。
Can I visit you tomorrow?
— ええ、いつでも来てください。
— *Sure, you can come at any time.*

(g) あなたのためなら、どこ(に)でも行きます。何でもします。ですから、結婚してください。
If it is for you, I will go anywhere. I will do anything. So, please marry me.

For negating a statement with these phrases, another phrase, namely, 〜わけではありません, must be added at the end of the sentence. For example, if you want to negate だれでもできます *Anyone can do (it)*, (h) is appropriate, but (i) is not.

(h) だれでもできるわけではありません。
It is not the case that anyone can do it.

(i) だれでもできません。(✗)
(Ungrammatical)

3 〜ても: Even if 〜; even though 〜

A clause that ends in a verb or an adjective in the te-form plus the particle も means *even if ~* or *even though ~*.

(a) いっしょうけんめい勉強しても、100点は取れませんでした。
I couldn't get 100 points even though I studied very hard.

(b) 弟は父が話しても、聞きません。
Even if my father talks (to him), my brother doesn't listen (to him).

(c) いいじしょなら、高くても買います。
If it is a good dictionary, I will buy it even if it is expensive.

(d) 高いなら、便利でも買いません。
If it is expensive, I will not buy it even if it is convenient.

4 なにを / だれが〜ても: No matter 〜

When a clause that ends in a verb or an adjective in the te-form plus も contains a question word, it means *no matter* 〜.

(a) どこを探しても、見つからなかったんです。

No matter where I searched, it could not be found.

(b) 何度探しても見つからなかったんです。

No matter how many times I searched for it, it could not be found.

(c) 私の姉はやせています。何を食べても太りません。

My sister is thin. She does not gain weight no matter what she eats.

(d) 兄は自分のベッドでしか眠れませんが、私はどこでねても、よく眠れます。

My brother can sleep only in his own bed, but I can sleep no matter where I sleep.

(e) 私の弟はだれが話しても聞きません。

No matter who talks (to him), my brother does not listen.

(f) いくらがんばっても 100 点はとれません。

No matter how hard I try, I cannot get 100 points.

(g) 子供のためなら、いくら高くても買います。

If it is for my child, I will buy it no matter how expensive it is.

5 なかなか (〜ない): (Not) easily 〜

When the adverb なかなか is used with a negative verb, it means *(not) easily*.

(a) この漢字は難しくて、なかなか覚えられません。

This kanji character is difficult, and I cannot memorize it very easily.

(b) この赤ちゃんはなかなか寝ません。

This baby does not sleep very easily.

6 しかたがない: Cannot be helped

仕方がない literally means that there is no method, and expresses one's reconciliation (a) or disappointment (b):

(a) お金がないので、車が買えないんです。

Because I do not have money, I cannot buy a car.

— 仕方がないですね。

— *You cannot be helped. (I'm sorry.)*

(b) ギリギリにならないと、宿題ができないんです。

I cannot start my homework until it's the last minute.

— 本当に仕方がないですね。

— *Oh, you are really hopeless, aren't you?*

7 〜れば: If 〜 [Condition]

The conditional form with れば is created by adding **reba** or **eba** at the end of a verb in the root form: **reba** for a **ru**-verb and **eba** for an **u**-verb, and by adding **kereba** at the end of an i-type adjective in the stem form. The verbs する and くる as well as the adjective いい pattern irregularly, as shown in the table. (The simple conditional form with れば is unavailable for na-type adjectives and the copula だ / です. The equivalent form for them is 〜であれば as in まじめであれば and 学生であれば.)

Dictionary Form	れば Conditional Forms
たべる *to eat*	tabe-reba たべれば
みる *to watch*	mi-reba みれば
かく *to write*	kak-eba かけば
およぐ *to swim*	oyog-eba およげば
はこぶ *to carry*	hakob-eba はこべば
よむ *to read*	yom-eba よめば
しぬ *to die*	shin-eba しねば
まつ *to wait*	mat-eba まてば
はなす *to speak*	hanas-eba はなせば
つくる *to make*	tsukur-eba つくれば
かう *to buy*	ka-eba かえば *w at the end of the root is deleted before **eba**.
する *to do*	sureba すれば *irregular
くる *to come*	kureba くれば *irregular
たかい *expensive*	taka-kereba たかければ
いい *good*	yo-kereba よければ *irregular

The れば clause expresses **generic**, **temporal**, **hypothetical** or **counterfactual conditions**, just like the たら clause. Just note that the predicate in a ば clause must not express an action or an event when the main clause expresses a command, request, or suggestion.

(a) 朝になれば明るくなります。

Whenever it becomes morning, it becomes bright.

(b) 7時になれば父が帰ります。

When it is seven (Lit. becomes seven), my father will be back.

(c) 宿題が難しければ、やらなくてもいいです。

If the homework is difficult, you don't have to do it.

(d) 犬と話せれば楽しいと思います。

If I could talk with dogs, I think it would be fun.

Unlike たら, れば cannot relate two succeeding events that actually happened in the past.

(e) 本屋に行ったら、ポールさんに会いました。

（✔）

When I went to the bookstore, I met Paul.

(f) 本屋に行けば、ポールさんに会いました。

（✘）　　　　　　　(Ungrammatical)

The conditional clauses with 〜たら and 〜れば can express one's regret over the past event or situation if the main clause includes phrases like よかったんです and よかったのに.

(g) またお金がないんですか。パチンコをしなければよかったんですよ。

You don't have money again? You should not have played pachinko games.

(h) もっと早く始めたらよかったのに。本当に仕方がありませんね。

You should have started much earlier. Really, nothing can help you.

(i) 車のじゅうたいにあったんですか。電車に乗ればよかったんですよ。

Oh, you got into a traffic jam? You should have taken the train.

(j) 中川さんと結婚すればよかったなあ。

I should have gotten married to Mr. Nakagawa!

(k) 大阪空港に行ったんですか。成田空港に行けばもっと早く着けたと思いますよ。

Oh, you went to Osaka Airport? If you have gone to Narita Airport, I think you would have been able to arrive (here) much earlier.

(l) もっと安ければよかったんですが。

It would have been nice, if it were much cheaper, but ...

(m) JRパスを使えば安かったと思いますよ。

If you have used a JR Pass, it would have been cheaper.

8 　〜そうだ: I heard that 〜 [Hearsay]

〜そうです is added at the end of a sentence and shows that the content of the sentence is the "report" of what the speaker heard or read. For example, 雨がふるそうです means *I heard that it will rain* or *they say that it will rain*. The verbs and adjectives that precede 〜そうです must be in the plain form.

(a) スミスさんは来月アメリカに帰るそうです。

I heard that Mr. Smith is returning to America next month.

(b) リーさんは社長とけんかをしたそうです。

I heard that Mr. Lee had a fight with the (company) president.

(c) 日本の牛肉は高いそうです。

I heard that beef in Japan is expensive.

(d) スミスさんはギターが上手だそうです。

They say that Mr. Smith is good at playing the guitar.

(e) マリーさんのお母さんは日本人だそうです。

I heard that Mary's mother is Japanese.

(f) マリーさんのお母さんはアメリカ人じゃないそうです。

I heard that Mary's mother is not American.

9 ～で: At, in [Location of events and incidents]

For expressing that there is / was some event or incident, the verb ある can be used. In this case, the location of the event or incident is marked by the particle で.

(a) 東京でジョブ・フェアーがあります。

There will be a job fair in Tokyo.

(b) 大阪で大きい地震がありました。

There was a large scale earthquake in Osaka.

10 ～ようだ: It seems that ～, it appears that ～ [General guess]

～ようです is added at the end of a sentence and shows that the fact expressed by the sentence is the speaker's conjecture. Unlike ～らしいです, ～ようです may be used in any context where one wants to express his conjecture, regardless of how careful, objective and logical the conjecture is. So, it can be used for intuitive guesses as well as for educated guesses. The verbs and adjectives that precede ようです must be in the pre-nominal form.

(a) あれっ、へんなあじですね。この牛乳は悪くなっているようですよ。

Oh, it tastes strange. This milk seems to be spoiled.

(b) あっ、あしおとがします。だれか来たようですね。

Oh, I hear footsteps. It appears that someone is coming.

(c) 返事が来ませんね。だめだったようですね。

They haven't responded to us. It seems that we have failed.

(d) スミスさんは来月アメリカに帰るようです。

It seems that Mr. Smith is returning to America next month.

(e) リーさんはもう中国に帰ったようです。

Mr. Lee seems to have returned to China.

(f) 日本の牛肉は高いようです。

Japanese beef seems to be expensive.

(g) スミスさんはギターが上手なようです。

Mr. Smith appears to be good at playing the guitar.

(h) マリーさんのお母さんは日本人のようです。

Mary's mother seems to be Japanese.

(i) マリーさんのお母さんはアメリカ人じゃないようです。

Mary's mother does not seem to be American.

When ～ようです follows a noun, its meaning is ambiguous. For example, sentence (h) means either that *Mary's mother seems to be Japanese* or that *Mary's mother is just like a Japanese person.*

11 ～らしい: It seems that ～, it appears that ～ [Educated guess]

～らしいです is added at the end of a sentence and shows that the fact expressed by the sentence is the speaker's objective, logical, careful, and non-intuitive conjecture based on what he heard, saw, or read. The verbs and adjectives that precede ～らしいです must be in the plain form, except that だ that appears at the end of a copula and at the end of a na-type adjective must be deleted.

(a) スミスさんは来月アメリカに帰るらしいです。

It seems that Mr. Smith is returning to America next month.

(b) 何かあったらしいですね。

It seems that something has happened.

(c) 日本の牛肉は高いらしいです。

Japanese beef seems to be expensive.

(d) スミスさんはギターが上手らしいです。

Mr. Smith seems to be good at playing the guitar.

(e) マリーさんのお母さんは日本人らしいです。

Mary's mother seems to be Japanese.

(f) マリーさんのお母さんはアメリカ人じゃないらしいです。

Mary's mother does not seem to be American.

When ～らしいです follows a noun, its meaning is ambiguous. For example, sentence (e) means either that *Mary's mother seems to be Japanese*, or that *Mary's mother is a typical Japanese.*

Unlike ～ようです, ～らしいです cannot be used for an intuitive or instant guess based on one's five

CHAPTER TWENTY-FIVE | Culture | Kanji List

senses. For example, in the following sentences, よう is appropriate, but らしい is not:

(g) あれっ、へんなあじですね。この牛乳（ぎゅうにゅう）は悪（わる）くなっている (らしい (✗)・よう (✔)) ですよ。

Oh! It tastes strange. This milk seems to be spoiled.

(h) あっ、動（うご）きませんよ。死（し）んでいる (らしい (✗)・よう (✔)) です。

Oh! He is not moving. He seems to be dead.

(i) あっ。足音（あしおと）がきこえます。だれか来（く）る (らしい (✗)・よう (✔)) ですね。

Oh! I hear footsteps. It sounds like someone is coming.

(j) あっ。山田さんが泣（な）いていますよ。ボーイフレンドとけんかをした (らしい (✗)・よう (✔)) ですね。

Oh! Ms. Yamada is crying. She seems to have had an argument with her boyfriend.

– Culture –

Ⓐ わがし (Japanese sweets)

和菓子（わがし）are traditional Japanese confections, and they are typically made from various beans, grains and sugar. They are sweet, but do not usually contain butter or oil. The shapes, colors, and designs of 和菓子（わがし）are often delicate and elegant, and reflect the season and beauty of nature, and you certainly can enjoy a tasty part of traditional Japanese culture. Different geographic areas in Japan have different 和菓子（わがし）that they are proud of and famous for.

– Kanji List –

苦い・太る・空港・結婚・間違える・火事・事故・平均点・中間試験・期末試験・週末・人気・集まる・死ぬ

苦 くる-しい・にが-い・ク bitter	一 十 艹 芒 芏 苦 苦 苦 [8]
	Example: 苦（にが）い bitter, 苦（くる）しい distressful, 苦手（にがて）だ not good at
太 ふと-い・ふと-る・タイ fat, big	一 ナ 大 太 [4]
	Example: 太（ふと）る to gain weight
空 そら・あ-く・あ-ける・から・クウ sky, air, empty, vacant	⺊ ⺊ 宀 宀 空 空 空 空 [8]
	Example: 空港（くうこう）airport, 空（そら）sky
港 みなと・コウ port, harbor	⺀ ⺀ ⺀ 氵 汁 汫 浐 浐 洪 洪 港 港 [12]
	Example: 空港（くうこう）airport, 港（みなと）harbor, port
結 むす-ぶ・ケツ・ケッ connect, conclude	⺔ 纟 纟 纟 糸 糸 紶 結 結 結 結 結 [12]
	Example: 結婚（けっこん）marriage
婚 コン wedding	⺰ 乄 女 奵 奵 奵 妶 婚 婚 婚 婚 [11]
	Example: 結婚（けっこん）marriage
間 あいだ・ま・カン between, interval	⎸ ⎹ ⺆ ⺆ 門 門 門 門 門 間 間 間 [12]
	Example: 間違（まちが）える to make a mistake, 時間（じかん）time, 車（くるま）と車（くるま）の間（あいだ）between cars

– 170 –

違 ちが-う・イ differ	ノ ナ キ キ キ キ キ キ キ キ 韋 違 [13] 違
	Example: 違う *to differ*, 間違える *to make a mistake*

火 ひ・カ fire	丶 丷 少 火 [4]
	Example: 火事 *fire*, 火曜日 *Tuesday*

事 こと・ごと・ジ affair, fact, engagement	一 一 戸 戸 写 写 写 事 [8]
	Example: 火事 *fire*, 事故 *accident*, 仕事 *job, work*

故 コ・ゆえ old and dear, late, obstacle	一 十 古 古 古 古 故 故 [9]
	Example: 事故 *accident*

平 たい-ら・ひら・ヘイ・ビョウ plain, flat, even	一 一 丆 立 平 [5]
	Example: 平均点 *average point*

均 ひと-しい・キン average	一 十 土 土 圴 均 均 [7]
	Example: 平均点 *average point*

点 テン point, score	丨 卜 占 占 占 点 点 点 [9]
	Example: 平均点 *average point*, 100点 *100 points*

中 なか・チュウ・ジュウ middle, inside	丨 口 口 中 [4]
	Example: 中間試験 *mid-term exam*, 部屋の中 *inside the room*

試 こころ-みる・ため-す・シ try, test	丶 亠 言 言 言 言 言 試 試 試 試 [13] 試
	Example: 試験 *exam*

験 ケン proof, examine	丨 厂 厂 厂 严 馬 馬 馬 馬 馬 駒 駒 駒 駒 駒 験 験 [18]
	Example: 試験 *exam*

期 キ term, period, expect	一 十 甘 甘 甘 甘 其 其 期 期 期 期 [12]
	Example: 期末試験 *final exam*, 今学期 *this academic term*

末 すえ・マツ・バツ end, tip	一 二 キ 末 末 [5]
	Example: 期末試験 *final exam*, 週末 *weekend*

週 シュウ week	丿 月 月 月 冑 冑 周 周 周 週 週 [11]
	Example: 週末 *weekend*, 毎週 *every week*, 来週 *next week*

人 ひと・ジン・ニン person	ノ 人 [2]
	Example: 人気 *popularity*, あの人 *that person*, 日本人 *Japanese person*

気 キ spirit, mind, air, atmosphere	丿 二 气 気 気 気 [6]
	Example: 人気 *popularity*, 病気 *sickness*, 天気 *weather*, 元気 *healthy, fine*

集 あつ-まる・あつ-める・シュウ collect, assemble	ノ イ イ イ 仟 什 隹 隹 隹 集 集 集 [12]
	Example: 集まる *to gather*

死 し-ぬ・シ death	一 ア ア 歹 死 死 [6]
	Example: 死ぬ *to die*

– Review –

Q1. *Write the readings of the following kanji phrases, and state what is common among the members of each set.*

1. 事故・3 枚・教える・数学
2. 集まる・難しい・日曜日
3. 集まる・楽しい・薬
4. 空港・宿題・病院・教室・家内・安い・漢字

Q2. *Fill in the blanks.*

1. こんなかんたんな 問 題 は ＿＿＿＿＿＿＿＿
   でもわかるでしょう。
2. 兄は魚が好きです。魚なら、＿＿＿＿＿＿＿
   ＿＿＿＿＿＿＿＿＿＿。
3. いくら勉強 ＿＿＿＿＿＿＿＿ も、ぜんぜん
   わかりません。
4. 勉強 ＿＿＿＿＿＿＿＿ も、わかります。
5. ＿＿＿＿＿＿＿＿ に行っても、安いホテル
   にとまります。
6. 父に ＿＿＿＿＿＿＿ を言っても、わかってく
   れません。
7. また私の電話ばんごうを 忘 れたんですか。
   ＿＿＿＿＿＿＿＿＿＿＿＿ ばよかったのに。
8. あれ。あそこに人が集まっていますよ。
   ＿＿＿＿＿＿＿＿＿＿＿＿＿ ようですね。
9. 山田さんから 聞 いたんですが、スミスさんは
   ＿＿＿＿＿＿＿＿＿＿＿ そうですよ。
10. 日本は今 ＿＿＿＿＿＿＿＿＿＿＿＿＿＿
    らしいですよ。

Q3. *Rephrase each of the underlined parts using an item in the box.*

> ～ようです
> ～らしいです
> ～そうです

1. 日本円は今 <u>高い</u>です。
2. あっ、ぜんぜん 動 きませんよ。<u>死んでいま
   すね</u>。
3. スミスさんはギターが<u>上手</u>です。

Tips and Additional Knowledge: Colloquial Phrases for Praising Others

すごい means *Great!* or *Super!*, and you hear it very often in colloquial conversations. You can use it whenever you are impressed by someone's great achievements and impressive characteristics. Other phrases you can use for praising others in an informal context are:

> さすが!
> *You are great as usual!*
>
> なかなかですね!
> *You are quite good!*
>
> かっこいい!
> *Cool!*

CHAPTER TWENTY-SIX
Perspective

花がリスに食べられました **Passive**

Notes Relating to This Lesson	
Grammar and Usage	
1 (〜の) せいで....182	2 (〜の) おかげで..182

 Basic Vocabulary and Kanji

にわ	庭	*n. yard, garden*
ことば⌐	言葉	*n. word*
じ⌐	字	*n. character, letter*
さく	*k-u* 咲く・咲かない・咲き・咲いて	*v. to bloom, to blossom*
ほめ⌐る	*e-ru* 褒める・褒めない・褒め・褒めて	*v. to praise*
しかる	*r-u* 叱る・叱らない・叱り・叱って	*v. to scold*
たた⌐く	*k-u* たたく・たたかない・たたき・たたいて	*v. to hit, to spank*
だま⌐す	*s-u* だます・だまさない・だまし・だまして	*v. to deceive, to trick*
ぬす⌐む	*m-u* 盗む・盗まない・盗み・盗んで	*v. to steal*
しょ⌐うたいする	*irr.* 招待する	*v. to invite*
からか⌐う	*w-u* からかう・からかわない・からかい・からかって	*v. to tease, to make fun of*
(〜の) せいで		*due to ~* 1
(〜の) おかげで		*thanks to ~* 2

Newly introduced kanji:

字・客 (customer)・知っている (to know)

客	⸍ ⸍⸍ 宀 宀 宀 客 客 客
知	ノ ⸍ ⸌ 矢 矢 知 知 知

 Dialog

John Smith is talking to Yoko Yamada about the rose bushes in his New York house.

スミス : ぼくのニューヨークのうちのにわには、バラがたくさんあるんですよ。
(バラ *rose*)

山田 : ああ、そうですか。いいですね。

スミス : となりのおばあさんがバラのことをよく知っていて、いろいろ教えてくれたんです。そのおばあさんのおかげで、毎年 きれいなバラがさくようになったんです。

山田 : へえ。

スミス : でも、最近 ① バラの花がよくリスに食べられるんですよ。
(リス *squirrel*)

山田 : えっ、本当に？②リスが花を食べるんですか。

スミス : ええ。リスのせいで、たくさんのバラが だめになってしまいました。

Guess and Try 1

Choose the appropriate option in the parentheses. 1 2

1. 田中さんの (おかげで・せいで) 車がこわれました。
2. 田中さんの (おかげで・せいで) 部屋がきれいになりました。

Guess and Try 2

State the difference between the two underlined parts, ① and ② , in the above dialog. 3

Guess and Try 3

Choose the appropriate option in the parentheses. ☐3

1. どろぼうがネックレスを (ぬすみました・ぬすまれました)。
2. ネックレスが (ぬすみました・ぬすまれました)。
3. ネックレスがどろぼう (が・に) ぬすまれました。

Guess and Try 4

Fill in the blanks. ☐3

食べる → 食べられる　　書く→ 書かれる

見る → 1. _____　　知る → 2. _____

読む → 3. _____　　運ぶ → 4. _____

使う → 5. _____　　する → 6. _____

🗣 Drill 1: Conjugation

だます ⟶ だまされる・だまされました

1. たたく
2. からかう
3. ぬすむ
4. 使う
5. ほめる
6. しかる
7. 見る
8. しょうたいする

🗣 Drill 2: Formation

客をだます ⟶ 客がだまされました

1. 子供をしかる
2. スミスさんをほめる
3. 名前を知る
4. 学生をたたく
5. 弟をからかう
6. お金をぬすむ
7. マリーさんをしょうたいする

📑 Task: Group Work

Answer the following questions, then talk about them in your group.

1. あなたの国ではどの日本人が一番知られていますか。
2. あなたの国ではどのことばが一番使われていますか。
3. 日本ではどのことばが一番使われていますか。
4. ひらがなではどの字が一番使われていますか。

📖 Short Reading

　私はアメリカで日本語を2年勉強して、日本の大学に留学しました。日本語を使って、生活するのが楽しみでした。しかし、日本に行くと、大学の友達も、寮の友達も私と英語で話したがりました。講義も英語で受けました。アルバイトは英会話の教師だったので、やはり、英語ばかり使いました。それで、ぜんぜん日本語が上達しませんでした。思い切って、半年後に寮を出て、大学から遠い古いアパートに引っ越しました。隣には、一人暮らしのおばあさんが住んでいました。そのおばあさんは暇だったので、毎日私と日本語で話しました。一緒に料理をしたり、買い物をしたりしました。おばあさんは英語がぜんぜん分からなかったので、もちろん英語はぜんぜん使いませんでした。そのおばあさんのおかげで、やっと日本語がうまく話せるようになりました。今は、友達とも日本語で話します。おばあさんには本当に感謝しています。

(生活する *to live*, 楽しみでした *was looking forward to ~*, 講義 *lecture*, やはり (= やっぱり), 英会話 *English conversation*, 上達する *to make progress*, 思い切って～する *dare to do ~*, 半年後 *after a half year*, 引っ越す *to move*, 一人暮らし *living alone*, おばあさん *old lady*, ～に感謝する *to be grateful to ~*)

✏️ Writing

Write about someone to whom you feel grateful even until now.

雨に降られました Annoying Incidents

Notes Relating to This Lesson	
Grammar and Usage 4 〜られ 183	

Basic Vocabulary and Kanji

ろんぶん	論文	*n. academic paper, thesis*
いや˥(な)	嫌だ・嫌じゃない	*adj. annoying, unpleasant*
かなしい	悲しい・悲しくない	*adj. sad*
ふむ	*m-***u** 踏む・踏まない・踏み・踏んで	*v. to step on*
ひはんする	*irr.* 批判する	*v. to criticize*
いえで(を)する	*irr.* 家出(を)する	*v. to run away from home*
かえり˥に	帰りに	*on the way home earlier (than ~)*
さきに	先に	*beforehand, in advance*
また		*adv. again*
はらがたつ	腹が立つ	*to become upset*
わるぐちをいう	悪口を言う	*to say bad things about a person behind his back*

Newly introduced kanji:

悲(かな)しい・家出(いえで)をする・先(さき)に・悪口(わるぐち)・降(ふ)る (fall)・降(お)りる (to get off)・手紙(てがみ) (letter)

悲	丿 ㇆ ヨ ヨ 㔾 非 非 非 非 悲 悲 悲
降	㇇ 阝 阝 阝 阝 阝夂 陊 降 降 降
紙	𠃋 幺 幺 糸 糸 糸 糸 紅 紙 紙

Dialog

Yoshio Tanaka is complaining about yesterday's rain to Yoko Yamada.

田中：昨日、アルバイトの帰りに雨が降って、シャツもズボンもビショビショになってしまったんですよ。

山田：またですか。田中さんは先週も雨に降られましたよね。

田中：ええ、ぼくはよく<u>雨に降られる</u>んですよ。

山田：じゃあ、今日も雨に降られるかもしれませんね。

田中：いいえ、今日はだいじょうぶですよ。

Guess and Try 1

Was Mr. Tanaka happy about the fact he stated in the underlined part? 4

Guess and Try 2

State the difference between the following sentences. 4

1. 兄が私の手紙を読みました。
2. 兄に私の手紙を読まれました。

Guess and Try 3

State what the following sentences mean. 4

1. 私は子供に死なれました。
2. 昨日犬ににげられて、たいへんでした。
3. 私は昨日どろぼうに入(はい)られました。

Guess and Try 4

Fill in the blanks. 4

1. 100点を取ったら、みんながびっくりしました。
   → 100点を取ったら、みんな ____ びっくりされました。

2. せんぱいがうちに来ました。
→ せんぱい ___ うちに _____ 。

🗣 Drill: Formation

母が死にました ➡ 私は母に死なれました

1. 友達が私の悪口を言いました
2. 弟が先に卒業しました
3. どろぼうがネックレスをぬすみました
4. 先生がろんぶんをひはんしました
5. 子供が外国に行きました
6. 子供が家出をしました
7. だれかが足をふみました

🔧 Task: Pair Work

Answer the following questions, then talk about them with your partner.

1. When do or did you feel annoyed at home? (For example: 弟に先に卒業された時、ちょっといやでした。)
2. When do or did you feel annoyed or disturbed at a public location? (For example: レストランでたばこをすわれた時、とてもはらがたちました。)
3. When do you think your parents would be sad? (For example: 私に病気になられる時、悲しいでしょう。)

📖 Short Reading

私の祖母は若い時苦労をたくさんしました。小さい時に母親に死なれて、叔母の養女になりました。叔母はとても厳しかったので、いつも叔母の顔色をうかがいながら育ちました。成績はいつもクラスで一番でした。それで、いつも友達がたくさんいて、みんなに尊敬されていました。21才の時にとてもハンサムで金持ちの男性と結婚しました。私の祖父です。しかし、祖父の会社が倒産して、祖父は病気になって、半身不随になってしまいました。その時、子供が4人いました。前まで仲良くしてくれていた人達はだんだん来なくなりました。祖母は小さいレストランを作って、一生懸命働いて、子供たちを育てました。

(苦労 suffering; hardship; difficulty, 養女 adopted daughter, 顔色をうかがう to judge someone's feelings from his expression, 育つ to grow up, 尊敬する to respect, 倒産 bankruptcy, 半身不随 paralysis of one side of the body, 前まで until recently, 仲良くする to be good friends with, だんだん little by little, 育てる to bring up; to raise)

✏️ Writing

Write about someone who had a hard time in the past.

むりやりに食べさせます **Parenting**

Notes Relating to This Lesson	
Grammar and Usage	**Writing**
5 ～させ 184	Ⓐ じゅく 185
	Ⓑ そろばん 186

📖 Basic Vocabulary and Kanji

さら	皿	*n. plate, dish*
じゅ⌐く	塾	*n. private tutoring school* Ⓐ
じゅけん	受験	*n. exam taking*
そろばん	算盤	*n. abacus* Ⓑ
しゅうじ	習字	*n. calligraphy*
ながで⌐んわ	長電話	*n. long telephone conversation*
むりやり	無理やり	*adv. forcefully*
ふく	*k-u* 拭く・拭かない・拭き・拭いて	*v. to wipe*
とまる	*r-u* 泊まる・泊まらない・泊まり・泊まって	*v. to stay, to lodge* (ホテルに泊まる *to stay at a hotel*)

Newly introduced kanji:

<ruby>受<rt>じゅ</rt></ruby><ruby>験<rt>けん</rt></ruby>・<ruby>習<rt>しゅう</rt></ruby><ruby>字<rt>じ</rt></ruby>・

<ruby>長<rt>なが</rt></ruby><ruby>電<rt>でん</rt></ruby><ruby>話<rt>わ</rt></ruby>・<ruby>練<rt>れん</rt></ruby><ruby>習<rt>しゅう</rt></ruby> する (to practice)

練	⺈ 𠂉 幺 幺 幺 糸 糸 糽 糽 紳 絈 絈 絈 練
	練練

そろばん *abacus*

🎧 💬 Dialog

Two mothers are discussing children's discipline.

林 ：うちは主人がきびしいんです。子供にむりやりにやさいを食べさせるし、勉強させるし。それに、テレビは見させないし、マンガは読ませないし。

石田：うちは、子供にテレビも見させるし、マンガも読ませますよ。

Guess and Try 1

What do the following sentences mean? 5

1. きらいでも子供にやさいを食べさせます。

2. 少しなら子供にチョコレートを食べさせます。

Guess and Try 2

Fill in the blanks. 5

見る ⟶ 見させる 　　飲む ⟶ 飲ませる
書く ⟶ 1.＿＿＿＿＿ 　　話す ⟶ 2.＿＿＿＿＿
買う ⟶ 3.＿＿＿＿＿ 　　取る ⟶ 4.＿＿＿＿＿
運ぶ ⟶ 5.＿＿＿＿＿ 　　する ⟶ させる
来る ⟶ 来させる

Guess and Try 3

Fill in the blanks and state what the sentences mean. 5

1. 父はきびしいです。父はいつも私＿＿＿＿＿5時間数学＿＿＿＿＿勉強させます。

2. 母はやさしいです。母はいつも私＿＿＿＿＿好きなもの＿＿＿＿＿食べさせてくれます。

Note: If an intransitive verb is used in a causative sentence, the action performer is marked by the particle を. 5

Guess and Try 4

Rephrase the sentences following the example. 5
For example:

私はやさいを食べました。 ⟶
母は私にやさいを食べさせました。

1. 妹はさらを洗いました。 ⟶
   母は _____。

2. 弟はテレビを見ました。 ⟶
   母は _____。

Guess and Try 5

What does the following sentence mean? 5

ちょっと休ませてくださいませんか。

🗣 Drill 1: Conjugation

食べる ⟶ 食べさせる・食べさせます

1. やめる   2. はしる
3. 行く   4. 休む
5. 習う   6. 話す
7. 練習する   8. 来る

🗣 Drill 2: Formation

やさいを食べる ⟶ やさいを食べさせる

1. にわをそうじする   2. 受験勉強をする
3. さらを洗う   4. ゆかをふく
5. くつをみがく   6. じゅくに行く
7. そろばんと習字を習う   8. ピアノを練習する
9. コンピューターゲームをやめる

🗣 Drill 3: Formation

日本に行く ⟶ 日本に行かせてくれました

1. テレビを見る   2. ゆっくり休む
3. 長電話をする   4. アルバイトをする
5. 友達と遊ぶ   6. 友達のうちにとまる
7. お酒を飲む   8. 好きなことをする

📖 Task: Group Work

Discuss whether you would allow your children to do the activities listed in the box when they are under 18 years old.

┌─────────────────────────────────────┐
• アルバイトをする   • 長電話をする
• ゲームセンターに行く
• 友達のうちにとまる
• たばこをすったり、お酒を飲んだりする
• ？？？ (your choice)
└─────────────────────────────────────┘

For example:
A： B さんが親になったら、子供にアルバイト
　　をさせますか。
B： いいえ、させません。／ はい、させます。
C： どうしてですか。
B： 勉強ができなくなるからです。／ アルバイ
　　トは勉強になるからです。

📖 Short Reading

　私の父はとても厳（きび）しい人です。門限（もんげん）は 9 時です。友達のうちに泊（と）まらせてくれません。もちろん、たばこをすったり、お酒を飲んだりさせてくれません。長電話をすると、大きい声（こえ）で怒鳴（どな）ります。とても恥（は）ずかしいです。毎日そうじと洗濯（せんたく）をさせます。そろばんや習字も習わせました。とても嫌でした。でも、大学に入（はい）った時、好きな学科（がっか）を専攻（せんこう）させてくれました。私は歴史（れきし）が好きだったので、歴史を専攻にしました。私が親になったら、子供に自由（じゆう）に遊（あそ）ばせてあげると思います。門限もつくりません。大学の専攻は父のように子供に決めさせてあげると思います。

(門限（もんげん） *curfew; locking-up time*, 声（こえ） *voice*, 怒鳴（どな）る *to yell; to shout*, 恥（は）ずかしい *embarrassing*, 学科（がっか） *(academic) subject*, 〜を専攻（せんこう）する *to major in ~*, 自由（じゆう）に *freely*)

✏️ Writing

Write about how your parent(s) raised you, and how you would raise your children if you become a parent in the future.

ろうかに立たせられました Punishment / Training

Notes Relating to This Lesson	
Grammar and Usage	
6 ～させられ 185	

 Basic Vocabulary and Kanji

ろうか	廊下	*n. hallway*
こうちょ^うしつ	校長室	*n. principal's office*
うでたてふ^うせ	腕立伏せ	*n. push-up*
かわいそ^う（な）	可哀相だ・可哀相じゃない	*adj. poor, pitiable, pitiful*

Newly introduced kanji:

校長室・空手(karate)
<ruby>校長室<rt>こうちょうしつ</rt></ruby>・<ruby>空手<rt>からて</rt></ruby>

 Dialog

Yoko Yamada and John Smith are talking about the typical punishments in schools.

山田　：アメリカの小学校では学生が悪いことをすると、どうなりますか。

スミス：悪い学生は校長室に行かせられます。

山田　：へえ。

スミス：日本の小学校は。

山田　：日本の小学校では、悪い学生はろうかに立たせられます。

スミス：ああ、そうですか。ちょっとかわいそうですね。

Guess and Try 1

Fill in the blanks so the two sentences in each set become equivalent. 6

1. A. 父は私に勉強させました。
   B. 私は父に勉強＿＿＿＿＿＿＿ました。

2. A. 空手の先生は私にうでたてふせを50回させました
   B. 私は空手の先生＿＿＿うでたてふせを50回させられました。

3. A. 母は私にやさいを食べ＿＿＿＿＿＿＿。
   B. 私は母にやさいを食べさせられました。

Guess and Try 2

Fill in the blanks using the verb in the parentheses. 6

1. シンデレラは継母 (stepmother) に＿＿＿＿＿＿＿＿＿＿＿＿＿＿＿＿＿。（そうじをする）

2. しらゆきひめ (Snow-white) はおばあさんにりんごを＿＿＿＿＿＿＿＿＿＿＿＿＿＿＿。（食べる）

3. ぼくはガールフレンドに2時間＿＿＿＿＿＿＿＿＿＿＿＿＿＿＿＿＿。（待つ）

Drill 1: Conjugation

食べる ➡ 食べさせる・食べさせられる

1. 見る　　　　　　2. 書く
3. 飲む　　　　　　4. 待つ
5. 持つ　　　　　　6. 洗う
7. てつだう　　　　8. 運ぶ
9. する　　　　　　10. 来る

Drill 2: Formation

漢字を書きました・先生 ➡ 先生に漢字を書かせられました

1. 車を洗いました・父
2. 名前を書きました・けいさつかん
3. コピーをとる・社長

4. 車を買いました・セールスマン

5. 二時間待ちました・ガールフレンド

Task 1: Group Work

Talk about punishments for students in elementary schools, middle schools and high schools in different countries.

For example:

A ： 中国では 学生はよくたたかれます。

B ： アメリカでは休み時間を少なくさせられます。

C ： 日本ではろうかに立たせられます。

Punishment at School
居残りをさせられる *to be kept after school*
廊下に立たせられる *to be forced to stand in the hallway*
休み時間をとられる *to be deprived of one's recess*
棒で手をたたかれる *to be hit in the palm with a stick*
停学させられる *to be suspended from school*
漢字を 100 回書かせられる *to be forced to write a kanji character 100 times.*
腕立伏せを 50 回させられる *to be forced to do pushups 50 times*
校長室に行かせられる *to be forced to go to the principal's office*
トラックを 20 周 走らせられる *to be forced to run around the track 20 times*

Task 2: Pair Work

Have you ever undertaken any training at a job or at a school? Talk about what you had to do.

For example:

A ： からての学校に行ったことがあります。

B ： どうでしたか。

C ： うでたてふせを一日に 100 回させられました。それから、…

Short Reading

私の兄はすし屋の板前です。18 歳の時に東京のすし屋で修業を始めました。最初の三年は皿洗いや、配達や、掃除ばかりさせられました。それから、毎日閉店後に少しずつ、魚のさわり方や、切り方を教えてもらえるようになりました。お客さんがいない時にだけ、すしを握る練習をしました。25 歳の時にやっとカウンターですしを握らせてもらえました。

(板前 *a cook specialized in Japanese cuisine,* 修業 *skill-learning; training,* 最初 *beginning,* 配達 *delivery,* 閉店後 *after the business hours of a restaurant / store,* さわり方 *handling method,* 切り方 *cutting method,* すしを握る *to make a piece of sushi by hand*)

Writing

Write about your training experience.

– Grammar and Usage –

1 (～の) せいで: Due to ～ [The cause of failure]

～のせいで specifies the cause of a failure or an undesirable situation, or the person who should be blamed for it.

(a) 雨のせいで BBQ パーティーが中止^{ちゅうし}になりました。

Due to the rain, the BBQ party was cancelled.

(b) エンジンオイルを交換しなかったせいで、エンジンが悪^{わる}くなってしまいました。

Because I didn't change the engine oil, the engine went bad.

(c) 田中^{たなか}さんのせいで車^{くるま}がこわれました。

Because of Mr. Tanaka, the car broke down. (Because of Mr. Tanaka's carelessness, the car broke down.)

(d) 車がこわれたのは田中さんのせいです

The damage of the car is due to Mr. Tanaka.

2 (～の) おかげで: Thanks to ～ [The cause of success]

～のおかげで specifies the cause of a success or a desirable situation, or the person who should get the credit for it.

(a) 奨学金制度^{しょうがくきんせいど}のおかげで卒業^{そつぎょう}できました。

Thanks to the scholarship program, I could graduate.

(b) 田中^{たなか}さんのおかげで部屋^{へや}がきれいになりました。

Thanks to Mr. Tanaka, the room became clean.

(c) 田中さんのおかげで洋服^{ようふく}を安^{やす}く買^かうことができました。

Thanks to Mr. Tanaka, I could buy clothes cheap.

3 ～られ: To be ～ ed [Direct passive]

The same situation can be expressed differently depending on the speaker's perspective. For example, when your father scolded your brother, you can say either (a) or (b), depending on whether your major concern is your father (a) or your brother (b):

(a) 父^{ちち}が弟^{おとうと}をしかりました。

My father scolded my brother.

(b) 弟が父にしかられました。

My brother was scolded by my father.

Sentences like (a), where the action performer is the subject, are called "active sentences", whereas sentences like (b), where the action receiver is the subject, are called "direct passive sentences".

The first step to convert an active sentence into a direct passive sentence is to convert the verb into a passive verb. You can do so by adding the passive suffix **(r)are** at the end of the verb in the root form: **rare** for a **ru**-verb, as in **tabe-rare** (食べられ); **are** for an **u**-verb, as in **kak-are** (書かれ). The resulting form can be treated as a newly created **ru**-verb in the root form, and can be followed by other suffixes such as **ru**, **nai** and **masu**, as in **tabe-rare-ru** (食べられる), **tabe-rare-nai** (食べられない) and **tabe-rare-masu** (食べられます). The passive forms of two major irregular verbs, する and くる, are される and こられる, respectively. The following table summarizes these:

Verbs in the Dictionary Form	Verbs in the Root Form	Passive Verbs in the Dictionary Form
たべる *to eat* tabe-ru	たべ tabe	たべられる *to be eaten* tabe-rare-ru
みる *to look* mi-ru	み mi	みられる *to be looked at* mi-rare-ru
かく *to write* kak-u	か k kak	かかれる *to be written* kak-are-ru
はぐ *to peel off* hag-u	は g hag	はがれる *to be peeled off* hag-are-ru
はこぶ *to carry* hakob-u	はこ b hakob	はこばれる *to be carried* hakob-are-ru
よむ *to read* yom-u	よ m yom	よまれる *to be read* yom-are-ru
しぬ *to die* shin-u	し n shin	しなれる * shin-are-ru

Verbs in the Dictionary Form	Verbs in the Root Form	Passive Verbs in the Dictionary Form
まつ *to wait* mats-u	ま t mat	またれる *to be kept waiting* mat-are-ru
かくす *to hide* kakus-u	かく s kakus	かくされる *to be hidden* kakus-are-ru
つくる *to make* tsukur-u	つく r tsukur	つくられる *to be made* tsukur-are-ru
かう *to buy* ka-u	か w kaw	かわれる *to be bought* kaw-are-ru
する *to do* suru	—	される *to be done* sare-ru
くる *to come* kuru	—	こられる * korare-ru

* makes sense only in indirect passive (Grammar and Usage note 4 in this chapter)

The next step is to make the direct object of the active sentence the subject of the direct passive sentence, and make the original subject as a part of the agent phrase marked by the particle に. Comparing sentences (a) and (b) will help you understand these changes. The following are additional examples of direct passive sentences:

(c) 子供がたたかれました。
The child was hit.

(d) スミスさんは先生にほめられました。
Mr. Smith was praised by the teacher.

(e) 私の部屋が使われました。
My room was used.

(f) マリーさんは先生に食事に誘われました。
Mary was invited for dinner by the teacher.

4 ～られ: [Indirect (adversative) passive]

The passive verbs are used not only for altering the speaker's perspective, but also for expressing a situation where one is negatively affected, annoyed, disturbed, or bothered by some incident. The latter use

of passive verbs is called "indirect passive" or "adversative passive", and it is not always easily translated into English. For example, the sentence 雨が降りました means *It rained*, and its indirect passive counterpart 雨に降られました means that the speaker was caught by the rain and was unhappy, which can be translated as *It rained on me*.

In indirect passive, the direct object remains as the direct object, being marked by the particle を, and the person who is affected becomes the subject. The performer of the action is marked by the particle に in indirect passive, just like in direct passive.

(a) 私は母に日記を読まれました。
My mother read my diary, (and I was unhappy about it).

(b) 私は子供に死なれました。
My child died, (and I am sad).

(c) 息子に家出をされました。
My son ran away, (and I am sad).

(d) 私は昨日犬ににげられて、たいへんでした。
My dog escaped yesterday, and I had a hard time.

(e) 田中さんは昨日ガールフレンドに泣かれて、困りました。
Mr. Tanaka's girlfriend cried yesterday, and he was in trouble.

(f) 私は隣の猫に金魚を食べられました。
My neighbor's cat ate my goldfish, (and I was upset).

(g) 私は昨日どろぼうに入られました。
My house was burglarized yesterday, (and I was upset).

(h) 私は弟に先に卒業されて、ちょっと恥ずかしかったです。
My younger brother graduated earlier than me, and I was a bit embarrassed.

(i) 私はスミスさんに論文を批判されて、ちょっと悲しかったです。
Mr. Smith criticized my paper, and I was a bit sad.

(j) 私が 100 点を取ったと言ったら、スミス
さんにびっくりされました。

*When I said that I got 100 points, Mr. Smith
was surprised, (and I was annoyed by it).*

The indirect passive may not be used for negative
verbs. For example, the following sentence is
ungrammatical:

(k) ルームメートに部屋をそうじされなくて、
いやでした。(**✗**)

(Ungrammatical) Intended meaning: *My
roommate didn't clean the room, and I was
annoyed by it.*

⑤ 　〜させ: To make / let someone do 〜
[Make-causative and let-causative]

The causative suffix **(s)ase** follows a verb in the root
form, and means *to make someone do something*
(*make*-causative) or *to let someone do something*
(*let*-causative). For example, 食べる means *to eat*,
but 食べさせる (tabe-sase-ru) means either *to make
someone eat* or *to let someone eat*. Whether it is
make-causative or *let*-causative depends on the context, or it depends on whether the action is done
according to the performer's will.

The causative suffix is **sase** for a **ru**-verb, as in
tabe-sase (食べさせ), but it is **ase** for an **u**-verb,
as in **kak-ase** (書かせ). The resulting form can be
treated as a newly created **ru**-verb in the root form,
and can be followed by other suffixes such as **ru**,
nai and **masu**, as in **tabe-sase-ru** (食べさせる),
tabe-sase-nai (食べさせない) and **tabe-sase-ma-
su** (食べさせます). The causative forms of two
major irregular verbs, する and くる, are させる
and こさせる, respectively. These are summarized
in the following table:

Verbs in the Dictionary Form	Verbs in the Root Form	Causative Verbs in the Dictionary Form
たべる *to eat* tabe-ru	たべ tabe	たべさせる *to make someone eat* tabe-sase-ru
みる *to look* mi-ru	み mi	みさせる *to make someone look at something* mi-sase-ru
かく *to write* kak-u	か k kak	かかせる *to make someone write* kak-ase-ru
およぐ *to swim* oyog-u	およ g oyog	およがせる *to make someone swim* oyog-ase-ru
はこぶ *to carry* hakob-u	はこ b hakob	はこばせる *to make someone carry something* hakob-ase-ru
よむ *to read* yom-u	よ m yom	よませる *to make someone read* yom-ase-ru
しぬ *to die* shin-u	し n shin	しなせる * shin-ase-ru
まつ *to wait* mats-u	ま t mat	またせる *to make someone wait* mat-ase-ru
はなす *to speak* hanas-u	はな s hanas	はなさせる *to make someone speak* hanas-ase-ru
つくる *to make* tsukur-u	つく r tsukur	つくらせる *to make someone make something* tsukur-ase-ru
かう *to buy* ka-u	か w kaw	かわせる *to make someone buy something* kaw-ase-ru
する *to do* suru	—	させる *to make someone do something* sase-ru
くる *to come* kuru	—	こさせる *to make someone come* kosase-ru

---

* makes sense only in *let*-causative (Grammar and
Usage note 6 in this chapter)

The action performer is always marked by the particle に if the verb is a transitive verb:

(a) 嫌いでも子供に野菜を毎日食べさせます。

I make my children eat vegetables every day even though they hate them.

(b) 少しなら子供にチョコレートを食べさせます。

I let my children eat chocolate if it is a little bit.

On the other hand, when the verb is intransitive, the action performer is marked by を:

(c) 私はテニス部の後輩をうちに来させました。

I made my juniors in the tennis club come to my house.

(d) コメディアンは客を笑わせました

The comedians made the guests laugh.

Let-causative is often used when one seeks permission very politely. All of the following sentences mean *Could I take a rest?* or *Please let me take a rest.*

(e) ちょっと休ませていただきたいんですが。

(f) ちょっと休ませていただけませんか。

(g) ちょっと休ませてくださいませんか。

(h) ちょっと休ませてください。

Let-causative can also be used for offering help very politely:

(i) 私に手伝わせてくださいませんか。

Could you let me help you?

(j) 私にその荷物を運ばせてください。

Please let me carry the baggage (you are holding).

6 〜させられ: **To be made to do 〜**
   [Causative-passive]

The combination of a causative suffix and a passive suffix **(s)ase-rare** expresses the situation where one is made to do something. For example, 父は私に勉強させました means *My father made me study*, but 私は父に勉強させられました means *I*

was made to study by my father. The person who is made to do something becomes the subject, and the person who makes him / her do it, is marked by the particle に.

(a) シンデレラは継母に掃除をさせられました。とてもかわいそうでた。

Cinderella was made to clean (the rooms) by her stepmother. It was pitiful.

(b) 白雪姫はおばあさんにりんごを食べさせられました。

Snow White was made to eat an apple by an old lady.

(c) 私はガールフレンドに二時間待たせられました。

I was made to wait for two hours by my girlfriend.

The causative-passive suffix **(s)ase-rare** often contracts to **(s)asare** in colloquial Japanese for u-verbs whose dictionary forms do not end in す. For example, とらせられる and 待たせられる can contract to とらされる and 待たされる, respectively.

– Culture –

Ⓐ じゅく: **Tutoring school / cram school**

塾 is a special private school that offers highly organized lessons conducted after regular school hours and on weekends for pre-college students. It helps students who are falling behind, who want to improve test scores, or who want to satisfy individual needs. Parents often believe that these schools can help their children get into the colleges of their preference.

Ⓑ そろばん: **Abacus**

The Chinese abacus and its operational technique were introduced to Japan in the fifteenth century. The Japanese then developed a smaller abacus and a distinct operation method which was different from the original Chinese method. The current Japanese standard abacus has one five-unit counter and four one-unit counters on each rod as you can see in the photograph, and its operation method is taught in the curriculum of Japanese compulsory education as well as in private abacus schools.

Many believe that practicing abacus improves their concentration, memory and skills in mental calculation and information process.

– Kanji List –

字・客・知っている・悲しい・家出を
する・先に・悪口・降る・降りる・手紙・
受験・習字・長電話・練習する・校長室・
空手

字 ジ letter, character	﹅ ﹅ ﹅ 宀 宁 字 [6]
	Example: 字 letter, character, 漢字 Chinese characters
客 キャク guest, customer	﹅ ﹅ 宀 宁 宁 灾 客 客 [9]
	Example: 客 customer
知 し-る・チ know, aware, intelligence	﹅ ﹅ 二 午 矢 知 知 知 [8]
	Example: 知っている to know, 知識 knowledge
悲 かな-しい・ かな-しむ・ ヒ sorrow	﹅ ﹅ ﹅ ﹅ ﹅ 非 非 非 非 悲 悲 悲 [12]
	Example: 悲しい sad, 悲しむ to feel sad

家 いえ・や・ うち・カ・ ケ house	﹅ ﹅ 宀 宁 宁 宇 宇 家 家 家 [10]
	Example: 家 house, 家内 one's own wife, 家出をする to run away from home
出 で-る・だ- す・シュツ / シュツ come, go out	﹅ 十 屮 出 出 [5]
	Example: 出る to come out, 出す to hand in, to take out, 家出をする to run away from home
先 さき・セン forgoing, previou	﹅ ﹅ 牛 生 先 先 [6]
	Example: 先に ahead, 先生 teacher
悪 わる-い・ア ク bad, ill	﹅ ﹅ 宀 亘 甲 亜 亜 亜 悪 悪 悪 [11]
	Example: 悪い bad, 悪口を言う to speak ill of a person
口 くち・-ぐち・ コウ mouth	﹅ 口 口 [3]
	Example: 口 mouth, 悪口を言う to speak ill of a person
降 ふ-る・ お-りる・ お-ろす・コ ウ descend	﹅ ﹅ 阝 阝 阝 阼 阼 降 降 降 [10]
	Example: 降る to fall (rain, snow, etc.), 降りる to get off
手 て・シュ hand	﹅ 二 三 手 [4]
	Example: 手紙 letter, 手 hand, 上手 skillful, 下手 unskillful
紙 かみ・シ paper, journal	﹅ ﹅ ﹅ ﹅ ﹅ 糸 紅 紅 紙 紙 [10]
	Example: 紙 paper, 手紙 letter
受 う-ける・ う-かる・ ジュ receive	﹅ ﹅ ﹅ ﹅ 四 四 严 受 受 [8]
	Example: 受ける to take (an exam), 受験 exam taking

験 ケン proof, examine	丨丨丆丏丐馬馬馬馬馬駽 駖駖駖駖験験 [18] Example: 試験(しけん) exam, 受験(じゅけん) exam taking
習 なら-う・シュウ practice	フフヨヨ羽羽羽羽習習習 [11] Example: 習字(しゅうじ) calligraphy, 練習(れんしゅう)する to practice, 習(なら)う to learn, 復習(ふくしゅう)する to review
長 なが-い・チョウ long, eldest, chief	一丆丆丆丨丨長長 [8] Example: 校長(こうちょう) principal, 長(なが)い long, 長電話(ながでんわ) long telephone conversation
電 デン electricity	一丆戸雨雨雨雨雪雪電電電 [13] Example: 電気(でんき) electricity, 長電話(ながでん わ) long telephone conversation
話 はな-す・はなし・ワ talk	丶丶亖亖言言言計計計話 話 [13] Example: 話(はな)す to talk, 長電話(ながでんわ) long telephone conversation
練 ね-る・レン knead	乙幺幺糸糸糸紅紅紀紳紳 紳練 [14] Example: 練習(れんしゅう)する to practice
校 コウ school	一十才木木杧杧杧校校 [10] Example: 学校(がっこう) school, 高校(こうこう) high school
室 シツ room, house	丶丶宀宀宀宔宔室室 [9] Example: 教室(きょうしつ) classroom
空 そら・クウ・から sky	丶丶宀宀宄空空空 [8] Example: 空手(からて) karate, 空(そら) sky, 空港(くうこう) airport

– Review –

Q1. *Write the reading of the following kanji phrases, and state what is common among the members of each set.*

1. 悲しい・忘れる・思う
2. 紙・結婚・3級・練習・絵
3. 降る・大阪・病院

Q2. *Choose the appropriate option in the parentheses.*

1. 父が兄を (しかりました・しかられました・しからせました)。
2. 兄が父に (しかりました・しかられました・しからせました)。
3. 父が兄に弟を (しかりました・しかられました・しからせました)。
4. てんいんは客に高いものを (買われました・買わせました・買わせられました)。
5. 私は友達にお酒をたくさん (飲まれて・飲ませて・飲ませられて)、気分が悪くなって、はいてしまいました。(はく to vomit)

Q3. *Complete the following sentences.*

1. 父は弟 _____ 英語を勉強させました。
2. 私はどろぼうにネックレス _____ ぬすまれました。
3. うちでは子供 _____ テレビを見させません。
4. シンデレラは継母(ままはは) _____ そうじをさせられました。

Q4. *Convert the following sentences as in the example.*

Part A, example: 先生が学生をほめました。
→ 学生が先生にほめられました。

1. リスが花を食べました。
→ 花が _____。
2. アメリカ人が日本語を話しています。
→ 日本語が _____。

Part B, example:

昨日雨が降って、父は困りました。

　→ 父は昨日雨に降られました。

1. 電車の中で女の人が私の足をふみました。
　→ 私は ＿＿＿＿＿＿＿＿＿＿＿＿＿＿＿。
2. 小さい時に父が外国に行って、さびしかっ
　たです。
　→ 私は ＿＿＿＿＿＿＿＿＿＿＿＿＿＿＿。

Part C, example:

子供がやさいを食べました。

　→ 私は子供にやさいを食べさせました。

1. 弟がさらを洗いました。
　→ 私は ＿＿＿＿＿＿＿＿＿＿＿＿＿＿＿。
2. 妹がハワイに行きました。
　→ 私は ＿＿＿＿＿＿＿＿＿＿＿＿＿＿＿。

Part D, example:

父は私にやさいを食べさせました。

　→ 私は父にやさいを食べさせられました。

1. 兄は弟に車を洗わせました。
　→ ＿＿＿＿＿＿＿＿＿＿＿＿＿＿＿＿＿。
2. 先生は私に漢字を 100 回書かせました。
　→ ＿＿＿＿＿＿＿＿＿＿＿＿＿＿＿＿＿。

Q5. *What would you say in Japanese in the situations below?*

1. You are about to ask the company president for leave to go on a vacation next month. (休みをと る *to take a vacation*)
2. Your teacher is holding three big dictionaries and you would like to help her by holding them.

Tips and Additional Knowledge: Formal Speech Style

社長がお書きになりました / 私がお書きしました

In addition to the plain / informal and polite / neutral speech styles, Japanese has a super polite speech style called the "formal speech style". In the formal speech style, the honorific form (尊敬語) is used for describing the action of one's social superior and the humble form (謙譲語) is used for describing one's own action in front of his / her social superior. They are manifested most prominently with verb forms.

The general formula for creating honorific and humble verb forms is as follows:

Honorific form: お + **verb stem** + に + なる

For example: 社長がお書きになりました

Humble form: お + **verb stem** + する

For example: 私がお書きしました

Another way of creating an honorific verb form is to add **(r)are** to the verb root, just like creating a passive verb discussed in this chapter:

Honorific form: **verb root** + **(r)are** + る

For example: 社長が書かれました

Some frequently used verbs have their own special honorific / humble forms and the above general formulas do not apply to them. The table below lists some of them.

Dictionary Form	Honorific Form	Humble Form
行く *to go*	いらっしゃる	参^{まい}る
来^くる *to come*		
いる *to exist*	いらっしゃる	おる
だ *to be*	でいらっしゃる	でござる
する *to do*	なさる	致^{いた}す
食^たべる *to eat*	召^めし上^あがる	頂^{いただ}く
飲^のむ *to drink*		
見^みる *to look*	ご覧^{らん}になる	拝見^{はいけん}する
言^いう *to say*	おっしゃる	申^{もう}す
知^しっている *to know*	ご存知^{ぞんじ}だ	存^{ぞん}じておる
あげる *to give*	(general formula)	差^さし上^あげる
くれる	下^{くだ}さる	(Not applicable) *to give to me*
もらう *to receive*	(general formula)	頂^{いただ}く

The following are two sample conversations. Can you identify the honorific / humble forms?

Dialog 1

Mrs. Yamada picks up the phone at her home.

山田 ： 山田でございます。
田中 ： 田中と申しますが、よう子さんはいらっしゃいますか？
山田 ： 今、ちょっと出かけておりますが。
田中 ： それでは、またこちらからお電話をおかけ致^{いた}します。

Yamada : This is Yamada's resident.
Tanaka : This is Mr. Tanaka speaking. Is Yoko there?

Yamada : She is out now.
Tanaka : Then, I will call (her) again.

Dialog 2

Ms. Yamada talks to the president of the company in the morning.

山田 ： コーヒーをお入^いれしました。
社長 ： ああ、どうも。
山田 ： お砂糖^{さとう}はお入れになりますか。
社長 ： いいえ、いいです。
山田 ： あのう、今朝の新聞をご覧^{らん}になりましたか。
社長 ： いいえ。
山田 ： 田中電機^{でんき}の社長が辞任^{じにん}されたそうです。
社長 ： えっ、本当ですか。ちょっとその新聞を見せてくれませんか。
山田 ： はい。すぐに持って参^{まい}ります。

Yamada : I have made coffee for you.
President : Oh, thank you.
Yamada : Would you like to add sugar?
President : No, thank you.
Yamada : Ummm, did you see this morning's newspaper, Sir?
President : No.
Yamada : It said that the president of Tanaka Electric, Inc. has resigned.
President : Oh, really? Could you show me the newspaper?
Yamada : Yes. I will bring it right away.

CHALLENGE
(Chapter Fifteen to Chapter Twenty-six)

🎧 Challenge 1

The following conversation is between Ms. Kato, a Japanese student who is studying in the United States and Mr. Smith, a physics major graduate student who is studying Japanese in the same college. Listen to the online audio and answer the questions that follow. You may encounter some unfamiliar words, but you should be able to answer the questions.

加藤　：　スミスさんは日本に行ったことがありますか。

スミス：　いいえ、まだありません。でも、今年の夏に行くつもりです。富山の大学で物理の研究をするんです。

加藤　：　ああ、そうですか。よかったですね。

スミス：　富山はどんなところですか。

加藤　：　富山は東京から電車で５時間ぐらいのところにあります。よく雪が降るところで、スキー場がたくさんあります。富山には立山というきれいな山もあります。それに、きれいな海岸もたくさんあって、おいしいものもたくさんあります。近くに金沢というところがあります。金沢は日本風の古い建物がたくさんあって、とてもきれいなところです。

スミス：　ああ、そうですか。じゃあ、金沢にも行きます。東京と京都にも行くつもりですが。

加藤　：　そうですか。東京は今、日本の首都です。昔は京都が日本の都でした。京都は東京より古くて、静かです。まわりに、山がたくさんあって、きれいです。東京は京都よりずっと大きくて、人も車もずっと多いです。

スミス：　じゃあ、東京には行きません。私はうるさいところは嫌いですから。

1. What kind of place is Kanazawa?
2. How different are Tokyo and Kyoto?
3. Which cities does Mr. Smith decide to go after the conversation with Ms. Kato? List all of them.

Challenge 2

The following letter was written by a Japanese high school student, Tomoko, to her pen pal, Leslie, who is studying Japanese in an American high school. Read the letter and answer the questions that follow.

Glossary: 絵葉書 *picture postcard*
雪祭り *snow festival*
避暑に行く *to go somewhere to avoid summer heat*

レスリーさんへ

　日本は今桜の花でいっぱいですが、レスリーさんはお元気ですか。私は元気です。この間はロングアイランドの地図と絵葉書を送って下さって、ありがとうございました。ロングアイランドはとてもきれいなところですね。私の町、札幌もきれいなところですよ。冬は雪祭りを見たり、スキーをしたりすることができます。夏はすずしいので、たくさんの人が避暑に来ます。レスリーさんもいつか遊びに来て下さいね。

　日本では四月から新しい学期が始まりました。私は高校三年生になりました。三年生は大学に入るためにいっしょうけんめい勉強しなくてはいけません。これからとても忙しくなりそうです。レスリーさんも高校での日本語の

勉強、頑張って下さい。

　それではまたお手紙書きますね。

お元気で。

高橋友子

1. What did Leslie send to Tomoko?
2. Where does Tomoko live? What kind of place is it?
3. Why does Tomoko have to study hard this year?

Challenge 3

Pretend that you have just found a Japanese pen pal, write a letter to him / her.

Challenge 4

The following essay was written by a student of Japanese, who had studied in Japan for a year before. Read it carefully, using a dictionary, and state the five characteristics of Japan and the Japanese people described in it.

私の目から見た日本と日本人

チアン・チョン

日本というと、まず思い浮かべるのは富士山です。飛行機から見た富士山はとてもきれいでした。日本に一年住んで、日本人の不思議なところや、いいところがたくさん分かりました。

日本に着いたとたんに、静かだと感じました。電車の中ではほとんどの人はしゃべりません。本を読んだり、寝たりしています。日本に来たばかりの外国人はよく大きい声で話すのでちょっと目立ちます。私が住んでいたアパートは3階建てでした。あまり人の声がしませんでした。はじめの1ヶ月は静かすぎて、ちょっと怖かったです。とても不思議でしたが、後で友達から日本人は他の人に迷惑をかけないようにいつも静かにしているのだと聞きました。

先輩と後輩の関係は日本社会の至るところで見られます。日本では、会社や学校に入ると、すぐに先輩と後輩の関係が作られてしまいます。能力に関係なく、早く入った人は先輩で、後に入った人は後輩になります。日本人の会話を聞くと、どちらが先輩で、どちらが後輩かすぐ分かります。ちょっと軍隊のようだと思いました。

日本のサラリーマンは仕事をしている時は静かですが、仕事の後、居酒屋でお酒を飲むと、急に明るくなって、よくしゃべり始めます。お酒を飲んで、人間関係や仕事のストレスを解消します。会社の不満を上司に言ったり、大声で話したりできるからです。日本のサラリーマンは夜いくら飲んでも、次の日の朝遅刻もしないで、会社に行き、また、きちんと仕事をします。とても不思議です。

日本は時間厳守の国です。人と約束をする時は必ず時間を守ります。日本の電車や、地下鉄はほとんど時刻表通りです。日本人は他の人の時間を無駄にしないようにいつも気をつけています。これは素晴らしいことだと思いました。

日本のお店やレストランではお客さんが神様のように大切に扱われます。お客さんがレストランに入ると、店員さんは必ず「いらっしゃいませ」と言って、優しく迎えてくれます。席に着くと、すぐおしぼりと、お水かお茶を出してくれます。とても丁寧な言葉を使ってくれます。食べ物はおいしいだけではなく、とても美しいです。本当に関心しました。

日本への留学は私にとって、とてもいい経験でした。常識とは国によって違うのであり、不思議だと思うことにも歴史的、社会的な理由があるのだということがよく分かりました。

(〜とたんに *just at the moment* 〜, 〜の至ると
ころ *throughout* 〜, 関係 *relationship; connection,*
ストレスを解消する *to get rid of stress,* 時間
厳守 *very punctual,* 時刻表通りです *to be the*
same as in the timetable, おしぼり *a small (hot)*
damp towel roll)

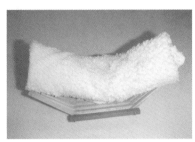

おしぼり

Challenge 5

The following passage is about "snoring". Read it
carefully, using a dictionary, and answer the questions that follow in English.

　イビキで困っている人は意外に多いようだ。
太っている人はイビキをかきやすい。また、顎
が小さい人や、顎がひっこんでいる人、扁桃
腺が大きい人もイビキをかきやすいようだ。

イビキをかいている間に気道が閉塞してし
まうこともある。そうすると、無呼吸 (apnea)
になる。無呼吸を繰り返しながら睡眠すると、
朝起きたとき頭が重く、昼間も眠気がして、
集中力がなくなる。記憶力も悪くなる。
無呼吸になる人は、寝つきは非常にいい。し
かし、長い時間眠っても熟睡した気がしな
い。

　イビキを防ぐためには、横を向いて寝るこ
とや、お酒を飲まないこともいいかもしれない。
マスクや、マウスピースも役立つこともあるが、
外科手術が必要なこともある。

1. What kinds of people are likely to snore?

2. What problems arise from apnea?

3. What can we do to prevent snoring?

Particles

Particles are short elements that follow words, phrases and sentences, and they themselves do not conjugate. They are classified into grammatical particles, pragmatic particles, connective particles and sentence-final particles.

- **Grammatical particles**: Follow nouns and express the relationship between the noun and the verb or adjective of a sentence or between nouns in the same sentence. For examples: が, を, に, で and と.
- **Pragmatic particles** (discourse particles): Follow not only nouns, but also verbs, adjectives, and some grammatical particles, and express sentence-external pragmatic information such as the speaker's knowledge and understanding. For examples: は, も, and ばかり.
- **Connective particles**: Follow verbs, adjectives and nouns, and create adverbial phrases / clauses or embedded clauses. For examples: と and ながら.
- **Sentence-final particles**: Placed at the end of a sentence and specify the function of the sentence or show the speaker's attitude or subtle implications. For examples: か and ね.

Particle / Translation	Function	Category	Examples	
～か [1] ~ or	disjunction	grammatical particle	日本語か、中国語か、韓国語を勉強します。 *I will study Japanese, Chinese or Korean.*	CH 11
～か [2] whether or not ~ ～か [2] if ~ (what, who, where, etc.)	embedded question	connective particle	アメリカの大学はいいか分かりません。 *I do no know whether or not American universities are good.*	CH 23
			お金はどこにあるか教えて下さい。 *Please let me know where the money is.*	CH 23
～か [3]	question	sentence-final particle	これはペンですか。 *Is this a pen?*	CH 2
～が [1]	subject	grammatical particle	スミスさんが来ました。 *Mr. Smith came.*	CH 6
			明日はテストがあります。 *I have a test tomorrow.*	CH 8
			日本語は漢字が難しいです。 *As for Japanese, kanji characters are difficult.*	CH 11

Particle / Translation	Function	Category	Examples
〜が [1]	subject	grammatical particle	私はアイスクリームが好きです。 *I like ice cream.* 兄は手品ができます。 *My brother can do magic.* CH 11
〜が [2] *~, but* *although ~* *~, and*	contrast, conflict, continuation	connective particle	私はアメリカ人ですが、母は日本人です。 *I'm American, but my mother is Japanese.* (contrast) 私は日本人ですが、すしがきらいです。 *I'm Japanese, but I do not like sushi.* (conflict) 日本食はおいしいが、高い。 *Japanese food is delicious, but expensive.* (contrast) 車をかりたいんですが、いいですか。 *I'd like to borrow your car, but is it okay?* (continuation) もしもし。スミスですが、 よう子さんはいらっしゃいますか。 *Hello. I'm Mr. Smith, but is Yoko available?* (continuation) CH 11
〜かどうか *whether or not* *~* *if ~*	embedded question	connective particle	アメリカの大学はいいかどうか分かりません。 *I do not know whether American universities* *are good.* CH 23
〜から [1] *from ~*	starting point	grammatical particle	どちらからですか。 *Where are you from?* (origin, CH 2) 大学から駅まで歩きます。 *I walk from the university to the railway station.* (Starting location, CH 7) 2時から、3時まで勉強した。 *I studied from 2 o'clock to 3 o'clock.* (Starting time) あの店は食べ物から、車まで売っている。 *That store sells various things from foods to cars.* (Starting point in diversity) 酒は米から作る。 *Sake is made from rice.* (Ingredients, cf. で)
〜から [2] *because ~*	reason / cause	connective particle	私は日本人だから、はしで食べる。 *Because I am Japanese, I eat with chopsticks.* 私は日本人ですから、はしで食べます。 *Because I am Japanese, I eat with chopsticks.* CH 15

Particle / Translation	Function	Category	Examples
〜から³ *after 〜*	time adverbial	connective particle	宿題をしてから、テレビを見ます。 *I will watch the TV after doing my homework.* CH 18
〜こそ	emphasis	pragmatic particle	こちらこそ。 *That's me (who should say that).* スミスさんこそ、頭がいいですよ。 *That's you, Mr. Smith, who is smart.* CH 1
〜さえ *even 〜*	least expected example	pragmatic particle	こんな簡単な漢字さえ知りません。 *(He) doesn't even know such an easy kanji.*
〜し *and 〜*	emphatic listing	connective particle	マイクさんは、頭がいいし、まじめだし、 よく働くし。 *Mike is smart, diligent, work very hard, (and ...)* CH 20
〜しか *only 〜*	only	pragmatic particle	10ドルしかないので、この本は買えません。 *I have only 10 dollars, so I cannot buy this book.* この植物はこの島にしかありません。 *This plant exists only in this island.* CH 22
〜ずつ *each 〜*	distributive	pragmatic particle	学生は1万円ずつもらいました。 *Students received 10,000 yen each.* CH 19
〜だけ *just 〜*	just	pragmatic particle	10ドルだけ頂きます。 *I'll accept just 10 dollars.* この本を返したかっただけです。 *I just wanted to return this book.* マリーさんはきれいなだけです。 *Mary is just pretty.* CH 18
〜たら *when 〜* *whenever 〜* *if 〜*	consequence / condition	a form of a verb	この薬を飲んだら、よくなりました。 *When I took this medicine, I got better. (Sporadic consequence)* このボタンをおしたら、きっぷが出ます。 *If you press this button, you will get a ticket.* (Automatic consequence / Generic condition) この映画が終わったら、宿題をします。 *When this movie is over, I will do my homework.* (Temporal condition) 高かったら、買いません。 *If it is expensive, I will not buy it. (Hypothetical condition)* 私が鳥だったら、空をとびます。 *If I were a bird, I would fly over the sky.* (Counterfactual condition) CH 24

Particle / Translation	Function	Category	Examples
〜たり *to do ~, etc.*	example-listing	a form of a verb	昨日^{きのう}は、食^たべたり、飲^のんだり、歌^{うた}ったりしました。 *Yesterday, I ate, drink, sing, and so on.*　　　CH 22
〜で *with ~* *by ~* *in ~* *at ~* *using ~*	background	grammatical particle	車^{くるま}で行^いきます。 *I go (there) by car.* (Transportation, CH 6) はしで食^たべます。 *I eat with chopsticks.* (Tool, CH 6) 図書館^{としょかん}で勉強^{べんきょう}します。 *I study in the library.* (Location of activity, CH 6) 日本語^ごで話^{はな}した。 *I spoke in Japanese.* (Means) テレビで見^みた。 *I watched (it) on TV.* (Means) 全部^{ぜんぶ}で30ドルです。 *It's 30 dollars all together.* (Basis, CH4) 一人^{ひとり}で日本に行^いった。 *I went to Japan alone.* (Circumstantial condition, CH 12) 家族^{かぞく}でレストランに行^いった。 *I went to a restaurant with my family.* (Circumstantial condition, CH 12) 台風^{たいふう}で屋根^{やね}がこわれた。 *The roof broke because of the typhoon.* (Reason, CH 12) ふじ山^{さん}は日本で一番高^{いちばんたか}い山^{やま}だ。 *Mt. Fuji is the tallest mountain in Japan.* (Basis, CH 17) 5才^{さい}で泳^{およ}げるようになった。 *I became able to swim at the age of five.* (Time, CH 21) 裸足^{はだし}で歩^{ある}いた。 *I walked barefoot.* (Circumstantial condition) 割引^{わりびき}で買^かった。 *I bought (it) with a discount.* (Circumstantial condition) 酒^{さけ}は米^{こめ}で作^{つく}る。 *Sake is made from rice.* (Ingredients)

Particle / Translation	Function	Category	Examples
〜と¹ 〜 and with 〜	equal status	grammatical particle	日本と、中国と、韓国に行きます。 *I will go to Japan, China and Korea.* (Listed items, CH 4) 父と日本に行きます。 *I will go to Japan (together) with my father.* (Accompany, CH 8) 父とけんかをした。 *I fought with my father.* (Partner / Opponent, CH 12) トラックとぶつかった。 *(My car) collided with a truck.* (Partner / Opponent, CH 25) よう子さんと結婚しました。 *I got married to Yoko.* (Partner, CH 25)
〜と² *that* 〜	embedded sentence, quotation	connective particle	アメリカの大学はいいと思います。 *I think that American universities are good.* (Embedded sentence, CH 15) 「いただきます」と、言いました。 *(I) said, "Itadakimasu."* (Quotation, CH 18)
〜と³ *if* 〜 *when* 〜	consequence	connective particle	このボタンをおすと、きっぷが出ます。 *If you press this button, you will get a ticket.* (Automatic consequence) 値段が高いと、売れません。 *If the prices are high, things don't sell very well.* (Automatic consequence) ドアを開けると、男の人が立っていました。 *When I opened the door, a man was standing.* (Sporadic consequence)　　　　　　　　CH 21
〜とか 〜, *etc.*	example-listing	grammatical particle	もう少しピアノを練習するとか、数学を勉強するとかしなさいよ。 *Do things like practicing the piano and studying mathematics.* ピザとか、スパゲッティーとかが大好きだ。 *I like pizza, spaghetti, etc.*　　　　　　　CH 12
〜ながら *while* 〜*ing*	accompanying action	connective particle	テレビを見ながら、食べます。 *I eat while watching TV.*　　　　　　　CH 18

Particle / Translation	Function	Category	Examples
～なら *if* ~	supposition / condition	connective particle*	日本に行くなら、日本語を勉 強して下さい。 *If you are going to Japan, please study Japanese.* 日本に３年いたなら、日本語が上手でしょう。 *If you stayed in Japan for three years, your Japanese must be good, right?* このコースが 難 しいなら、どのコースも難しいでしょう。 *If you find this course difficult, any course will be difficult for you.* 学 生がまじめなら、先 生もうれしいでしょう。 *If the students are studious, their teacher will be happy.* CH 24
～に[1] *to* ~ *in* ~ *on* ~ *against* ~ *by* ~ *from* ~	target	grammatical particle	日本に行きます。 *I will go to Japan.* (Target of movement / Destination, CH 5) 月に一回カラオケ・バーに行きます。 *I go to karaoke bars once a month.* (Interval, CH 5) ふじ山は日本にあります。 *Mt. Fuji is in Japan.* (Location of existence, CH 7) 兄は医者になった。 *My brother became a doctor.* (Target of change, CH 11) 月曜日に行きます。 *I will go (there) on Monday.* (Absolute time, CH 12) ビタミン A は目にいいです。 *Vitamin A is good for the eyes.* (Target of pros and cons, CH 13) タバコは肺に悪いです。 *Cigarettes are bad for lungs.* (Target of pros and cons, CH 13) 東 京 に住んでいます。 *I live in Tokyo.* (Location of existence, CH 14) トラックにぶつかった。 *(My car) hit a truck.* (Target of movement, CH 25)

Particle / Translation	Function	Category	Examples
〜に[1] *to ~* *in ~* *on ~* *against ~* *by ~* *from ~*	target	grammatical particle	ガールフレンドに花^{はな}をあげた。 *I gave flowers to my girlfriend.* (Recipient, CH 20) 卒業^{そつぎょう}のお祝^{いわ}いにネクタイをあげた。 *I gave (him) a tie as a congratulation gift for graduation.* (Occasion, CH 20) 祖父^{そふ}にネクタイをもらった。 *I received a tie from my grandfather.* (Source, CH 20) 弟^{おとうと}が父^{ちち}に叱^{しか}られた。 *My brother was scolded by my father.* (Agent of the action in passive sentences, CH 26) 妹^{いもうと}に皿^{さら}を洗^{あら}わせた。 *I made my sister wash the dishes.* (Agent of the action in causative sentences, CH 26) 壁^{かべ}にカレンダーをはった。 *I posted the calendar on the wall.* (Target surface) 弟^{おとうと}は父^{ちち}に似^にている。 *My brother resembles my father.* (Target of resemblance)
（〜に[1]）	time adverbial	connective particle	食事^{しょくじ}の時^{とき}に、話^{はな}します。 *I will tell (him) at mealtime.* 日本^にに行^いく前^{まえ}に、日本語^{にほんご}を勉強^{べんきょう}します。 *I will study Japanese before going to Japan.* ご飯^{はん}を食^たべた後^{あと}に、日本語^ごを勉強^{べんきょう}します。 *I will study Japanese, after eating.* 父^{ちち}が会社^{かいしゃ}で働^{はたら}いている間^{あいだ}に、母^{はは}は買^かい物^{もの}に行^いきます。 *While my father is working, my mother goes shopping.* お金^{かね}があるうちに、買^かいましょう。 *While we have money, let's buy it.* 父^{ちち}が帰^{かえ}らないうちに、テレビを見^みます。 *I will watch TV before my father returns.* 明^{あか}るいうちに、帰^{かえ}りましょう。 *Let's go home while it is bright.* CH 18
〜に[2] *(to go / come to somewhere)* *to do ~*	purpose of coming and going	connective particle	牛乳^{ぎゅうにゅう}を買^かいに、スーパーマーケットに行^いきました。 *I went to the supermarket to buy milk.* CH 13

Particle / Translation	Function	Category	Examples
〜ね ~, isn't it?	confirmation, agreement elicitor	sentence-final particle	この建物は図書館ですね。 *This building is a library, correct?* (Confirmation) あの女の人はきれいですね。 *That lady is pretty, isn't she?* (Agreement elicitor, CH 3)
〜の ~'s of	attribute	grammatical particle	これは私の本です。 *This is my book.* (Owner) 兄は日本語の学生です。 *My brother is a student of Japanese.* (Modifier)　　　CH 3
〜ので therefore	reason	connective particle**	母は日本人なので、すしが大好きです。 *My mother is Japanese, so she likes sushi very much.* 明日試験があるので、勉強します。 *As there will be an exam tomorrow, I will study.*　　　CH 20
〜のに ~, but although ~	conflict	connective particle**	母は日本人なのに、すしがきらいです。 *My mother is Japanese, but she does not like sushi.* 勉強したのに、0点を取りました。 *Although I studied, I got 0 points.*　　　CH 20
〜は as for ~ speaking of ~	topic, contrast	pragmatic particle	これは何ですか。 *What is this?* (Topic, CH 2) カラオケ・バーにはよく行きますか。 *As for to karaoke bars, do you often go (there)?* (Topic, CH 5) 私は日本語は話します。でも、英語は話しません。 *I speak Japanese. But I do not speak English.* (Contrast, CH 11) 見はしますが、買いはしません。 *I will see it, but I wouldn't buy it.* (Contrast) テキストを読んではおきましたが、単語は覚えませんでした。 *I read the textbook in advance, but I didn't memorize vocabulary.* (Contrast) 大きくは書けますが、きれいには書けません。 *I can write big, but I cannot write neatly.*

Particle / Translation	Function	Category	Examples
〜ばかり *nothing but ~*	exclusiveness	pragmatic particle	ピザばかり食べています。 *I eat nothing but pizza.* ゲームセンターにばかり行っています。 *(He) goes nowhere but arcades.* 兄はねてばかりいます。 *He does nothing but sleep.* CH 14
〜へ *to ~* *toward ~*	direction	grammatical particle	日本へ行きます。 *I will go to Japan.* CH 12
〜ほど… *not as ... as ~*	unreachable	pragmatic particle	九州は北海道ほど広くありません。 *Kyushu is not as large as Hokkaido.* CH 17
〜まで *up to ~* *until ~*	ending point	grammatical particle	大学から駅まで歩きます。 *I walk from the university to the railway station.* (Ending point in distance, CH 7) 2時から、3時まで勉強します。 *I study from 2 o'clock to 3 o'clock.* (Ending point in time) あの店は食べものから、車まで売っている。 *That store sells various things from foods to cars.* (Ending point in diversity)
〜までに *by ~*	deadline	grammatical particle	金曜日までに宿題を出してください。 *Please hand in your homework by Friday.* CH 16
〜も *also* *too* *both* *all* *no*	addition	pragmatic particle	これは英和辞典です。あれも英和辞典です。 *This one is an English-Japanese dictionary.* *That one is an English-Japanese dictionary, too.* CH 2 本屋にもよく行きます。 *I also go to bookstores often.* CH 5 どちらも好きです。 *I like both.* CH 17 何も食べませんでした。 *I ate nothing.* CH 12
〜（て）も・ 〜（で）も *even if ~* *even though ~* *no matter ~*	concession	connective particle	安くても、買いません。 *Even if it is cheap, I will not buy it.* 勉強しても、100点はとれません。 *Even if I study, I will not be able to get 100 points.* いくら勉強しても、100点はとれません。 *No matter how hard I study, I will not be able to get 100 points.* CH 25

Particle / Translation	Function	Category	Examples
〜や ~, etc.	example-listing	grammatical particle	日本語や、中国語や、韓国語を勉強します。 *I will study Japanese, Chinese, Korean, etc.*　　CH 11
〜よ ~, I tell you ~, you know?	emphasis	sentence-final particle	日本語は簡単ですよ。 *Japanese is easy, I tell you.*　　CH 2
〜より *than ~*	comparison	grammatical particle	プールで泳ぐ方が海で泳ぐより好きです。 *I like swimming in a swimming pool better than swimming in the ocean.* 母は父よりやさしいです。 *My mother is kinder than my father.*　　CH 17
〜れば (-reba /-eba) for verbs 〜ければ for i-type adjectives *if ~*	condition	connective particle	おいしければ、食べます。 *If it is delicious, I'll eat it.* 天気がよければ、テニスをしましょう。 *If the weather is nice, let's play tennis.* 薬を飲めば、よくなりますよ。 *If you take medicine, you will get better.* よくねれば、よくなりますよ。 *If you sleep well, you'll get better.*　　CH 25
〜わ	mild emphasis used only by female	sentence-final particle	私が行くわよ。 *I'll go there.* きれいだわ。 *It's beautiful.* きれいですわ。 *It's beautiful.*　　(CH 23, Tips)
〜を	direct object	grammatical particle	本を読みます。 *I will read a book.*　　CH 6 この道をまっすぐ行って下さい。 *Go straight on this road.*　　CH 10 彼女は東京を何時に出たんですか。 *What time did she leave Tokyo?*　　CH 23

* だ that appears at the end of the preceding copula and *na*-type adjective is deleted.

** だ that appears at the end of the preceding copula and *na*-type adjective becomes な.

APPENDIX TWO
Predicate Formatives

Predicate formatives are the auxiliaries, suffixes, and other elements that follow verbs, adjectives and nouns to form a predicate with additional meanings, implications and nuances. Unlike particles (see Appendix One), predicate formatives do conjugate.

Predicate Formative / Translation	Function	Preceding Item	Examples
～ある *to have been done ~*	resulting state of things	te-form (verb)	部屋にテレビがおいてあります。 *A TV is placed in the room.* CH 19
～いく *to go on ~ing* *to continue ~ing* *to start ~ing*	continuation from the time of speech	te-form (verb)	子供はちゃんと育って行きます。 *Children will continue to grow properly.* 中学生になった時から、意見をはっきり言うようになって行った。 *From the time he became a middle school student, he started to state his opinion very clearly.*
～いる *to be ~ing* *to have ~ed*	state (progressive, habitual and resulting)	te-form (verb)	今、食べています。 *I am eating now.* (Progressive state) 毎日ご飯を食べています。 *I eat rice every day.* (Habitual state) 兄は結婚しています。 *My brother is married.* (Resulting state) ドアがあいています。 *The door is open.* (Resulting state) CH 14
～おく *to do ~ for future convenience*	preparation	te-form (verb)	ご飯を作っておきます。 *I will cook rice (in advance).* CH 19
～おわる *to finish ~ing*	finishing	stem-form (verb)	昨日レポートを書きおわりました。 *I finished writing a report yesterday.* CH 19
～かもしれない (～かもしれません polite version) *it is possible that ~*	possibility	plain form (verb / adjective)*	マリーさんは来るかもしれません。 *Mary may come.* マリーさんは来ないかもしれません。 *Mary may not come.* おもしろいかもしれません 。 *It may be interesting.* CH 15

Predicate Formative / Translation	Function	Preceding Item	Examples
〜かもしれない (〜かもしれません polite version) *it is possible that ~*	possibility	plain form (verb / adjective)*	便利かもしれません。 *It may be convenient.* いいかもしれません。 *It may be good.* CH 15
〜からだ *it is because ~*	reason, cause	plain form (verb / adjective)	どうして日本に行くんですか。 *Why are you going to go to Japan?* — 日本が好きだからです。 *— Because I like Japan.* CH 15
〜がる *to show the signs of~*	the third person's feelings	stem form (adjective)	弟 はお金をほしがっています。 *My brother wants money.* 妹 は勉 強 を嫌がります。 *My sister does not like to study.* CH 22
〜ください *do ~, please*	request	te-form (verb)	早く食べて下さい。 *Please eat.* CH 10
〜くる *to come about ~ to come to ~ to begin to ~*	continuation up to the time of speech	te-form (verb)	妹 は最近背が高くなって来ました。 *My sister started to become tall these days.* 今日までいっしょうけんめい 働 いて来ました。 *I have worked very hard up to now.*
〜ことがある *to have occasions of ~ /to have an experience of ~*	habit / experience	plain form (verb)	カラオケ・バーに行くことがあります。 *There are occasions that I go to karaoke bars.* カラオケ・バーに行ったことがあります。 *I have been to karaoke bars.* CH 12
〜ことにする *to decide to ~*	decision	plain form (verb)	日本に行くことにしました。 *I decided to go to Japan.* CH 21
〜ことになる *to be decided that ~*	decision	plain form (verb)	日本に行くことになりました。 *It has been decided that I go to Japan.* CH 21
〜させ -(s)ase *make someone do ~ let someone do ~*	causative	root form (verb)	子供に 魚 を食べさせました。 *I made my child eat fish.* 子供にビールを飲ませました。 *I let my child drink beer.* CH 26

Predicate Formative / Translation	Function	Preceding Item	Examples
〜しまう to complete ~ing	completion	te-form (verb)	車をこわしてしまいました。 *I broke the car, (and I regret it).* 宿題をしてしまいました。 *I completed my homework, (and I'm happy).* コーヒーを飲んでしまいます。 *I will finish this coffee.* CH 19
〜すぎる to do ~ too much	extreme	stem form (verb / adjective)	すしを食べすぎました。 *I ate too much sushi.* この部屋は広すぎます。 *This room is too spacious.* スミスさんはまじめすぎます。 *Mr. Smith is too serious.* パークさんは頭がよすぎて困る。 *Mr. Park is too smart, and it is a problem.* CH 19
〜そうだ they say that ~ I heard that ~	hearsay	plain form (verb / adjective)	このホテルは静かだそうです。 *They say that this hotel is quiet.* 事故があったそうです。 *I heard that there was an accident.* このネックレスは高いそうです。 *I heard that this necklace is expensive.* CH 25
〜そうだ to appear to be ~ to be about to do ~	appearance	stem form (verb / adjective)	ボタンが落ちそうです。 *The button is about to fall off.* このネックレスは高そうです。 *This necklace looks expensive.* このホテルは静かそうですね。 *This hotel appears quiet.* この車はよさそうです。 *This car appears to be good.* CH 22
〜たい to want to ~	desire	stem form (verb)	すしが食べたいです。 *I want to eat sushi.* コーヒーが飲みたい。 *I want to drink coffee.* CH 11

Predicate Formative / Translation	Function	Preceding Item	Examples
〜だろう (polite version: 〜でしょう) *it is probably the case that* ~	probability	plain form (verb / adjective)*	雨が降るだろう。 *It will probably rain.* 車は便利だろう。 *Cars are convenient, I guess.* デパートのものは高いだろう。 *The items at a department store are probably expensive.* 雨が降るでしょう。 *It will probably rain.* アメリカでは車が必要でしょう。 *Cars are necessary in the United States.* 明日の天気はいいでしょう。 *Tomorrow's weather will probably be good.* CH 15
〜つもりだ *it is planned that* ~	plan	plain form (verb)	明日パーティーに行くつもりです。 *I plan to go to the party tomorrow.* 明日パーティーに行かないつもりです。 *I plan not to go to the party tomorrow.* 僕は大学には行かないつもりだ。 *I plan not to go to college.* CH 6
〜なさい *do* ~	polite command	stem-form (verb)	早く食べなさい。 *Eat quickly.* 本を読みなさい。 *Read books.* CH 23
〜にくい *to be difficult to* ~	difficult	stem-form (verb)	ステーキは食べにくいです。 *Steaks are hard to eat.* この辞書は使いにくい。 *This dictionary is hard to use.* CH 19
〜のようだ *to be just like* ~	simile	noun	母は男のようです。 *My mother is just like a man.* 母は男のような人です。 *My mother is a person who is just like a man.* CH 22
〜はじめる *to start* ~*ing*	starting	stem-form (verb)	昨日レポートを書きはじめました。 *I started to write a report yesterday.* CH 19

Predicate Formative / Translation	Function	Preceding Item	Examples
〜はずだ *it is supposed to be the case that ...*	objective expectation	pre-nominal form (verb / adjective)	飛行機は2時に着くはずです。 *The plane is supposed to arrive here at 2 o'clock.* 飛行機は2時に着いたはずです。 *The plane is supposed to have arrived here at 2 o'clock.* 飛行機は2時に着いたはずでした。 *The plane was supposed to have arrived here at 2 o'clock.* 賞品は車のはずです。 *The prize is supposed to be a car.* この時計は正しいはずです。 *This watch is supposed to be correct.* 図書館は静かなはずだ。 *The library is supposed to be quiet.* CH 23
〜べきだ *it should be the case that ~*	subjective expectation	plain present affirmative form (verb)	もっと野菜を食べるべきです。 *You should eat more vegetables.* 先生は学生にきびしくするべきです。 *Teachers should be strict to the students.* カンニングはするべきじゃありません。 *One should not cheat (on the exam).* CH 23
〜ほしい *to want someone to do something*	desire for the third person	te-form (verb)	私はボーイフレンドに泳げるようになってほしいです。 *I want my boyfriend to become able to swim.* CH 21
〜ましょう (see 〜よう for the plain version) *let's ~*	volition (polite)	stem-form (verb)	手紙を書きましょう。 *Let's write a letter.* CH 5
〜ます (present negative: 〜ません, past affirmative: 〜ました, past negative: 〜ませんでした)	polite suffix	stem-form (verb)	日本に行きます。 *I will go to Japan.* 今日はクラスに行きません。 *I will not go to the class today.* 昨日はレストランに行きました。 *I went to a restaurant yesterday.* 昨日はぜんぜんねませんでした。 *I didn't sleep at all yesterday.* CH 5 and CH 6
〜ませんか *why don't we ~?*	suggestion	stem-form (verb)	カラオケに行きませんか。 *Why don't we go to karaoke?* CH 5

Predicate Formative / Translation	Function	Preceding Item	Examples
〜みたいだ *to be just like ~*	simile	noun	母は 男 みたいです。 *My mother is just like a man.* 母は男みたいな 人 です。 *My mother is a person who is just like a man.*　　CH 22
〜みる *to try ~ing / do ~ and see*	trial	te-form (verb)	ちょっと着てみます。 *I'll try it on.*　　CH 19
〜やすい *to be easy to ~*	easy	stem-form (verb)	サンドイッチは食べやすいです。 *Sandwiches are easy to eat.*　　CH 19
〜よう -(y)ō (see 〜ましょう for the polite version) *let's ~*	volition (plain)	root form (verb)	すしを食べよう。 *Let's eat sushi.* 手紙を書こう。 *Let's write a letter.*　　CH 24
〜よう -(y)ō と おもう *to think of doing ~*	volitional plan	root form (verb)	来 年日本に行こうと 思 っています。 *I am thinking of going to Japan next year.*　　CH 24
〜よう -(y)ō と する *to attempt to ~*	attempt	root form (verb)	どろぼうがにげようとしましたが、 警 察 が来ました。 *The thief attempted to run away, but the police came.*　　CH 24
〜ようだ *it seems / appears that ~*	general guess	pre-nominal form (verb / adjective)	だれかいるようだ。 *It seems that someone is there.* この 車 は便 利なようです。 *This car seems to be convenient.* あの人は日本人のようです。 *That person appears to be a Japanese.* あのコースは 難 しいようです。 *That course seems to be difficult.*　　CH 25
〜ようにする *to try to do ~ / to make an arrangement*	making an effort /making a change	plain form (verb)	野 菜 をできるだけ食べるようにしています。 *I am trying to eat vegetables as much as I can.* このまどが 開 くようにしました。 *I made it so this window will open.*　　CH 21
〜ようになる *to become ~*	getting a change	plain form (verb)	弟 は早く起きるようになりました。 *My younger brother started to wake up early in the morning.* 弟は早く起きられるようになりました。 *My younger brother became able to wake up early in the morning.*　　CH 21

Predicate Formative / Translation	Function	Preceding Item	Examples
〜らしい¹ *it seems / appears that ~*	educated guess	plain form (verb / adjective)*	リーさんは大学をやめるらしい。 *It seems that Mr. Lee is going to quit college.* あのコースは難しいらしいです。 *That course seems to be difficult.* 日本語の先生は山田先生らしいです。 *It seems that the instructor of the Japanese course is Professor Yamada.*　CH 25
〜らしい² *ideal model of ~, typical ~*	typicality	noun	私のボーイフレンドはとても男らしいです。 *My boyfriend is a manly man.*　CH 22
〜られ -(r)are¹ *to be ~ed*	passive	root form (verb)	金魚が猫に食べられました。 *A goldfish was eaten by a cat.* 先生にしかられました。 *I was scolded by my teacher.*　CH 26
〜られ -(r)are²	honorific	root form (verb)	社長はもう出られました。 *The president has already left here.*　(CH 26 Tips)
〜られ -(rar)e	potential *can ~*	root form (verb)	食べられます。 *I can eat.* 飲めます。 *I can drink.* まだ専攻を決められない。 *I still cannot decide my major.*　CH 11
〜ろ -ro / -e (see 〜なさい for the polite version) *do ~*	plain command	root form (verb)	早く食べろ。 *Eat quickly.* 本を読め。 *Read books.* このボタンを押せと書いてあります。 *It is written that we should press this button.*　CH 23
〜んです *it is the case that ~*	response elicitor	plain form (verb / adjective)**	来月結婚するんです。 *I am going to get married next month.* この辞書はとても便利なんです。 *This dictionary is very convenient.*　CH 6

* だ that appears at the end of a copula and at the end of a *na*-type adjective is deleted.
** だ that appears at the end of a copula and at the end of a *na*-type adjective becomes な.

APPENDIX THREE
Kanji List

	New Kanji Words and Compounds	New Kanji Characters	Writing Notes Related to Kanji
Chapter Two	私・〜人・日本人・何・ぶん 学・すう学・本・山田・川口・ 人・犬・学生・先生・車	私 人 日 本 何 学 山 田 川 車 犬 生 先	Kanji strokes Kanji readings
Chapter Three	母・お母さん・父・お父さん・ 兄・お兄さん・大学・大学いん・ 男の人・女の人	母 父 兄 大 男 女	Kanji components ひとあし：儿 ちから：力
Chapter Four	一・二・三・四・五・六・ 七・八・九・十・今・ 〜月・〜月生まれ・〜年生・ 〜時・何時・〜分・高い・安 い・百・千・万・〜円	一 二 三 四 五 六 七 八 九 十 今 月 年 時 分 高 安 百 千 万 円	Conjugational endings ひとがしら：人 なべぶた：亠 うかんむり：宀
Chapter Five	今日・明日・行く・来る・来ます・ 来ない・帰る・山・安田・田中	明 行 来 帰 中	ひへん：日
Chapter Six	でん車・じてん車・歩いて・ 〜時間・〜分(間)・食べる・飲む・ 書く・朝・昼・晩・昨日・今朝・ 今晩・作る・使う・買う・見る	歩 間 食 飲 書 朝 昼 晩 昨 作 使 買 見	もんがまえ：門 しょくへん：飠 にんべん：イ
Chapter Seven	木・間・近く・上・下・中・ 右・左・月曜日・火曜日・ 水曜日・木曜日・金曜日・ 土曜日・日曜日	木 近 上 下 右 左 曜 火 水 金 土	しんにょう：辶 おのづくり：斤
Chapter Eight	〜本・〜枚・〜冊・〜台・姉・ お姉さん・妹・兄弟・ 弟・〜匹・〜人・勉強する	枚 冊 台 姉 妹 弟 匹 勉 強	きへん：木 ぼくづくり：攵 おんなへん：女 ゆみへん：弓

	New Kanji Words and Compounds	New Kanji Characters	Writing Notes Related to Kanji
Chapter Nine	大きい・小さい・新しい・古い・明るい・暗い・広い・近い・日本語・文・作文・文ぽう・文学	小 新 古 暗 広 語 文	まだれ：广 ごんべん：言
Chapter Ten	言う・話す・読む・聞く・立つ・出す・入る・見せる・早い・速い・習う・れん習・ふく習・道・曲がる・東・西・南・北	言 話 読 聞 立 出 入 早 速 習 道 曲 東 西 南 北	
Chapter Eleven	口・目・耳・足・手・背・長い・短い・多い・少ない・少し・国・中国・かん国・来月・食べもの・読書・好き・大好き・上手・下手・名前・運転・教える・お金・休む・社長・会社・社会学・会社いん・働く	目 耳 足 手 背 長 短 多 少 国 好 名 前 運 転 教 休 社 会 働	くにがまえ：口 しめすへん：ネ
Chapter Twelve	春・夏・秋・冬・夏休み・会う・会話・今年・去年・来年・学期・〜日・〜年・前・外国・〜度・今度	春 夏 秋 冬 去 期 外 度	なつあし：夂 ふゆがしら：夂
Chapter Thirteen	言語学・楽しい・楽です・漢字・難しい・洗う・洗たく・乗る・買いもの・薬・〜点	楽 漢 字 難 洗 乗 薬 点	ふるとり：隹 さんずいへん：氵 くさかんむり：艹 よつてん：灬

	New Kanji Words and Compounds	New Kanji Characters	Writing Notes Related to Kanji
Chapter Fourteen	お茶・学校・学長・校長・小学校・中学校・高校・英語・石田・林・子供・化学・遊ぶ・住む・着る	茶子着 校供化 英遊石林住	
Chapter Fifteen	思う・天気・雨・雪・電話・電気・電車・出る・病気・元気だ・病院・痛い・問題・質問・宿題・文化・本当です	思電問 天病題 気元質 雨院宿 雪痛当	こころ：心 あめかんむり：雨 やまいだれ：疒
Chapter Sixteen	教室・気をつける・困る・部屋・〜屋・覚える・仕事・便利だ・不便だ・毎日・毎週・毎月・毎年・探す	室仕毎 困事週 部便探 屋利 覚不	おおざと：阝 しかばね：尸 のぎへん：禾 てへん：扌
Chapter Seventeen	北海道・本州・九州・四国・土地・地下・人口・同じ・〜の方・森田・川・湖・海・泳ぐ・肉・魚・色・一番	海森色 州湖番 地泳 同肉 方魚	さかなへん：魚
Chapter Eighteen	食事・出かける・地図・〜時・新聞・卒業する・入学する・前・後・後ろ・午前・午後・主人・お酒・ご飯	図主 卒酒 業飯 後 午	ぎょうにんべん：彳
Chapter Nineteen	重い・入れる・動く・持つ・物・動物・食べ物・苦しい・始める・終わる・〜個・竹下・待つ・忘れる・映画・絵・開ける・閉める	重始忘閉 動終映 持個画 物竹絵 苦待開	いとへん：糸
Chapter Twenty	花・友達・よう子・時計・泣く・送る・祖父・祖母・住所	花送 友祖 達所 計 泣	

	New Kanji Words and Compounds	New Kanji Characters	Writing Notes Related to Kanji
Chapter Twenty-One	自分・自転車・運動する・運ぶ・最近・取る・申す・音楽・音・数学・お願いする・鳥	自 最 取 申 音 数 願 鳥	とり：鳥
Chapter Twenty-Two	気が強い・気が弱い・天使・大人・親・父親・母親・親切だ・切手・虫・人間	弱 親 切 虫	むしへん：虫
Chapter Twenty-Three	部長・〜部・仕方・正しい・悪い・着く・東京・大阪・奥さん・妻・家内・家・夫・決める・考える・違う・専攻・専門	正 悪 京 阪 奥 妻 家 内 夫 決 考 違 専 攻 門	こざとへん：阝
Chapter Twenty-Four	受ける・申しこむ・〜級・試験・金持ち・若い・図書館・映画館・名古屋・京都・店・高級だ・〜的	受 級 試 験 若 館 都 店 的	うまへん：馬
Chapter Twenty-Five	苦い・太る・空港・結婚・間違える・火事・事故・平均点・中間試験・期末試験・週末・人気・集まる・死ぬ	太 空 港 結 婚 故 平 均 末 集 死	
Chapter Twenty-Six	字・客・知っている・悲しい・家出をする・先に・悪口・降る・降りる・手紙・受験・習字・長電話・練習する・校長室・空手	客 知 悲 降 紙 練	

APPENDIX FOUR
Basic Vocabulary List

adj.	: adjective	**n.**	: noun
adv.	: adverb	**pn.**	: proper noun
aux.	: auxiliary	**pron.**	: pronoun
c.	: counte	**prt.**	: particle
con.	: conjunction	**q.**	: question word
cop.	: copula	**v.**	: verb
interj.	: Interjection		

No category mark: phrases, suffixes or prefixes

あ

あいさつ **n.** 挨拶 greeting (挨拶をする to greet) CH 21

あいだ **n.** 間 the position between (two items) 3 CH 7

〜あいだ(に)　〜間(に) during ~ 9 CH 18

あう **v.** w-u 会う・会わない・会い・会って to meet (田中さんに会う to meet Mr. Tanaka) 1 CH 12

あお **n.** 青 blue color 1 CH 8

あか **n.** 赤 red color 1 CH 8

あかちゃん **n.** 赤ちゃん baby CH 22

あかるい **adj.** 明るい・明るくない bright, cheerful CH 9

あき **n.** 秋 autumn, fall CH 12

あきはばら **pn.** 秋葉原 Akihabara (name of aplace) CH 24

あく **v.** k-u 開く・開かない・開き・開いて to open (ドアが開く The door opens.) (cf. 開ける v. to open) CH 14

あける **v.** e-ru 開ける・開けない・開け・開けて to open (ドアを開ける to open the door) CH 19

あげる **v.** e-ru 上げる・上げない・上げ・上げて to give 1 CH 20

〜あげる **aux.** e-ru 〜あげる・〜あげない・〜あげ・〜あげて to do something for someone (本を読んであげる to read a book (for someone)) 3 CH 20

あさ **n.** 朝 morning 7 CH 6

あさごはん **n.** 朝御飯 breakfast CH 6

あさって **n.** 明後日 the day after tomorrow CH 8

あし **n.** 足 foot, leg CH 1

あした **n.** 明日 tomorrow 5 CH 5

あそこ **pron.** over there 10 CH 5

あそびにいく　/　遊びに行く to visit somewhere or someone for fun CH 11

あそびにくる　/　遊びに来る to be visited by someone CH 11

あそぶ **v.** b-u 遊ぶ・遊ばない・遊び・遊んで to enjoy oneself, to play (子供が公園で遊んでいる Children are playing in the park.) 6 CH 14

あたたかい **adj.** 暖かい・暖かくない warm (weather) 4 CH 15

あたま **n.** 頭 head CH 11

あたらしい **adj.** 新しい・新しくない new CH 9

あつい **adj.** 暑い・暑くない hot (weather) 4 CH 15

あつまる **v.** r-u 集まる・集まらない・集まり・集まって to gather CH 25

あつめる **v.** e-u 集める・集めない・集め・集めて to collect (cf. 集まる v.) CH 10

〜あと(に)　/　〜後(に) after ~ 9 CH 18

あなた **pron.** 貴方 you (2nd person pronoun) 2 CH 2

あに・おにいさん **n.** 兄・お兄さん older brother 1 CH 3

あね・おねえさん **n.** 姉・お姉さん older sister 1 CH 3

あの〜　/　that ~ over there 11 CH 2

アパート **n.** apartment CH 6

あぶない **adj.** 危ない・危なくない dangerous CH 17

あまい **adj.** 甘い・甘くない sweet CH 25

あまり(〜ない) **adv.** (not) often, (not) much 14 15 CH 5

あめ **n.** 雨 rain CH 15

アメリカ **n.** the United States of America CH 2

あらう **v.** *w-u* 洗う・洗わない・洗い・洗って
to wash　CH 13

ある **v.** *r-u* ある・ない＊・あり・あって
to exist 1　CH 7

〜ある **aux.** *r-u* 〜ある・〜ない・〜あり・
〜あって to have been ~ed (ドアが開けてある
The door is left opened.)　CH 19

あるいて 歩いて on foot, by walking　CH 6

あるく **v.** *k-u* 歩く・歩かない・歩き・歩いて
to walk　CH 6

アルバイト **n.** part-time job (the German word,
Arbeit)　CH 8

あれ **pron.** that one (over there) 11　CH 2

あんぜん (な) **adj.** 安全だ・安全じゃない safe　CH 17

い

いい **adj.** *irr.* いい・よくない fine, good　CH 4

いいえ no, wrong 3　CH 2

いう **vt.** *w-u* 言う・言わない・言い・言って
to say (こたえを言う to say the answer)　CH 10

いえ **n.** 家 house　CH 9

いえで (を) する **v.** *irr.* 家出 (を) する to run
away from home　CH 26

いかが **q.** how (the respectful form of どう)　CH 21

いく **vi.** *k-u* 行く・行かない・行き・行って
to go(東京に行く to go to Tokyo) 6　CH 5

いくら **q.** how much 4　CH 4

いけばな **n.** 生け花 flower arrangement /
flower arranging　CH 15

いざかや **n.** 居酒屋 izakaya bar
(casual Japanese-style bar) **E**　CH 5

いしゃ・おいしゃさん **n.** 医者・お医者さん
medical doctor　CH 11

いじわる (な) **adj.** 意地悪だ・意地悪じゃない
mean, nasty　CH 12

いす **n.** 椅子 chair　CH 2

いそがしい **adj.** 忙しい・忙しくない busy　CH 13

いたい **adj.** 痛い・痛くない painful
(あたまが痛い to have a headache)　CH 13

いただきます　頂きます a set phrase used
right before eating 5　CH 18

いただく **v.** *k-u* 頂く・頂かない・頂き・頂いて
to (modestly) receive 8　CH 20

〜いただく **aux.** *k-u* 〜頂く・〜頂かない・〜頂き・
〜頂いて to (modestly) have someone do ~ 3　CH 20

いち **n.** 一 one　CH 1

いちばん **adv.** 一番 the most, the best　CH 11

いつ **q.** when 6　CH 12

いっしょうけんめい (に) **adv.** 一生懸命 (に)
hard　CH 25

いっしょに **adv.** 一緒に together　CH 1

いってください　言って下さい Please say (it).　CH 1

いってきます　行ってきます a set phrase used
before leaving one's home for work or school　CH 18

いつも **adv.** always, all the time 1　CH 6

いとこ **n.** 従兄弟 cousin　CH 8

いぬ **n.** 犬 dog　CH 2

いま **n.** 今 now　CH 4

イーメール **n.** electric mail (cf. E メール・電子
(でんし) メール)　CH 21

いもうと・いもうとさん **n.** 妹・妹さん
younger sister 1　CH 3

いや (な) **adj.** 嫌だ・嫌じゃない annoying,
unpleasant　CH 26

いらっしゃる **v.** *r-u* いらっしゃる・
いらっしゃらない・いらっしゃい＊・
いらっしゃって to exist (honorific) 1　CH 7

いる **v.** *i-ru* いる・いない・い・いて to exist 1 CH 7

いる **v.** *r-u* 要る・要らない・要り・要って
to be required, to be needed (単位がいる (I)
need credits.)　CH 15

いれる **v.** *e-u* 入れる・入れない・入れ・入れて
to put (かばんに本を入れる *to put a book in the bag*) ⬚1 　　CH 19

いろ **n.** 色 *color* 　　CH 19

いろいろ **adj.** 色々 *for all sorts of things* 　　CH 21

う

うえ **n.** 上 *top part, above* ⬚3 　　CH 7

うける **v.** *e-ru* 受ける・受けない・受け・受けて
to receive, to take (an exam) 　　CH 24

うごく **v.** *k-u* 動く・動かない・動き・動いて
to move 　　CH 19

うしろ **n.** 後 *behind* ⬚3 　　CH 7

うそ **n.** 嘘 *lie, untruth* (うそをつく *to tell a lie*) 　　CH 12

うそをつく 　嘘をつく *to tell a lie* 　　CH 24

うた **n.** 歌 *song* 　　CH 11

うたう **v.** *w-u* 歌う・歌わない・歌い・歌って
to sing 　　CH 5

うち **n.** 家 *house, home* 　　CH 5

〜うちに 　*before 〜, while 〜* (子供がねている
うちに *while the children are sleeping*) ⬚7 　　CH 23

うでたてふせ **n.** 腕立伏せ *pushups* 　　CH 26

うなぎ **n.** 鰻 *eel* Ⓒ 　　CH 1

うまく **adv.** *well, skillfully* 　　CH 15

うみ **n.** 海 *sea, ocean* 　　CH 5

うるさい **adj.** うるさい・うるさくない *noisy* 　　CH 8

うわさ **n.** 噂 *rumor* 　　CH 25

うんてんする **v.** *irr.* 運転する *to drive*
(車を運転する *to drive a car*) 　　CH 11

うんどうする **v.** *irr.* 運動する *to do exercise* 　　CH 21

え

え **n.** 絵 *picture, painting, drawing, illustration* 　　CH 19

えいが **n.** 映画 *movie, film* 　　CH 6

えいがかん **n.** 映画館 *movie theater* 　　CH 5

えいご **n.** 英語 *English language* 　　CH 2

えいわじてん **n.** 英和辞典 *English-Japanese
dictionary* 　　CH 2

えき **n.** 駅 *railway station* 　　CH 7

〜えん **c.** 〜円 *〜yen* (¥) Ⓓ 　　CH 4

えんぴつ **n.** 鉛筆 *pencil* 　　CH 2

えんりょ **n.** 遠慮 *hesitation, reservation*
(遠慮(を)する *to hesitate*) 　　CH 18

お

おいしい **adj.** 美味しい・美味しくない
delicious, tasty 　　CH 11

おいわい **n.** お祝い *celebration* Ⓐ 　　CH 20

おおい **adj.** 多い・多くない *many, a lot* ⬚1 　　CH 11

おおきい **adj.** *irr.* 大きい・大きくない *big*
(大きな *variation*) 　　CH 9

おおさか **pn.** 大阪 *Osaka* (*name of a place*) 　　CH 1

おかあさん **n.** お母さん *mother* 　　CH 1

(〜の)おかげで 　*thanks to 〜* ⬚2 　　CH 26

おかね **n.** お金 *money* 　　CH 11

おきる **vi.** *i-ru* 起きる・起きない・起き・
起きて *to wake up* 　　CH 12

おく **vt.** *k-u* 置く・置かない・置き・置いて
to put 　　CH 19

〜おく **aux.** *k-u* 〜おく・〜おかない・〜おき・
〜おいて *to do 〜 in advance* (本を読んでおく
to read a book in advance) ⬚8 　　CH 19

おくさん **n.** 奥さん *someone else's wife* ⬚3 　　CH 23

おくる **v.** *r-u* 送る・送らない・送り・送って
to send 　　CH 20

おくれる **v.** *e-ru* 遅れる・遅れない・遅れ・遅れて
to be late (クラスに遅れる *to be late for class*) 　　CH 13

おこる **v.** *r-u* 怒る・怒らない・怒り・怒って
to get angry 　　CH 14

おじ・おじさん **n.** 叔父 / 伯父・叔父さん / 伯父さん *uncle*	CH 20
おしえる **v.** *e-ru* 教える・教えない・教え・教えて *to teach* (子供に日本語を教える *to teach children Japanese*)	CH 11
おじゃまします　お邪魔します *I'll come in* (lit. I am going to disturb you) [7]	CH 9
おす **v.** *s-u* 押す・押さない・押し・押して *to press*	CH 21
おせいぼ **n.** お歳暮 *year-end present* **B**	CH 20
おそい **adj.** 遅い・遅くない *late, slow*	CH 12
おちゃ **n.** お茶 *(Japanese) tea*	CH 14
おちる **vi.** *i-ru* 落ちる・落ちない・落ち・落ちて *to fall*	CH 22
おっと **n.** 夫 *one's own husband* [3]	CH 23
おと **n.** 音 *sound, volume*	CH 10
おとうさん **n.** お父さん *father*	CH 1
おとうと・おとうとさん **n.** 弟・弟さん *younger brother* [1]	CH 3
おとこのひと **n.** 男の人 *man* [5]	CH 3
おとす **v.** *s-u* 落とす・落とさない・落とし・落として *to let something fall, to lose*	CH 12
おとな **n.** 大人 *adult*	CH 22
おどる **v.** *r-u* 踊る・踊らない・踊り・踊って *to dance*	CH 11
おなか **n.** お腹 *abdomen, stomach*	CH 15
おなかがすいている　*hungry*	CH 14
おなじ　同じ *same* [3]	CH 17
おに **n.** 鬼 *ogre*	CH 22
おにいさん **n.** お兄さん *older brother*	CH 1
おねえさん **n.** お姉さん *older sister*	CH 1
おねがい **n.** お願い *favor*	CH 20
おねがいする **v.** *irr.* お願いする *to ask a favor of someone*	CH 10

おば・おば さん **n.** 叔母 / 伯母・叔母さん / 伯母さん *aunt*	CH 20
おひめさま **n.** お姫様 *princess*	CH 22
おぼえる **v.** *e-ru* 覚える・覚えない・覚え・覚えて *to memorize*	CH 16
おみやげ **n.** お土産 *souvenir*	CH 11
おもい **adj.** 重い・重くない *heavy*	CH 19
おもう **v.** *w-u* 思う・思わない・思い・思って *to think* (〜と思う *to think that ~*) [1]	CH 15
おもしろい **adj.** 面白い・面白くない *funny, interesting, amusing*	CH 8
おや **n.** 親 *parent*	CH 22
おやすみなさい　お休みなさい *Good night!*	CH 18
およぐ **v.** *g-u* 泳ぐ・泳がない・泳ぎ・泳いで *to swim*	CH 6
おりがみ **n.** 折り紙 *origami*	CH 1
おりる **v.** *i-ru* 降りる・降りない・降り・降りて *to get off, to come down* (バスをおりる *to get off a bus*)	CH 14
おわり **n.** 終わり *ending*	CH 20
おわる **v.** *r-u* 終わる・終わらない・終わり・終わって *to be over, to end*	CH 18
〜おわる **aux.** *r-u* 〜終わる・〜終わらない・〜終わり・〜終わって *to finish ~ing* (食べ終わる *to finish eating*) [2]	CH 19
おんがく **n.** 音楽 *music*	CH 11
おんなのひと **n.** 女の人 *woman* [5]	CH 3

か

〜か **prt.** *sentence-final question particle* [7]	CH 2
〜か **prt.** *or* (A か B *A or B*) [4]	CH 11
〜か **c.** 〜課 *~ section ~ division, Lesson ~*	CH 20
〜が **prt.** *subject marker* [11]	CH 6
〜が **con.** *but* [7]	CH 11
〜かい **c.** 〜階 *~th floor*	CH 7
がいこく **n.** 外国 *foreign country*	CH 12

がいこくご **n.** 外国語 *foreign language* CH 9

かいしゃ **n.** 会社 *company* CH 11

かいしゃいん・かいしゃいんさん **n.** 会社員・会社員さん *company employee* CH 11

かいだん **n.** 階段 *stairs, stairway* CH 21

かいもの **n.** 買(い)物 *shopping* (買い物をする *to shop / to go shopping*) CH 13

かいわ **n.** 会話 *conversation* CH 9

かう **v.** *w-u* 買う・買わない・買い・買って *to buy* (くつを買う *to buy shoes*) CH 6

かえす **v.** *s-u* 返す・返さない・返し・返して *to return* CH 18

かえりに 帰りに *on the way home* CH 26

かえる **v.** *r-u* 帰る・帰らない・帰り・帰って *to return to one's home, country or base* ⑥ CH 5

かお **n.** 顔 *face* CH 13

かがく **n.** 化学 *chemistry* CH 14

かかる **v.** *r-u* かかる・かからない・かかり・かかって *to cost, to take* CH 6

かぎ **n.** 鍵 *key* CH 3

かく **v.** *k-u* 書く・書かない・書き・書いて *to write* (手紙を書く *to write a letter*) CH 6

がくい **n.** 学位 *academic degree* CH 24

がくしゃ **n.** 学者 *scholar* CH 22

がくせい **n.** 学生 *student* CH 1

がくちょう・がくちょうさん **n.** 学長・学長さん *school president* CH 14

かける **v.** *e-ru* 掛ける・掛けない・掛け・掛けて *to wear* (eyeglasses), *to hang* ⑫ CH 14

かさ **n.** 傘 *umbrella* CH 3

かし・おかし **n.** 菓子・お菓子 *sweets, confectionery* CH 20

かじ **n.** 火事 *fire* CH 25

かす **v.** *s-u* 貸す・貸さない・貸し・貸して *to loan, to lend* (弟に本をかした (*I*) *loaned a book to my brother.*) CH 10

かぜをひく 風邪を引く *to catch a cold* CH 13

かぞく **n.** 家族 *family members* CH 12

〜かた **n.** 〜方 *person* (polite) (*cf.* 人) CH 2

〜かた 〜方 *the way of ~, the manner of ~* (食べ方 *the way of eating*) ⑤ CH 22

かたづける **v.** *e-ru* 片付ける・片付けない・片付け・片付けて *to put things in order, to tidy up* (へやを片付ける *to tidy up the room*, おもちゃを片付ける *to put toys in order*) CH 23

〜がつ **c.** 〜月 *months of the year* (一月 *January*) CH 4

〜がつうまれ 〜月生まれ *a person born in the month of ~* CH 4

がっき **n.** 学期 *academic term* CH 12

かっこいい **adj.** かっこいい・かっこよくない *good looking* (mainly for young men and boys) CH 14

がっこう **n.** 学校 *school* CH 1

かつよう **n.** 活用 *conjugation* CH 15

かど **n.** 角 *corner* CH 10

〜かどうか *whether or not ~* (いいかどうか考える *to consider whether* (*it*) *is good or not*) ⑧ CH 23

かない **n.** 家内 *one's own wife* ③ CH 23

かなしい **adj.** 悲しい・悲しくない *sad* CH 26

かならず **adv.** 必ず *without fail, by all means* CH 24

かねもち **n.** 金持ち *rich person* CH 24

かのじょ **pron.** 彼女 *her, she* CH 11

かばん **n.** 鞄 *bag* CH 2

かびん **n.** 花瓶 *vase* CH 19

カフェテリア **n.** *cafeteria* CH 2

かぶる **v.** *r-u* かぶる・かぶらない・かぶり・かぶって *to wear* (items such as hats and caps) ⑫ CH 14

かべ **n.** 壁 *wall* CH 19

かみ **n.** 髪 *hair of the head* CH 11

かみさま **n.** 神様 *god* CH 22

カメラ **n.** *camera*   CH 4

〜かもしれ ない   *It may be the case that ~.* (*polite / neutral form:* 〜かもしれません) [7]   CH 15

かようび **n.** 火曜日 *Tuesday* [6]   CH 7

〜から **prt.** *from ~*   CH 2

〜から **prt.** *after ~* [9]   CH 18

からい **adj.** 辛い・辛くない *(hot) spicy*   CH 25

カラオケ **n.** *karaoke*   CH 5

からかう **v.** *w-u* からかう・からかわない・からかい・からかって *to tease, to make fun of*   CH 26

からて **n.** 空手 *karate*   CH 1

〜からです   *It is because ~.* [10]   CH 15

かりる **v.** *i-ru* 借りる・借りない・借り・借りて *to borrow* ((*I) borrowed a bag from my brother.*)   CH 11

〜がる   *r-u* 〜がる・〜がらない・〜がり・〜がってりた (兄はお金をほしがっている *My brother wants money.*) [8]   CH 22

かれ **pron.** 彼 *he, him*   CH 11

かわ **n.** 川 *river*   CH 17

かわいい **adj.** 可愛い・可愛くない *cute*   CH 3

かわいそう（な）**adj.** 可哀相だ・可哀相じゃない *poor, pitiable, pitiful*   CH 26

かんがえる **v.** *e-ru* 考える・考えない・考え・考えて *to consider, to think* (山田さんのことを考える *to think about Ms. Yamada*)   CH 23

かんこう **n.** 観光 *sightseeing*   CH 24

かんこく **n.** 韓国 *Korea*   CH 2

かんごし・かんごしさん **n.** 看護士・看護士さん *nurse*   CH 14

かんじゃ **n.** 患者 *patient*   CH 15

かんたん（な）**adj.** 簡単だ・簡単じゃない *easy*   CH 2

がんばる **v.** *r-u* 頑張る・頑張らない・頑張り・頑張って *to try one's best*   CH 13

き

き **n.** 木 *tree*   CH 7

きがつよい   気が強い *strong-willed, hardheaded*   CH 22

きがよわい   気が弱い *coward, timid*   CH 22

ききとり **n.** 聞き取り *listening comprehension*   CH 9

きく **v.** *k-u* 聞く・聞かない・聞き・聞いて *to listen, to inquire, to ask* (おんがくをき *to listen to the music*) (先生にきく *to ask the teacher*)   CH 10

きせつ **n.** 季節 *season*   CH 17

きた **n.** 北 *north* [3]   CH 7

きたない **adj.** 汚い・汚くない *dirty*   CH 9

きって **n.** 切手 *stamp*   CH 8

きっぷ **n.** 切符 *ticket*   CH 18

きのう **n.** 昨日 *yesterday*   CH 6

きびしい **adj.** 厳しい・厳しくない *strict*   CH 10

きぶん **n.** 気分 *feeling* (気分がいい *to be in a good mood,* 気分がわるい *to be in a bad mood*)   CH 18

きまつしけん **n.** 期末試験 *final exam*   CH 25

きめる **v.** *e-ru* 決める・決めない・決め・決めて *to decide* (せんこうを決める *to decide on one's major*)   CH 23

きもの **n.** 着物 *kimono*   CH 1

きゃく **n.** 客 *customer, guest*   CH 4

〜きゅう **c.** 〜級 *level ~*   CH 24

きゅう / く **n.** 九 *nine*   CH 1

きゅうきゅうしゃ **n.** 救急車 *ambulance*   CH 25

きゅうしゅう **pn.** 九州 *Kyushu* (*name of a Japanese island*)   CH 17

ぎゅうにゅう **n.** 牛乳 *milk*   CH 19

きゅうりょう **n.** 給料 *salary, wages, pay*   CH 13

きょう **n.** 今日 *today* [5]   CH 5

ぎょうぎ **n.** 行儀 *manners, behavior*   CH 18

ぎょうぎよく **adv.** 行儀よく *with good manners* CH 18

ぎょうざ **n.** 餃子 *(Chinese-style) dumpling* Ⓐ CH 19

きょうし・せんせい **n.** 教師・先生 *teacher* CH 11

きょうしつ **n.** 教室 *classroom* CH 16

きょうじゅ **n.** 教授 *professor* CH 15

きょうだい・ごきょうだい **n.** 兄弟・御兄弟 *siblings* CH 8

きょうと **pn.** 京都 *Kyoto (name of a place)* CH 1

きょうみ 興味 *interest* (〜に興味がある *to be interested in ~*) CH 15

きょねん **n.** 去年 *last year* CH 12

きらい (な) **adj.** 嫌いだ・嫌いじゃない *hating* (*to hate ~*) CH 11

ギリギリに なる *to become close to the last minute* CH 25

きる **v.** *i-ru* 着る・着ない・着・着て *to wear, to put on (one's clothes)* CH 13

きれい (な) **adj.** 綺麗だ・綺麗じゃない *pretty, beautiful* [2] CH 3

きをつける 気をつける *to be careful* (車に気をつける *to watch out for cars*) [2] CH 16

ぎんこう **n.** 銀行 *bank* CH 5

きんちょうする **v.** *irr.* 緊張する *to become tense or nervous* CH 15

きんようび **n.** 金曜日 *Friday* [6] CH 7

く

くうこう **n.** 空港 *airport* CH 25

くさる **v.** *r-u* 腐る・腐らない・腐り・腐って *to spoil* CH 25

くしゃみ **n.** *sneeze* (くしゃみが出る / くしゃみをする *to sneeze*) CH 15

くすり **n.** 薬 *medicine* (薬をのむ *to take medicine* CH 13

くせになる 癖になる *to become a habit* CH 19

(〜て) ください 〜てください *please do ~* [4] CH 10

ください 下さい *give me~* (〜をください *give me ~*) [6] CH 4

くださる **v.** *r-u* 下さる・下さらない・下さい・下さって *to (kindly) give* [1] CH 20

〜くださる **aux.** *r-u* 〜ください・〜くださらない・〜ください・〜下さって *to (kindly) do something for me (us)* (書いて下さる *to kindly write something for me*) [3] CH 20

くだもの **n.** 果物 *fruit* CH 17

くち **n.** 口 *mouth* CH 1

くつ **n.** 靴 *shoes* CH 2

くつした **n.** 靴下 *socks* CH 14

くに **n.** 国 *country, home country* CH 11

くも **n.** 雲 *cloud* CH 15

くもる **v.** *r-u* 曇る・曇らない・曇り・曇って *to become cloudy* CH 15

くらい **adj.** 暗い・暗くない *dark, gloomy* CH 9

〜ぐらい / 〜くらい *approximately* (10 分ぐらいかかる *It takes about 10 minutes.*) [4] CH 6

クラス **n.** *class* CH 5

くる **v.** *irr.* 来る・来ない・来・来て *to come* [6] CH 5

くるしい **adj.** 苦しい・苦しくない *distressful, uncomfortable* CH 19

くるま **n.** 車 *car* CH 2

くれる **v.** *e-ru* くれる・くれない・くれ・くれて *to give* [1] CH 20

〜くれる **aux.** *e-ru* 〜くれる・〜くれない・〜くれ・〜くれて *to do something for me (us)* (書いてくれる *to write something for me*) [3] CH 20

くろ **n.** 黒 *black color* [1] CH 8

〜くん 〜君 *a friendly respectful title for boys and young men or a formal respectful title for ones subordinates* CH 14

け

けいえいする **v.** *irr.* 経営する *to run (a business)*
(レストランを経営する *to run a restaurant*) CH 11

けいけん **n.** 経験 *experience* CH 21

けいざいがく **n.** 経済学 *economics* CH 8

けいさつかん **n.** 警察官 *police officer* CH 14

けいたいでんわ **n.** 携帯電話 *cellular phone* CH 3

けいようし **n.** 形容詞 *adjective* CH 15

けが **n.** 怪我 *injury* (けがをする *to get injured*) CH 25

けさ **n.** 今朝 *this morning* CH 6

けしゴム **n.** 消しゴム *eraser* CH 8

けす **v.** *s-u* 消す・消さない・消し・消して
to turn off (テレビを消す *to turn off the TV*) CH 19

けっこんする **v.** *irr.* 結婚する *to get married* (田中さんと結婚する *to get married to Mr. Tanaka*) CH 14

げつようび **n.** 月曜日 *Monday* [6] CH 7

けんか **n.** 喧嘩 *fight, quarrel* (弟とけんかをする *to have a fight with one's younger brother*) CH 12

けんきゅう　　研究室 *university faculty's*

しつ **n.** *office, laboratory* CH 19

けんこう **n.** 健康 *health* CH 21

げんごがく **n.** 言語学 *linguistics* CH 13

けんどう **n.** 剣道 *kendo (Japanese fencing)* Ⓐ CH 1

こ

〜こ **c.** 〜個 *a counter for medium-sized inanimate objects* CH 19

ご **n.** 五 *five* CH 1

〜ご　　〜語 *~ language* (日本語 *Japanese language*) CH 2

こうえん **n.** 公園 *park* CH 5

こうきゅう（な）**adj.** 高級だ・高級じゃない
high grade, high class, fancy CH 24

こうこう **n.** 高校 *high school* CH 3

こうさてん **n.** 交差点 *intersection* CH 7

こうじょう **n.** 工場 *factory* CH 14

こうずい **n.** 洪水 *flood* CH 25

こうちょう・こうちょうせんせい **n.** 校長・校長先生 *school principal* CH 14

こうちょうしつ **n.** 校長室 *principal's office* CH 26

こうはい **n.** 後輩 *one's junior* CH 24

ここ **pron.** *here* [10] CH 5

ごご **n.** 午後 *p.m., afternoon* [3] CH 4

ごぜん **n.** 午前 *a.m.* [3] CH 4

ごぜんちゅう **n.** 午前中 *after dawn before noon (morning)* (*c.f.* ごぜん *a.m.*) CH 8

ごちそうさま　　ご馳走様 *a set phrase used right after eating* [5] CH 18

こちら **pron.** *this way, this side, this person* [1] CH 2

ことし **n.** 今年 *this year* CH 12

ことば **n.** 言葉 *word* CH 26

こども・こどもさん／おこさん **n.** 子供・子供さん／お子さん *child* [1] CH 3

この〜 *this ~* [11] CH 2

このあいだ　この間 *the other day* CH 12

ごはん **n.** ご飯 *cooked rice, meal* Ⓑ CH 6

こぼす **v.** *s-u* こぼす・こぼさない・こぼし・こぼして *to spill* CH 21

こまる **v.** *r-u* 困る・困らない・困り・困って *to be in trouble* [1] CH 16

ごみ **n.** ゴミ・ごみ *trash, garbage* CH 19

こむ **v.** *m-u* 混む・混まない・混み・混んで *to become crowded* CH 14

ごめんください *Hello!* (*used when one knocks on the door*) [2] CH 18

これ **pron.** *this one* [11] CH 2

〜ごろ 　〜頃 *approximately* (6 時ごろ *about 6 o'clock*) [7]　CH 12

こわい **adj.** 怖い・怖くない *scary, scared*　CH 22

こわす **v. s-u** 壊す・壊さない・壊し・壊して *to break* (カメラを壊す *to break a camera*)　CH 19

こわれる **v. e-ru** 壊れる・壊れない・壊れ・壊れて *to break* (車が壊れた *The car broke down.*)　CH 19

こんど **n.** 今度 *next time, this time* [5]　CH 11

こんな〜 　*this kind of 〜, such 〜* (*cf.* どんな〜)　CH 25

こんばん **n.** 今晩 *this evening, tonight*　CH 5

さ

〜さい **c.** 〜オ・〜歳 *a counter for age, 〜 years old*　CH 4

さいきん **adv.** 最近 *recently*　CH 21

さいふ **n.** 財布 *wallet*　CH 3

さがす **v. s-u** 探す・探さない・探し・探して *to search 〜, to search for 〜, to look for 〜*　CH 16

さかな **n.** 魚 *fish*　CH 17

さきに 　先に *earlier (than 〜), beforehand, in advance*　CH 26

さく **vi. k-u** 咲く・咲かない・咲き・咲いて *to bloom, to blossom*　CH 26

さくぶん **n.** 作文 *composition*　CH 9

さくら **n.** 桜 *cherry tree, cherry blossom*　CH 7

さけ・おさけ **n.** 酒・お酒 *rice wine, alcoholic beverage in general*　CH 11

さしあげる **v. e-ru** 差し上げる・差し上げない・差し上げ・差し上げて *to (modestly) give* [1]　CH 20

〜さしあげる **aux. e-ru** 〜差し上げる・〜差し上げない・〜差し上げ・〜差し上げて *to (modestly) do something for someone* [3]　CH 20

さしみ **n.** 刺身 *sliced raw fish* ⒸG　CH 1

〜さつ **c.** 〜冊 *a counter for bound objects such as books and magazines*　CH 8

ざっし **n.** 雑誌 *magazine*　CH 6

さとう **n.** 砂糖 *sugar*　CH 25

さびしい **adj.** 寂しい・寂しくない *lonely*　CH 8

さむい **adj.** 寒い・寒くない *cold (weather)* [4]　CH 15

さら **n.** 皿 *plates, dishes*　CH 26

さらあらい **n.** 皿洗い *dish-washing*　CH 16

さん **n.** 三 *three*　CH 1

ざんぎょう **n.** 残業 *overtime work*　CH 16

ざんねん (な) **adj.** 残念だ・残念じゃない *regrettable, disappointing*　CH 24

し

じ **n.** 字 *character, letter*　CH 26

〜じ **c.** 〜時 *〜 o'clock*　CH 4

しお **n.** 塩 *salt*　CH 25

〜しか (…ない) **prt.** *only* [2]　CH 22

しかし **con.** *but* (*cf.* でも)　CH 21

しかた **n.** 仕方 *method, way* (勉強の仕方 *the way of studying*)　CH 23

しかたがない 　仕方がない *cannot be helped* [6]　CH 25

しかる **v. r-u** 叱る・叱らない・叱り・叱って *to scold*　CH 26

じかん **n.** 時間 *time*　CH 11

〜じかん **c.** 〜時間 *〜 hours* [3]　CH 6

じきゅう **n.** 時給 *payment by the hour*　CH 16

しけん **n.** 試験 *exam, test* (試験をうける *to take an exam*)　CH 8

じこ **n.** 事故 *accident*　CH 25

しこく **pn.** 四国 *Shikoku (name of a Japanese island)*　CH 17

しごと **n.** 仕事 *job* (仕事をする *to work*)　CH 8

じしょ **n.** 辞書 *dictionary*　CH 7

じしん **n.** 地震 *earthquake*　CH 25

しずか（な）**adj.** 静かだ・静かじゃない *quiet*　　CH 9

した **n.** 下 *bottom part, below, under* ③　　CH 7

しっかりする **v.** *irr.* しっかりする *to become reliable, strong, responsible*　　CH 23

じつは **adv.** 実は *as a matter of fact*　　CH 11

しつもん **n.** 質問 *question*　　CH 1

しつれいします　　失礼します *I'll come in / I'll leave (Lit. I will be rude.)* ③　　CH 10

じてんしゃ **n.** 自転車 *bicycle*　　CH 6

じぶん **n.** 自分 *self* (自分で *by oneself*)　　CH 21

しまう **v.** *w-u* しまう・しまわない・しまい・しまって *to store, to put away* (ようふくをしまう *to store the clothes*)　　CH 19

〜しまう **aux.** *w-u* 〜しまう・〜しまわない・〜しまい・〜しまって *to complete ~ing* (食べてしまう *to complete eating something*) ⑥　　CH 19

じむいん **n.** 事務員 *office worker, clerk*　　CH 15

しぬ **v.** *n-u* 死ぬ・死なない・死に・死んで *to die*　　CH 25

しめきり **n.** 締め切り *deadline*　　CH 20

しめる **v.** *e-ru* 閉める・閉めない・閉め・閉めて *to close* (ドアを閉める *to close the door*)　　CH 19

じゃあ **interj.** *then* ⑫　　CH 2

〜じゃありません／〜ではありません **cop.** *not to be (polite / neutral present negative form of* 〜だ*)* ⑥　　CH 2

しゃかいがく **n.** 社会学 *sociology*　　CH 8

しゃしん **n.** 写真 *photograph*　　CH 7

しゃちょう・しゃちょうさん **n.** 社長・社長さん *company president*　　CH 11

シャワーを あびる　　シャワーを浴びる *to take a shower*　　CH 13

しゃべる **v.** *r-u* しゃべる・しゃべらない・しゃべり・しゃべって *to chat*　　CH 14

じゅう **n.** 十 *ten*　　CH 1

しゅうじ **n.** 習字 *calligraphy*　　CH 26

しゅうしかてい **n.** 修士課程 *master's program*　　CH 21

じゅうしょ **n.** 住所 *address*　　CH 20

しゅうしょく **n.** 就職 *employment*　　CH 13

しゅうしょくする **v.** *irr.* 就職する *to find employment*　　CH 24

じゅうたい **n.** 渋滞 *traffic jam*　　CH 25

じゅうたん **n.** carpet　　CH 16

じゅうどう **n.** 柔道 *judo (Japanese wrestling)* Ⓐ　　CH 1

しゅうまつ **n.** 週末 *weekend*　　CH 5

じゅぎょう **n.** 授業 *class, lesson*　　CH 15

じゅぎょうりょう **n.** 授業料 *tuition*　　CH 15

じゅく **n.** 塾 *private tutoring school* Ⓐ　　CH 26

しゅくだい **n.** 宿題 *homework*　　CH 1

じゅけん **n.** 受験 *exam taking*　　CH 26

しゅじん・ごしゅじん **n.** 主人・御主人 *husband*　　CH 18

しょうがっこう **n.** 小学校 *elementary school* Ⓐ　　CH 14

じょうず（な）**adj.** 上手だ・上手じゃない *skillful (to be good at ~)* ⑥　　CH 11

しょうたいする **v.** *irr.* 招待する *to invite*　　CH 26

じょうだん **n.** 冗談 *joke*　　CH 12

しょうらい **n.** 将来 *future*　　CH 11

しょくぎょう・ごしょくぎょう **n.** 職業・御職業 *occupation*　　CH 14

しょくじ **n.** 食事 *meal, dining* (食事をする *to dine*)　　CH 18

じょし **n.** 助詞 *particles*　　CH 15

じょせい **n.** 女性 *woman*　　CH 22

しょっぱい **adj.** しょっぱい・しょっぱくない *salty*　　CH 25

しる **v.** *r-u* 知る・知らない・知り・知って *to get to know* ⑨　　CH 14

〜じん　　〜人 *~person (nationality)* (日本人 *Japanese person*) ④　　CH 2

しんかんせん **n.** 新幹線 *Shinkansen (bullet train in Japan)*　　CH 24

しんけいしつ (な) **adj.** 神経質だ・神経質じ
ゃない *too sensitive, nervous, temperamental*　　CH 22

じんこう **n.** 人口 *population*　　CH 17

しんせき **n.** 親戚 *relative*　　CH 20

しんせつ (な) **adj.** 親切だ・親切じゃない
kind, thoughtful　　CH 12

しんぱいする **v.** *irr.* 心配する　*to worry (about ~)* CH 16

しんぶん **n.** 新聞 *newspaper*　　CH 6

す

すいせんじょう **n.** 推薦状 *recommendation letter*　CH 20

すいようび **n.** 水曜日 *Wednesday* 6　　CH 7

すう **v.** *w-u* 吸う・吸わない・吸い・吸って　*to inhale*
(タバコをすう *to smoke*)　　CH 14

すうがく **n.** 数学 *mathematics*　　CH 2

すき (な) **adj.** 好きだ・好きじゃない　*to be fond of ~*
(*to like ~*)　　CH 11

すきやき **n.** すき焼き　*sukiyaki* **C**　　CH 1

すぎる **v.** *i-ru* 過ぎる・過ぎない・過ぎ・過ぎて
to pass　　CH 10

～すぎる **aux.** *i-ru* ～過ぎ・～過ぎない・～過ぎ・
～過ぎて　*to overdo ~ing* (食べ過ぎる　*to eat
too much*) 2 4　　CH 19

すく **v.** *k-u* すく・すかない・すき・すいて
to become less crowded (おなかがすく
to become hungry)　　CH 14

すくない **adj.** 少ない・少なくない　*scarce, little,
few* 1　　CH 11

すこし **adv.** 少し　*a little, a few, slightly* 5　　CH 8

すし **n.** 鮨・寿司　*sushi* **C**　　CH 1

すずしい **adj.** 涼しい・涼しくない　*cool (weather)*
4　　CH 15

～ずつ **prt.** *each, at a time, by* (2 つずつ食べる
eat two pieces at a time) 5　　CH 19

ずっと **adv.** *by far*　　CH 17

すっぱい **adj.** 酸っぱい　*sour*　　CH 25

すてる **v.** *e-ru* 捨てる・捨てない・捨て・捨てて
to throw away (ゴミを捨 (てる　*to throw away
the garbage*)　　CH 19

スプーン **n.** *spoon*　　CH 6

ズボン **n.** *pants, trousers*　　CH 14

すむ **vi.** *m-u* 住む・住まない・住み・住んで　*to live*
(*somewhere*) (日本に住む　*to live in Japan*) 10　　CH 14

スリッパ **n.** *slippers* **A**　　CH 16

する **v.** *irr.* する・しない・し・して　*to do* 14　　CH 6

すわる **v.** *r-u* 座る・座らない・座り・座って　*to sit*
(いすにすわる *sit on the chair*)　　CH 10

せ

せ / せい **n.** 背 *height of people and animals*　　CH 11

せいせき **n.** 成績 *grade, score, performance*　　CH 23

(～の) せいで　　　*due to ~* 1　　CH 26

せかい **n.** 世界 *world*　　CH 17

せき **n.** 咳 *cough* (咳が出る / 咳をする
to cough)　　CH 15

せきにんかん **n.** 責任感 *a sense of responsibility*　CH 22

ぜったい (に) **adv.** 絶対 (に) *absolutely*
(絶対にいけません　*absolutely not permitted*)　　CH 16

せつやくする **v.** *irr.* 節約する *to save, to economize*
CH 21

せまい **adj.** 狭い・狭くない　*non-spacious,
narrow* (狭いへや　*a small room*)　　CH 9

せわ **n.** 世話　*care, aid* (～の世話をする
to take care of ~)　　CH 16

～せん / ぜん **n.** ～千 *one thousand*　　CH 4

せんこう **n.** 専攻 *academic major*　　CH 2

せんせい **n.** 先生 *teacher*　　CH 1

ぜんぜん (～ない) **adv.** (*not*) *at all* 14 15　　CH 5

せんたく **n.** 洗濯 *laundry* (洗濯をする
to do the laundry)　　CH 13

せんぱい **n.** 先輩 *one's senior*　　CH 24

ぜんぶで　全部で　*all together*　　CH 4

せんもん　**n.** 専門　*specialty* (*cf.* 専攻)　CH 2

せんもんがっこう　**n.** 専門学校
special (vocational) school　　CH 14

そ

〜そう (な)　　〜そうだ・〜そうじゃない
to look like ~ 1　　CH 22

そういえば　　そう言えば　*if you say so,*
it reminds me of that ~　　CH 22

そうじ　**n.** 掃除　*cleaning* (掃除をする　*to do cleaning*)
　　CH 13

そうすると　　*if* (*you do*) *so, in that case* 11　CH 10

〜そうだ　**aux.** 〜そうだ・〜そうじゃない
I heard that ~, they say that ~ 8　　CH 25

そうですか　　*Oh, I see. / Really?* ❹　CH 2

そこ　**pron.** *there* (*near you*) 10　CH 5

そして　**con.** *and then, and* (*cf.* それから)　CH 21

そつぎょうする　**v.** *irr.* 卒業する　*to graduate*　CH 18

その〜　　*that ~* (*near you*) 11　CH 2

そば　**n.** *vicinity* (*cf.* ちかく) 3　CH 7

そふ・おじいさん　**n.** 祖父・おじいさん
grandfather　　CH 8

そぼ・おばあさん　**n.** 祖母・おばあさん
grandmother　　CH 8

それ　**pron.** *that one* (*near you*) 11　CH 2

それか　**con.** *or* (*cf.* それとも) 15　CH 11

それから　**con.** *and then, in addition* 2　CH 6

それで　**con.** *as a result* 5　CH 13

それとも　**con.** *alternatively* (*cf.* それか) 8　CH 18

それに　**con.** *furthermore, moreover* 6　CH 9

そろばん　**n.** 算盤　*abacus* ❸　CH 26

た

〜たい　**aux.** 〜たい・〜たくない　*to want to do*
something (食べたい *to want to eat*) 13　CH 11

〜だい　**c.** 〜台　*a counter for mechanical objects*　CH 8

たいいくかん　**n.** 体育館　*gym*　CH 2

だいがく　**n.** 大学　*university*　CH 3

だいがくいん　**n.** 大学院　*graduate school*　CH 3

だいじょうぶです　　大丈夫です　*fine, not to*
worry, all right　　CH 15

だいすき (な)　**adj.** 大好きだ・大好きじゃない
to be extremely fond of ~　　CH 11

たいてい　**adv.** *usually, in general* 1　CH 6

だいどころ　**n.** 台所　*kitchen*　CH 16

たいふう　**n.** 台風　*typhoon*　CH 19

たいへん (な)　**adj.** 大変だ・大変じゃない
a lot of trouble, difficult task　　CH 6

たかい　**adj.** 高い・高くない　*expensive, tall, high*　CH 4

たくさん　**adv.** 沢山　*a lot*　CH 8

〜だけです　　*It's just that ~* (ちょっと会いた
かっただけです *I just wanted to see you.*) 4　CH 18

たしか　**adv.** 確か　*if I remember correctly, I suppose*
　　CH 23

だす　**v.** *s-u* 出す・出さない・出し・出して
to hand in, to take out (しゅくだいを出す
to hand in one's homework)　　CH 10

たすける　**v.** *e-ru* 助ける・助けない・助け・
助けて　*to rescue, to help, to save*　　CH 22

ただいま　　只今　*a set phrase used when one*
gets home　　CH 18

たたく　**v.** *k-u* たたく・たたかない・たたき・
たたいて　*to hit, to spank*　　CH 26

ただしい　**adj.** 正しい・正しくない　*correct, precise*
(正しいこたえ *correct answers*)　　CH 23

たたみ　**n.** 畳　*straw mat*　CH 16

〜たち　　　〜達 plural suffix for nouns (that denote people and animals) (私達 we, 学生 students)　CH 18

たつ **v.** *t-u* 立つ・立たない・立ち・立って *to stand up*　CH 10

たてもの **n.** 建物 *building*　CH 2

たとえば　　例えば *for example*　CH 12

たのしい **adj.** 楽しい・楽しくない *fun, entertaining, amusing*　CH 9

たのむ **v.** *m-u* 頼む・頼まない・頼み・頼んで *to ask, to request* (兄に頼む *to ask my brother (to do something)*)　CH 20

タバコ **n.** 煙草・タバコ *tobacco, cigarette* (タバコをすう *to smoke*)　CH 14

たぶん **adv.** 多分 *probably, maybe, perhaps*　CH 15

たべもの **n.** 食べ物 *food*　CH 11

たべる **v.** *e-ru* 食べる・食べない・食べ・食べて *to eat*　CH 6

たまご **n.** 卵・玉子 *egg*　CH 21

だます **v.** *s-u* だます・だまさない・だまし・だまして *to deceive, to trick*　CH 26

だめ (な) **adj.** 駄目だ・駄目じゃない *not good, hopeless*　CH 22

ためる **v.** *e-ru* 貯める・貯めない・貯め・貯めて *to save up, to accumulate* (お金を貯める *to save money*)　CH 19

だれ **q.** 誰 *who* [14]　CH 2

たんい **n.** 単位 *(academic) credit*　CH 15

たんご **n.** 単語 *word, vocabulary*　CH 9

たんじょうび **n.** 誕生日 *birthday*　CH 12

たんす **n.** 箪笥 *clothes chest*　CH 7

だんせい **n.** 男性 *man*　CH 22

ち

ちいさい **adj.** *irr.* 小さい・小さくない *small* (小さな *variation*)　CH 9

ちか **n.** 地下 *basement*　CH 7

ちかい **adj.** 近い・近くない *near* (*c.f.* 近く *vicinity*)　CH 9

ちがう **v.** *w-u* 違う・違わない・違い・違って *to be wrong, to be different* [13]　CH 14

ちかく **n.** 近く *vicinity* [3]　CH 7

ちかてつ **n.** 地下鉄 *subway*　CH 6

ちず **n.** 地図 *map*　CH 18

ちち・おとうさん **n.** 父・お父さん *father* [1]　CH 3

ちちおや **n.** 父親 *father*　CH 22

〜ちゃん　　　〜ちゃん *the respectful title for young children* (よう子ちゃん) [4]　CH 20

ちゃんと **adv.** *tidily, properly, perfectly, correctly*　CH 23

ちゅうがっこう **n.** 中学校 *junior high school* Ⓐ　CH 14

ちゅうかんしけん **n.** 中間試験 *mid-term exam*　CH 25

ちゅうごく **n.** 中国 *China*　CH 2

ちゅうしゃ　　　駐車場 *parking lot,*

じょう **n.** *parking garage*　CH 7

ちょくせつ **adv.** 直接 *directly*　CH 20

ちょっと **adv.** *slightly, a little* [9]　CH 2

ちらかる **v.** *r-u* 散らかる・散らからない・散らかり・散らかって *to become messy*　CH 21

つ

〜つ **c.** *a native counter for a variety of objects*　CH 8

つうきん **n.** 通勤 *travel to work, commute*　CH 16

つかう **v.** *w-u* 使う・使わない・使い・使って *to use* (ペンを使う *to use a pen*)　CH 6

つかれる **v.** *e-ru* 疲れる・疲れない・疲れ・疲れて *to get tired*　CH 13

つきあたり **n.** 突き当たり *dead-end*　CH 10

つぎの〜　　次の〜 *next ~*　CH 15

つく **v.** *k-u* 着く・着かない・着き・着いて *to arrive* (ニューヨークに着く *to arrive in New York*)　CH 23

つくえ **n.** 机 *desk*　CH 2

つくる **v.** *r-u* 作る・作らない・作り・作って
to make (すしを作る *to make sushi*)　　CH 6

つける **v.** *e-ru* つける・つけない・つけ・つけて
to turn on (テレビをつける *to turn on the TV*)　CH 19

つづける **v.** *e-ru* 続ける・続けない・続け・
続けて *to continue*　　CH 19

～つづける **aux.** *e-ru* ～続ける・～続けない・
～続け・～続けて *to continue ~ing* (食べ続ける
to continue eating) [2]　　CH 19

つなみ **n.** 津波 *tsunami, big wave*　　CH 25

つま **n.** 妻 *one's own wife* [3]　　CH 23

つまらない **adj.** 詰まらない・詰まらなくない
boring, uninteresting, unexciting　　CH 12

つまり **adv.** *in short, put simply*　　CH 22

～つもりです　　*I plan to do ~* [12]　　CH 6

つよい **adj.** 強い・強くない *strong, powerful*　CH 22

つれる **v.** *e-ru* 連れる・連れない・連れ・連れて
to take (someone) with [2]　　CH 20

て

て **n.** 手 *hand, arm*　　CH 1

～で **prt.** *by ~, in ~, at ~, with ~* [5]　　CH 6

ていしょく **n.** 定食 *set menu*　　CH 6

でかける **vi.** *e-ru* 出かける・出かけない・
出かけ・出かけて *to go out*　　CH 18

てがみ **n.** 手紙 *letter*　　CH 6

～てき(な) ～的だ・～的じゃない *typical ~,
like ~* (日本的だ *typical Japanese*) [8]　　CH 24

できる **v.** *i-ru* できる・できない・でき・できて
to be made, to be completed, to be able to do ~ [1]　CH 18

できるだけ **adv.** *as much as one can*　　CH 21

～でしょう　　*It is probably the case that ~.*
(*plain form:* ～だろう) [6]　　CH 15

～です **cop.** *to be* (*polite / neutral present
affirmative form of* ～だ) [6]　　CH 2

ですから **con.** *therefore, so* [4]　　CH 8

てつだう **v.** *w-ru* 手伝う・手伝わない・手伝い・
手伝って *to assist, to help* (宿題を手伝う
to assist (someone's) homework)　　CH 20

デート **n.** *date*　　CH 8

デパート **n.** *department store* Ⓐ　　CH 5

でも **con.** *but, however* [16]　　CH 5

～でも **prt.** *even* [1]　　CH 25

でる **v.** *e-ru* 出る・出ない・出・出て *to come out,
to attend, to leave* (くしゃみが出る *to sneeze*, セミナ
ーに出る *to attend the seminar*, レストランを出る
to leave the restaurant)　　CH 15

テレビ **n.** *television*　　CH 4

～てん **c.** ～点 *~ points*　　CH 13

てんいん **n.** 店員 *salesclerk*　　CH 4

でんき **n.** 電気 *electric light, electricity*　　CH 7

てんき **n.** 天気 *weather*　　CH 15

てんし **n.** 天使 *angel*　　CH 22

でんしゃ **n.** 電車 *(electric) train*　　CH 6

てんじょう **n.** 天井 *ceiling*　　CH 19

でんとう **n.** 伝統 *tradition*　　CH 24

てんぷら **n.** 天麩羅 *tempura* Ⓒ　　CH 1

でんわ **n.** 電話 *telephone*　　CH 4

でんわばんごう **n.** 電話番号 *telephone number*　CH 4

と

～と **prt.** *and* (ラジオとカメラ *a radio and a
camera*) [5]　　CH 4

～と **prt.** *embedded sentence particle, quotation
particle* [2]　　CH 15

～ど **c.** ～度 *times* [13]　　CH 12

～という　　*called ~* [12]　　CH 10

～ということは…ということだ　　*The fact that ~
means that ...* [2]　　CH 23

トイレ **n.** *toilet*　　CH 16

どう **q.** *how* [5] CH 9

とうきょう **pn.** 東京 *Tokyo (name of a place)* CH 1

どうし **n.** 動詞 *verb* CH 15

どうして **q.** *why* [9] CH 15

どうぶつ **n.** 動物 *animal* CH 2

どうぶつえん **n.** 動物園 *zoo* CH 5

とおい **adj.** 遠い・遠くない *far* CH 9

とおり **n.** 通り *street* CH 7

～どおり ～通り *~ street* (三番どおり (さんばんどおり) 3rd street) CH 7

～とか *etc.* CH 12

～とき (に) ～時 (に) *at the time of~* [6] CH 18

ときどき **adv.** 時々 *sometimes* [14] CH 5

とくい (な) **adj.** 得意だ・得意じゃない *skillful* [6] CH 11

どくしょ **n.** 読書 *reading* CH 11

とけい **n.** 時計 *watch, clock* CH 2

どこ **q.** *where* CH 5

ところ **n.** 所 *place* CH 11

～ところです *It is at the moment when* ~ (今食べているところです *I am in the middle of eating now.*) [3] CH 18

としょかん **n.** 図書館 *library* CH 2

とち **n.** 土地 *land* CH 17

どちら **q.** *which way, which direction* CH 2

とつぜん **adv.** 突然 *suddenly, abruptly* CH 18

とても **adv.** *very much* [9] CH 2

どなた **q.** *who (polite) (cf.* だれ*)* [14] CH 2

となり **n.** 隣 *next door, next position* [3] CH 7

とにかく **adv.** *anyway, in any case* CH 23

どの～ **q.** *which ~* [11] CH 2

とまる **v.** *r-u* 泊まる・泊まらない・泊まり・泊まって *to stay in ~, to sleep-over at ~* (ホテルに泊まる *to stay at a hotel*) CH 26

ともだち **n.** 友達 *friend* CH 3

どようび **n.** 土曜日 *Saturday* [6] CH 7

とり **n.** 鳥 *bird* CH 21

とりあい **n.** 取り合い *fight over taking something* CH 12

どりょく **n.** 努力 *effort* CH 21

とる **v.** *r-u* 取る・取らない・取り・取って *to take* (日本語をとる *to take a Japanese course*) CH 13

～ドル **c.** *~ dollars ($)* CH 4

どれ **q.** *which one* [11] CH 2

どれぐらい *approximately how long / much / many* CH 6

どろぼう **n.** 泥棒 *thief* CH 25

どんな **q.** *what kind of* [2] CH 9

な

なおす **v.** *s-u* 直す・直さない・直し・直して *to repair, to fix, to correct* CH 20

なか **n.** 中 *inside, middle* [3] CH 7

ながい **adj.** 長い・長くない *long (length)* CH 11

ながでんわ **n.** 長電話 *long telephone conversation* CH 26

なかなか (～ない) **adv.** *(not) easily* ~ (なかなか漢字が覚えられない *(I) cannot memorize kanji easily*) CH 25

～ながら **prt.** *while doing ~* [10] CH 18

なく **v.** *k-u* 泣く・泣かない・泣き・泣いて *to cry* CH 14

なくす **v.** *s-u* なくす・なくさない・なくし・なくして *to lose* (さいふをなくす *to lose one's purse*) CH 10

なくなる **v.** *r-u* なくなる・なくならない・なくなり・なくなって *to disappear, to run out* CH 14

なごや **pn.** 名古屋 *Nagoya (name of a place)* CH 24

～なさい *Do ~* (かたづけなさい *Tidy up!*) [5] CH 23

なつ **n.** 夏 *summer* — CH 12

なっとう **n.** 納豆 *fermented soybeans* Ⓐ — CH 21

なつやすみ **n.** 夏休み *summer vacation* — CH 12

なな／しち **n.** 七 *seven* — CH 1

なまえ・おなまえ **n.** 名前・お名前 *name* — CH 1

なまける **v. e-ru** 怠ける・怠けない・怠け・怠けて *to be lazy* — CH 14

〜なら　*if〜* [7] — CH 24

ならう **v. w-u** 習う・習わない・習い・習って *to learn* [7] — CH 10

なりた **pn.** 成田 *Narita (name of a place)* — CH 1

なる **v. r-u** なる・ならない・なり・なって *to become* (学生になる *to become a student*) — CH 11

なん／なに **q.** 何 *what* [8] — CH 2

に

に **n.** 二 *two* — CH 1

〜に **prt.** *to〜* [8] — CH 5

にがい **adj.** 苦い・苦くない *bitter* — CH 25

にがて（な）**adj.** 苦手だ・苦手じゃない *unskillful* [6] — CH 11

にぎやか（な）**adj.** にぎやかだ・にぎやかじゃない *bustling, cheerful, lively, crowded* — CH 11

にく **n.** 肉 *meat* — CH 17

〜にくい **aux.** 〜にくい・〜にくいです *to be difficult to 〜* (食べにくい *to be difficult to eat*) [2] [3] — CH 19

にげる **v. e-ru** 逃げる・逃げない・逃げ・逃げ・逃げて *to escape* — CH 24

にし **n.** 西 *west* [3] — CH 7

〜にち **c.** 〜日 *~th date* — CH 12

にちようび **n.** 日曜日 *Sunday* [6] — CH 7

にほん **n.** 日本 *Japan* — CH 1

にほんご **n.** 日本語 *Japanese language* — CH 1

にほんじん **n.** 日本人 *Japanese people* — CH 2

にゅうがくする **v. irr.** 入学する *to enter a school, to be admitted to a school* — CH 18

〜によって　*depending on 〜* (人によってちがう *to differ depending on the person*) [9] — CH 23

〜によると　*according to 〜* — CH 25

にわ **n.** 庭　*yard, garden* — CH 26

〜にん／り **c.** 〜人 *a counter for people* — CH 8

にんき **n.** 人気 *popularity* (人気がある *to be popular*) — CH 25

にんぎょう **n.** 人形 *doll* — CH 19

にんげん **n.** 人間 *human being* — CH 22

ぬね

ぬすむ **v. m-u** 盗む・盗まない・盗み・盗んで *to steal* — CH 26

〜ね **prt.** 〜, *isn't it* (きれいですね *It's beautiful, isn't it?*) [3] — CH 3

ねこ **n.** 猫 *cat* — CH 2

ねつ **n.** 熱 *fever, temperature* (熱がある *I have a fever.*) — CH 15

ねだん **n.** 値段 *price* — CH 10

ねぼうする **v. irr.** 寝坊する *to oversleep* — CH 13

ねむい **adj.** 眠い・眠くない *sleepy* — CH 18

ねる **v. e-ru** 寝る・寝ない・寝・寝て *to go to bed, to sleep* — CH 6

〜ねん **c.** 〜年 *~ years, ~th year* Ⓐ — CH 12

〜ねんせい **c.** 〜年生 *a counter for an academic year or grade* (一年生 *first grade, freshman*) — CH 4

の

〜の **prt.** *~'s, of ~* (私の兄 *my brother*) [4] — CH 3

のうりょく **n.** 能力 *ability, proficiency* — CH 24

〜のに **con.** *although 〜* (日本人なのに、日本語が話せません *Although he is a Japanese, he cannot speak Japanese.*) [12] — CH 20

〜ので **con.** *because* ~（日本人なので、日本語が話せます *He can speak Japanese because he is a Japanese.*) [11]   CH 20

ノート **n.** *notebook*   CH 8

のど **n.** 喉 *throat*   CH 15

のむ **v.** *m-u* 飲む・飲まない・飲み・飲んで *to drink*   CH 6

〜のよう（な）**n.** 〜のようだ・〜のようじゃない *just like ~* [3]   CH 22

のる **v.** *r-u*（乗る・乗らない・乗り・乗って *to ride, to take* (*a form of transportation*) (バスに乗る *to take / get on a bus* [3]   CH 13

のんびりする **v.** *irr.* のんびりする *to relax*   CH 18

は

は **n.** 歯 *tooth* (歯をみがく *to brush one's teeth*)   CH 13

〜は **prt.** *as for ~* (*topic marker*) *Exceptional pronunciation* (*wa*) [5]   CH 2

はい *yes, right* [3]   CH 2

はいる **v.** *r-u* 入る・入らない・入り・入って *to enter* (へやに入る *to enter the room*)   CH 10

はかせかてい **n.** 博士課程 *doctoral program*   CH 21

はく **v.** *k-u* はく・はかない・はき・はいて *to wear* (*items such as pants and shoes*) [12]   CH 14

はこ **n.** 箱 *box*   CH 21

はこぶ **v.** *b-u* 運ぶ・運ばない・運び・運んで *to transport, to carry*   CH 21

はし **n.** 橋 *bridge*   CH 10

はし・おはし **n.** 箸・お箸 *chopsticks*   CH 6

はじまる **v.** *r-u* 始まる・始まらない・始まり・始まって *to begin* (クラスが始まる *The class begins.*)   CH 14

はじめ **n.** 始め *beginning*   CH 20

はじめる **v.** *e-ru* 始める・始めない・始め・始めて *to start*   CH 19

〜はじめる **aux.** *e-ru* 〜始める・〜始めない・〜始め・〜始めて *to start ~ing* (食べ始める *to start eating*) [2]   CH 19

はしる **v.** *r-u* 走る・走らない・走り・走って *to run*   CH 17

はずかしい **adj.** 恥ずかしい・恥ずかしくない *embarrassing, shameful*   CH 12

〜はずだ **aux.** 〜はずだ・〜はずじゃない *I suppose that ~* [1]   CH 23

ハンサム（な）**adj.** ハンサムだ・ハンサムじゃない *handsome*   CH 3

はたらく **v.** *k-u* 働く・働かない・働き・働いて *to work* (レストランで働く *to work at a restaurant*) [14]   CH 11

はち **n.** 八 *eight*   CH 1

パチンコ **n.** *a Japanese pinball game* **B**   CH 14

はつおん **n.** 発音 *pronunciation*   CH 9

はな **n.** 鼻 *nose*   CH 1

はな・おはな **n.** 花・お花 *flower*   CH 20

はなす **v.** *s-u* 話す・話さない・話し・話して *to tell, to talk* (ともだちと話す *to talk with one's friend*)   CH 10

はは・おかあさん **n.** 母・お母さん *mother* [1]   CH 3

ははおや **n.** 母親 *mother*   CH 22

はやい **adj.** 早い・早くない *early* [6]   CH 10

はやい **adj.** 速い・速くない *fast, speed* [6]   CH 10

はらう **v.** *w-u* 払う・払わない・払い・払って *to pay* (授業料を払う *to pay for the tuition*)   CH 19

はらがたつ 腹が立つ *to become upset*   CH 26

はらじゅく **pn.** 原宿 *Harajuku* (*name of a place*) **A** CH 13

はる **n.** 春 *spring*   CH 12

はる **v.** *r-u* 貼る・貼らない・貼り・貼って *to post, to paste* (かべにポスターを貼る *to put up a poster on the wall*)   CH 19

はれる **v.** *e-u* 晴れる・晴れない・晴れ・晴れて *to become clear* (*sky*)   CH 15

〜はん **n.** 〜半 *half*   CH 4

ばん **n.** 晩 *evening, nigh* [7]   CH 6

ばんごはん **n.** 晩御飯 *supper, dinner*   CH 6

ひ

ひがし **n.** 東 *east* ③	CH 7
～ひき / びき / ぴき **c.** ～匹 *a counter for animals*	CH 8
ひきだし **n.** 引き出し *drawer*	CH 7
ひく **v.** *k-u* 弾く・弾かない・弾き・弾いて *to play string instruments and keyboards* (ピアノをひく *to play the piano*) ⑭	CH 6
ひくい **adj.** 低い・低くない *low, not tall*	CH 9
ひこうき **n.** 飛行機 *airplane*	CH 6
ひしょ **n.** 秘書 *secretary*	CH 19
ひだり **n.** 左 *left* ③	CH 7
びっくりする **v.** *irr.* びっくりする *to be surprised*	CH 21
ひと **n.** 人 *person* (*cf.* ～かた)	CH 2
ひとつ 一つ *one (piece)*	CH 6
ひとりっこ **n.** 一人っ子 *only one child*	CH 8
ひはんする **v.** *irr.* 批判する *to criticize*	CH 26
ひま (な) **adj.** 暇だ・暇じゃない *not busy, free*	CH 5
～ひゃく / びゃく / ぴゃく **n.** ～百 *one hundred*	CH 4
びょういん **n.** 病院 *hospital*	CH 5
びょうき **n.** 病気 *sickness, illness*	CH 15
ひる **n.** 昼 *noon, daytime* ⑦	CH 6
ひるごはん **n.** 昼御飯 *lunch*	CH 6
ひろい **adj.** 広い・広くない *spacious, wide*	CH 9

ふ

～ぶ ～部 *~ division, ~ club*	CH 23
ふうとう **n.** 封筒 *envelop*	CH 21
ふく **v.** *k-u* 吹く・吹かない・吹き・吹いて *to blow, to play (wind instruments)* (トランペットを吹く *to play the trumpet*) ⑭	CH 6
ふく **v.** *k-u* 拭く・拭かない・拭き・拭いて *to wipe*	CH 26
ふくしゅう (を) する **v.** *irr.* 復習 (を) する *to review*	CH 10
ふたつ 二つ *two (pieces)*	CH 6
ぶちょう 部長 *the head of a department, division, or club*	CH 23
ぶっか **n.** 物価 *prices of things in general*	CH 17
ぶつかる **v.** *r-u* ぶつかる・ぶつからない・ぶつかり・ぶつかって *to collide* (車にぶつかる *to crash into a car*, 車とぶつかる *to collide with a car*)	CH 25
ぶつり **n.** 物理 *physics*	CH 13
ふとる **v.** *r-u* 太る・太らない・太り・太って *to gain weight*	CH 25
ふとん **n.** 布団 *futon mattress* Ⓐ	CH 8
ふべん (な) **adj.** 不便だ・不便じゃない *inconvenient*	CH 9
ふむ **v.** *m-u* 踏む・踏まない・踏み・踏んで *to step on*	CH 26
ふゆ **n.** 冬 *winter*	CH 12
ふる **vi.** *r-u* 降る・降らない・降り・降って *to fall (rain/ snow)*	CH 15
プール **n.** *swimming pool*	CH 6
ふるい **adj.** 古い・古くない *old (for non-animate items)* ①	CH 9
ふろ・おふろ **n.** 風呂・お風呂 *bath*	CH 16
ぶん **n.** 文 *sentence*	CH 9
～ふん / ぷん **c.** ～分 *minutes*	CH 4
～ふん (かん) **c.** ～分 (間) ~ *minutes* (*the duration of time*) ③	CH 6
ぶんか **c.** 文化 *culture*	CH 15
ぶんがく **n.** 文学 *literature*	CH 2
ぶんぽう **n.** 文法 *grammar*	CH 9

へ

～へ **prt.** *to, toward (pronunciation is "e")* ②	CH 12
へいきんてん **n.** 平均点 *average point*	CH 25

～べきだ **aux.** ～べきだ・～べきじゃない
It should be the case that ~ (学生は勉強するべきだ
Students should study.) 4 CH 23

へた (な) **adj.** 下手だ・下手じゃない *unskillful*
(*to be not good at ~*) 6 CH 11

ベッド **n.** *bed* CH 8

べつに **adv.** 別に (*not*) *particularly* CH 11

へや **n.** 部屋 *room* CH 7

へん (な) **adj.** 変だ・変じゃない *strange, weird,*
unusual CH 14

べんきょう (を) する **v.** *irr.* 勉強 (を) する
to study 8 CH 6

べんごし・べんごしさん **n.** 弁護士・弁護士さん
lawyer CH 11

べんり (な) **adj.** 便利だ・便利じゃない
convenient (便利なじしょ *a convenient dictionary*) CH 9

ほ

～ほう 　～方 *side, direction* 1 CH 17

ぼうえき **n.** 貿易 *trading* (貿易会社
trading company) CH 11

～ほうがいい 　～方がいい *It is better to ~.*
(ねた方がいい *to be better to sleep*) 7 CH 19

ぼうし **n.** 帽子 *cap, hat* CH 2

ほか **n.** 他 *others* (他の車 *other cars*) CH 15

ぼく **pron.** 僕 *I, me* (*the first person pronoun*
for male) CH 8

ほしい **adj.** 欲しい・欲しくない *to want*
(*some items*) 12 CH 11

～ほしい **aux.** ～欲しい・～欲しくない
to want someone to do ~ 4 CH 21

ボタン **n.** *button* CH 21

ほっかいどう **pn.** 北海道 *Hokkaido*
(*name of a Japanese island*) CH 17

～ほど (…ない) **prt.** (*not*) *as ... as ~* 4 CH 17

ほめる **v.** *e-ru* 誉める・誉めない・誉め・誉めて
to praise CH 26

ほん **n.** 本 *book* CH 2

～ほん / ぼん / ぽん **c.** ～本 *a counter for*
cylindrical objects CH 8

ほんしゅう **pn.** 本州 *Honshu* (*name of a Japanese*
island) CH 17

ほんとうです 　本当です *It is true.* CH 15

ほんとうに **adv.** 本当に *truly* CH 15

ほんばこ **n.** 本箱 *bookcase* CH 7

ほんや **n.** 本屋 *bookstore* 9 CH 5

ま

まあ **interj.** *Oh dear!* (*used by female*) CH 18

まあまあ **adv.** *more or less* 9 CH 2

～まい **c.** ～枚 *a counter for flat objects* CH 8

まいしゅう **n.** 毎週 *every week* CH 16

まいつき **n.** 毎月 *every month* CH 16

まいとし **n.** 毎年 *every year* CH 16

まいにち **n.** 毎日 *every day* CH 16

まえ **n.** 前 *the previous time, the front position* CH 12

まえ **n.** 前 *front, front position* 3 CH 7

～まえ (に) 　～前 (に) *before ~* 9 CH 18

まがる **v.** *r-u* 曲がる・曲がらない・曲がり・
曲がって *to make a turn* CH 10

～ました 　*polite past affirmative suffix for*
verbs 10 CH 6

まじめ (な) **adj.** 真面目だ・真面目じゃない
serious, honest CH 10

～ます 　*polite present affirmative suffix for*
verbs 3 CH 5

まず **adv.** 先ず *first of all* (まず朝ごはんを食べる
to eat breakfast first) CH 23

まずい **adj.** まずい・まずくない *not delicious* CH 11

～ません 　*polite present negative suffix for verb* 3
CH 5

～ませんでした　*polite past negative suffix for verb* [10] CH 6

また **adv.** *again* CH 26

まだ **adv.** *(not ~) yet* (まだ始まっていない
(It) has not begun yet.) CH 14

まちがえる **v.** *e-ru* 間違える・間違えない・
間違え・間違えて　*to mix up, to make a mistake* CH 25

まつ **v.** *t-u* 待つ・待たない・待ち・待って
to wait (ガールフレンドを待つ *to wait for
one's girlfriend)* CH 19

まっすぐ **adv.** *straight* CH 10

～まで **prt.** *up to, until* [5] CH 7

～までに　*by ~ (deadline)* (9時までに帰り
ます *I will return by 9 o'clock.)* [6] CH 16

まど **n.** 窓 *window* CH 2

まるで **adv.** *just like, so to speak* CH 22

～まん **n.** ～万 *ten thousand* CH 4

まんが **n.** マンガ・漫画 *comic book* CH 14

み

みがく **v.** *k-u* 磨く・磨かない・磨き・磨いて
to polish CH 13

みぎ **n.** 右 *right* CH 7

みじかい **adj.** 短い・短くない *short (length)* CH 11

みずうみ **adj.** 湖 *lake* CH 17

みせ・おみせ **n.** 店・お店 *store* CH 24

みせる **v.** *e-ru* 見せる・見せない・見せ・
見せて *to show* CH 10

みそしる **n.** 味噌汁 *miso soup* CH 6

～みたい（な）　～みたいだ・～みたいじゃない
just like ~ [4] CH 22

みち **n.** 道 *street, road* CH 10

みなさん **n.** 皆さん *everyone, all of you* CH 21

みなみ **n.** 南 *south* [3] CH 7

みみ **n.** 耳 *ear* CH 1

みる **v.** *i-ru* 見る・見ない・見・見て *to watch,
to look* (テレビを見る *to watch TV)* CH 6

～みる **aux.** *i-ru* ～みる・～みない・～み・
～みて *to try ~ing* [9] CH 20

みんな **pron.** *everyone, everything* CH 23

む

むし **n.** 虫 *bug, insect* CH 22

むずかしい **adj.** 難しい・難しくない *difficult* CH 2

むすこ・むすこさん **n.** 息子・息子さん *son* CH 14

むすめ・むすめさん／おじょうさん **n.** 娘・
娘さん／お嬢さん *daughter* CH 14

むりやりに **adv.** 無理やりに *by force* CH 26

め

め **n.** 目 *eye* CH 1

～め **c.** ～目 *a counter for ordinal numbers*
（一つ目 *the first)* [13] CH 10

めいし **n.** 名詞 *noun* CH 15

めがね **n.** 眼鏡 *eyeglasses* CH 14

めんせつ **n.** 面接 *interview* CH 8

めんどう（な）**adj.** 面倒だ・面倒じゃない *troublesome* CH 18

めんどうをみる　面倒を見る *to take care of,
or look after a person or an animal* (こどもの
面倒を見る *to take care of the children)* CH 23

も

～も **prt.** *also* [13] CH 2

もう **adv.** *already* (もうだいじょうぶです
I am already fine) CH 13

もういちど　もう一度 *once more* CH 1

もうしこむ **v.** *m-u* 申し込む・申し込まない・
申し込み・申し込んで *to apply* CH 24

もうす **v.** *s-u* 申す・申さない・申し・申して
to (modestly) say (the humble form of 言う) CH 21

もうすこし **adv.** もう少し *a little more* CH 10

もくようび **n.** 木曜日 *Thursday* [6] CH 7

もし **adv.** *if* (*by any chance*)   CH 24

もしもし *Hello!* (*on the phone*)   CH 7

もちろん **adv.** 勿論 *surely, certainly*   CH 11

もつ **v.** *t-u* 持つ・持たない・持ち・持って *to hold or carry by hand* (かばんを持つ *to carry a bag*)   CH 19

もっていく 持って行く *to take* (*something*) (*there*) [2]   CH 10

もっている 持っている *to have, to possess* (車を持っている *to have a car*)   CH 19

もってくる 持って来る *to bring* (*something*) (*here*) [2]   CH 10

もっと **adv.** *more, some more* (もっと食べてください *Please eat some more.*)   CH 23

もどる **v.** *r-u* 戻る・戻らない・戻り・戻って *to return*   CH 21

もの **n** 物 *thing, item, object*   CH 11

もらう **v.** *w-u* もらう・もらわない・もらい・もらって *to receive*   CH 18

～もらう **aux.** *w-u* ～もらう・～もらわない・～もらい・～もらって *to have someone do ~* [3]   CH 20

もんく **n.** 文句 *complaint* (文句をいう *to complain*)   CH 21

もんだい **n.** 問題 *question, issue, problem*   CH 15

や

～や **prt.** *and so on, etc* [3]   CH 11

やきもちをやく *to be jealous*   CH 25

やくそく **n.** 約束 *personal appointment, promise* (*c.f.* 予約 (よやく) *reservation / business appointment*)   CH 23

やさい **n.** 野菜 *vegetable*   CH 17

やさしい **adj.** 優しい・優しくない *kind, nice*   CH 10

やすい **adj.** 安い・安くない *cheap, inexpensive*   CH 4

～やすい **aux.** ～やすい・～やすいです *to be easy to ~* (食べやすい *to be easy to eat*) [2][3]   CH 19

やすむ **v.** *m-u* 休む・休まない・休み・休んで *to rest, to take a day off, to be absent from ~*   CH 11

やせる **v.** *e-ru* 痩せる・痩せない・痩せ・痩せて *to lose weight*   CH 25

やちん **n.** 家賃 *rent for houses and apartments*   CH 9

やっと **adv.** *finally* (やっとおわりました *It finally ended.*)   CH 21

やっぱり **adv.** 箱 *expectedly* (*c.f.* やはり)   CH 21

やま **n.** 山 *mountain*   CH 5

やめる **v.** *e-ru* 辞める・辞めない・辞め・辞めて *to quit, to resign*   CH 13

やる **v.** *r-u* やる・やらない・やり・やって *to give something to one's subordinate* [1]   CH 20

～やる **aux.** *r-u* ～やる・～やらない・～やり・～やって *to do something for one's subordinate* [3]   CH 20

ゆ

ゆうがた **n.** 夕方 *early evening, dusk*   CH 5

ゆうき **n.** 勇気 *courage*   CH 22

ゆうびんきょく **n.** 郵便局 *post office*   CH 5

ゆうめい (な) **adj.** 有名だ・有名じゃない *famous*   CH 12

ゆか **n.** 床 *floor*   CH 19

ゆき **n.** 雪 *snow*   CH 15

ゆっくり **adv.** *slowly*   CH 1

よ

～よ **prt.** *sentence-final emphasis marker* [10]   CH 2

ようし **n.** 用紙 *form, sheet*   CH 20

～ようだ **aux.** ～ようだ・～ようじゃない *it seems to be ~* [10]   CH 25

ようふく **n.** 洋服 *clothes*   CH 6

よく **adv.** *often, well* [14]   CH 5

よこ **n.** 横 *side* [3]   CH 7

よむ **v.** *m-u* 読む・読まない・読み・読んで *to read* (本を読む *to read a book*)   CH 6

よやくする **v.** *irr.* 予約する *to make a reservation, to make an appointment* (ホテルを予約する *to make a reservation at a hotel*) CH 19

～より **prt.** *than* [2] CH 17

よる **n.** 夜 *night* CH 14

よろこぶ **v.** *b-u* 喜ぶ・喜ばない・喜び・喜んで *to become pleased* [1] CH 14

よわい **adj.** 弱い・弱くない *weak, not powerful* CH 22

よん / し **n.** 四 *four* CH 1

ら

らいげつ **n.** 来月 *next month* CH 11

らいねん **n.** 来年 *next year* CH 12

らく（な）**adj.** 楽だ・楽じゃない *easy* (*less labor intensive*) CH 13

～らしい　～らしい・～らしくない *to be a typical ~* (男らしい人 *a manly man*) [7] CH 22

～らしい **aux.** ～らしい・～らしくない *it seems to be ~* [11] CH 25

ラジオ **n.** *radio* CH 4

り

りっぱ（な）**adj.** 立派だ・立派じゃない *splendid, elegant, gorgeous, great* CH 9

りゅうがく **n.** 留学 *study abroad* CH 20

りょう **n.** 寮 *dormitory* CH 2

りょうしん・ごりょうしん **n.** 両親・御両親 *parents* CH 8

りょうり **n.** 料理 *cooking* CH 11

りょかん **n.** 旅館 *Japanese-style inn* CH 24

りょこう **n.** 旅行 *traveling* CH 11

りょこうがいしゃ **n.** 旅行会社 *travel agency* CH 24

る れ

れい / ゼロ **n.** 零・ゼロ・0 *zero* CH 4

れいぞうこ **n.** 冷蔵庫 *refrigerator* CH 8

れきし **n.** 歴史 *history* CH 13

レストラン **n.** *restaurant* CH 5

れんしゅう（を）する **v.** *irr.* 練習（を）する *to practice* CH 10

ろ

ろうか **n.** 廊下 *hallway* CH 26

ろく **n.** 六 *six* CH 1

ろんぶん **n.** 論文 *academic paper, thesis* CH 26

わ

わえいじてん **n.** 和英辞典 *Japanese-English dictionary* CH 2

わかい **adj.** 若い・若くない *young* CH 24

わかる **v.** *r-u* 分かる・分からない・分かり・分かって *to know, to understand* [7] CH 5

わすれる **v.** *e-ru* 忘れる・忘れない・忘れ・忘れて *to forget* (宿題を忘れる *to forget one's homework*) CH 19

わたし **pron.** 私 *I, me* (*1st person pronoun*) [2] CH 2

わたる **v.** *r-u* 渡る・渡らない・渡り・渡って *to cross, to cross over* CH 10

わらう **v.** *w-u* 笑う・笑わない・笑い・笑って *to laugh, to smile* CH 14

わるい **adj.** 悪い・悪くない *bad* CH 12

わるぐちをいう　悪口を言う *to say bad things about a person behind his back* CH 26

を

～を **prt.** *direct object marker* [9] CH 6

ん

～んです *it is the case that ~* [6] CH 6

APPENDIX FIVE
Note List

Grammar and Usage

Absolute time expressions	8	CH 12
Adjectives (高い, 高価な, etc.)	3	CH 9
Adverbial phrases for periods of time (〜まえに, etc.)	9	CH 18
Adverbs derived from adjectives (〜く and 〜に)	8	CH 10
An overview of verb conjugation	1	CH 5
Asking a favor politely (書いていただけないでしょうか, etc.)	13	CH 20
Auxiliaries	2	CH 19
Auxiliaries that mean to give or receive (〜あげる / 〜くれる / 〜もらう)	3	CH 20
Basic Japanese sounds	1	CH 1
Colors	1	CH 8
Counters	2	CH 4
Daily time frame (あさ, ばん, etc.)	7	CH 6
Degree adverbs (とても, ぜんぜん, まあまあ, etc.)	8	CH 9
Demonstrative pronouns for location	10	CH 5
Demonstratives (あれ, あの〜, etc.)	11	CH 2
Demonstratives for the items outside of the visual field (あれ, etc.)	4	CH 24
Direct Quote	7	CH 18
Family members (母, お母さん, etc.)	1	CH 3
Frequency (よく, ときどき, etc.)	14	CH 5
Genders (男の人, 女の人, etc.)	5	CH 3
Gratitude (ありがとうございます, etc.)	3	CH 1
Greetings (こんにちは, おはようございます, etc.)	7	CH 1

Imitating words (ワンワン, ネバネバ, etc.)	6	CH 8
Indefinite pronouns (なにか something, だれか someone, etc.)	4	CH 12
Interjections (あっ, ほら, etc.)	5	CH 15
Introduction (はじめまして, よろしく, etc.)	5	CH 1
Negative adverbs (あまり, ぜんぜん, etc.)	15	CH 5
Negative pronouns (なにも nothing, だれも no one, etc.)	5	CH 12
Number phrases [Numeral + counter]	3	CH 8
Numbers	1	CH 4
Occupation	5	CH 14
Particle combination (〜には, 〜にも, etc.)	17	CH 5
Parting (さようなら, etc.)	8	CH 1
Personal pronouns (私, あなた, etc.)	2	CH 2
Plain forms of verbs (食べる, 食べない, etc.)	2	CH 5
Plain past affirmative forms of verbs (〜た)	14	CH 12
Plain past forms of predicates	8	CH 15
Plain present forms of predicates	3	CH 15
Polite prefix (お〜 and ご〜)	16	CH 1
Present tense	4	CH 5
Proportional frequency (たいてい, いつも, etc.)	1	CH 6
Relative clauses	14	CH 14
Relative location	3	CH 7

Relative time (明日 , 昨日 , etc.)	5	CH 5
Relative time expressions	9	CH 12
Respectful titles (〜さん , 〜くん , etc.)	6	CH 1
Skills (とくい (な), にがて (な), etc.)	6	CH 11
Spouses	3	CH 23
Syllable structure in Japanese	7	CH 4
Te-form of verbs (〜て / で)	1	CH 10
Te-forms [Listing predicates]	1	CH 13
Temperature	4	CH 15
To give (あげる / くれる / さしあげる / くださる / やる)	1	CH 20
To live (すむ , せいかつする , いきる , etc.)	10	CH 14
To receive (もらう / いただく)	8	CH 20
To wear (きる , はく , かぶる , する , つける , etc.)	12	CH 14
To work (はたらく and つとめる)	14	CH 11
Transitive and intransitive verbs	1	CH 19
Verbs of existence (ある , いる and いらっしゃる)	1	CH 7
Verbs of going and coming (行く , 来る and 帰る)	6	CH 5
Verbs of learning (ならう , まなぶ , べんきょうする , etc.)	7	CH 10
Verbs of mental states (よろこぶ , etc.)	1	CH 14
Verbs that mean "to play"	14	CH 6
X という Y: Y called X [Introducing a new item with its proper name]	12	CH 10
あう : To meet / to see	1	CH 12
あそぶ : To play	6	CH 14
あっ : Oops! / oh! [Shock]	11	CH 1

あのう : Ummm, ... [Initiating talk]	13	CH 1
〜ある : To have been 〜 ed [The state of things]	9	CH 19
いいです : Good / no, thank you	10	CH 10
いくら : How much? [Question word for price]	4	CH 4
いただきます and ごちそうさま [Before and after eating]	5	CH 18
いちばん : The most 〜 [Superlative comparison]	7	CH 17
いつ : When? [Question word for time]	6	CH 12
いる : State	2	CH 14
〜うちに : While / before 〜 [The time adverbial that bears a threat]	7	CH 23
うちの〜 : Our 〜 / my 〜	7	CH 14
おおい , すくない : Numerous, scarce	1	CH 11
(〜の) おかげで : Thanks to 〜 [The cause of success]	2	CH 26
〜おく : To do 〜 in advance for future convenience [Preparation]	8	CH 19
おげんきですか : How are you?	15	CH 1
おじゃまします [When entering someone else's residence]	7	CH 9
おなじぐらい : As 〜 as ... [Equivalence]	3	CH 17
おねがいします : Please 〜 [Favor]	10	CH 1
おもう : To think	1	CH 15
〜か : Or [Disjunctive listing]	4	CH 11
〜か [Sentence final question particle]	7	CH 2
〜かた : The method / way of 〜 ing [Method / manner]	5	CH 22
〜か (どうか): If 〜 , whether (or not) 〜 [Embedded question]	8	CH 23
〜かもしれません : It is possibly the case that 〜 [Possibility]	7	CH 15

～から : Because ～ [Reasons]	10	CH 15	
～から : From ～ [Starting point]	4	CH 7	
～が : But [Conflict / contrast]	7	CH 11	
～が [Subject marker]	11	CH 6	
～がる : To show signs of ～ [The third person's feelings]	8	CH 22	
～かん [The duration of time]	3	CH 6	
き (気): Spirit	2	CH 16	
きれい (な): Beautiful, pretty, clean and neat	2	CH 3	
～くする , ～にする : To make something ～ / to make oneself ～ [Change]	9	CH 10	
～ください : Please do ～ [Requesting]	9	CH 1	
～くなる・～になる : To become ～	10	CH 21	
～ぐらい : Approximately ～	4	CH 6	
ございます : To have, to be	7	CH 7	
ごぜん , ごご : a.m., p.m.	3	CH 4	
こちら : This person	1	CH 2	
～ことができる : Can do ～ [Potential]	11	CH 11	
～ことにする vs. ～ことになる : I decided to ～ vs. it's been decided [Decision]	8	CH 21	
こまる (困る): To be in trouble	1	CH 16	
ごめんください: Hello! Is anyone there? / Goodbye!	2	CH 18	
～ごろ : Approximately	7	CH 12	
こんど : This time / next time	5	CH 11	
～させ : To make / let someone do ～ [Make-causative and let-causative]	5	CH 26	
～させられ : To be made to do ～ [Causative-passive]	6	CH 26	
～し : [Emphatic conjunction]	7	CH 20	

～しか (…ない): Only ～	2	CH 22	
しかたがない : Cannot be helped	6	CH 25	
しつれいします [Entering and leaving someone else's office]	3	CH 10	
～しまう : To complete ～ ing [Completion]	6	CH 19	
じゃあ : Then, in that case [Transition]	12	CH 2	
しる : To get to know	9	CH 14	
～じん [Nationality / citizenship / ethnic background of people]	4	CH 2	
～すぎる : To do ～ too much, to be too ～ [Extremity]	4	CH 19	
すこし : A few / a little / slightly [Quantity / amount / degree]	5	CH 8	
～ずつ : Each / at a time [Distributive marker]	5	CH 19	
すみません : Excuse me / I am sorry [Apology / attention catching]	12	CH 1	
～する [Verb formative]	8	CH 6	
(～の) せいで : Due to ～ [The cause of failure]	1	CH 26	
～そう (な): To look ～ , ～ -looking [Conjecture based on appearance]	1	CH 22	
そうすると : Then [Subsequent fact]	11	CH 10	
～そうだ : I heard that ～ [Hearsay]	8	CH 25	
それか : Or [Alternative idea]	15	CH 11	
それから : And then / in addition [Multiple events]	2	CH 6	
それで : As a result [Resulting fact]	5	CH 13	
それとも : Alternatively [Alternative yes-no questions]	8	CH 18	
それに : Furthermore [Additional fact]	6	CH 9	
～たい : To want to do ～ [Desire for action]	13	CH 11	

〜だけです : It is just that 〜	4	CH 18	〜てき (な): [Adjective formative]	8	CH 24
〜たことがある : I have 〜 ed [Experience]	15	CH 12	できる : To be able to do / to be completed / to be made	1	CH 18
〜たら、…した : After / when 〜 , ... [Sporadic consequence]	5	CH 24	〜てください (ませんか): Please do 〜 , could you do 〜 [Requesting]	4	CH 10
〜たら、…する : After / when / whenever / if 〜 , ... [Conditioned consequence]	6	CH 24	〜でした , 〜かったです [Past tense of noun and adjective predicates]	12	CH 12
〜たり : Do 〜 , etc. [Partial-list of activities]	6	CH 22	〜でしょう : It is probably the case that 〜 ; I guess 〜 [Likeliness]	6	CH 15
だれ , どなた : Who [Question word for people]	14	CH 2	〜です (だ): To be [Copula]	6	CH 2
ちがう : Wrong / different	13	CH 14	ですから : Therefore [Consequence]	4	CH 8
〜ちゃん [Respectful title for young children]	4	CH 20	でも : But [Conflict / contrast]	16	CH 5
ちょっと : A little bit [Expression softener]	14	CH 1	〜でも : Even 〜 [The least expected item]	1	CH 25
ちょっと : It's a little... [Declination]	13	CH 5	〜ても : Even if 〜 , even though 〜	3	CH 25
ちょっと , まあまあ : Slightly, more or less	9	CH 2	〜てもいい / 〜てはいけない [Permission / prohibition]	3	CH 16
〜つもりです : It is planned that 〜 [Plan]	12	CH 6	〜てもいい / 〜てはいけない [Permissible / impermissible]	4	CH 16
つれる : To take or bring someone	2	CH 20	〜と : And [Listing marker for nouns]	5	CH 4
〜で : At, in [Location of events and incidents]	9	CH 25	〜と : That 〜 [Embedded sentence marker]	2	CH 15
〜で : At, in [Time]	5	CH 21	〜と : With 〜 [Accompaniment]	7	CH 8
〜で : By, with, in, at [How the action takes place]	5	CH 6	〜と、…した : When 〜 , ... happened [Sporadic consequence]	11	CH 21
〜で : Due to [Cause / reason]	11	CH 12	〜と、…する : Whenever 〜 , ... happens [Automatic consequence]	9	CH 21
〜で : Under the condition such as 〜 [Circumstantial condition]	3	CH 12	〜ど vs 〜かい : 〜 times [The number of occasions]	13	CH 12
〜ている : To be in the middle of doing 〜 [Progressive state]	3	CH 14	〜ということは…ということです : 〜 means ... [Implication]	2	CH 23
〜ている : To do 〜 usually / always / often [Habitual state]	4	CH 14	どう : How [Question word for a property (predicate)]	5	CH 9
〜ている : To have done 〜 [Resulting state]	11	CH 14	どうしたんですか : What happened?	6	CH 13

どうして～んですか : Why ～? [Asking reasons and causes]	9	CH 15
どうぞ : Go ahead (and do ～), please (do ～) [Offering]	2	CH 1
どうも : Indeed [Gratitude / apology-intensifier]	4	CH 1
～とき (に): At the time when ～	6	CH 18
～ところです : It is at the moment when ～	3	CH 18
どちら : Which one of the two? [A question word for two-item-comparison]	1	CH 17
どんな : What kind of ～ [Question word for a property (prenominal)]	2	CH 9
～ないで : Without ～ ing	3	CH 21
なかなか (～ない): (Not) easily ～	5	CH 25
～ながら : While doing ～ [Accompanying activity]	10	CH 18
～なくてはいけない / ～なくてもいい [Obligation discretion]	5	CH 16
～なさい : Do ～ [Polite command]	5	CH 23
なに , なん : What [Question word for non-human items]	8	CH 2
なにを / だれが～ても : No matter ～	4	CH 25
～なら : If ～ / if you are talking about ～ [Supposition]	7	CH 24
なんでも・だれでも : Any ～ [Free-choice items]	2	CH 25
～に : At, on, in [Absolute time of an event]	10	CH 12
～に : For [Target (occasion)]	6	CH 20
～に : For [The target of pros and cons]	2	CH 13
～に : From [Target (source)]	10	CH 20
～に : To ～ [Target, destination]	8	CH 5
～に : To [Target (recipient)]	5	CH 20

～に , ～ために [Purpose]	4	CH 13
～にくい・～やすい : To be difficult / easy to do ～ [Toughness]	3	CH 19
～には… がある : There is an ... in ～ , I have an ... in ～ [Existence]	2	CH 8
～によって : Depending on ～ [Determinant factors]	9	CH 23
～ね : ～ , Isn't it? [Sentence final confirmation marker]	3	CH 3
～の [Noun-maker]	8	CH 11
～の [Noun-maker used in comparative sentences]	5	CH 17
～の : One [Pronominal element]	4	CH 9
～の : ～ 's [Modifier marker]	4	CH 3
～ので : Because ～ [Reasons and causes]	11	CH 20
～のに : Although ～ [Conflict and contradiction]	12	CH 20
のる : To ride, to take	3	CH 13
～は : As for ～ , speaking of ～ [Topic marker]	5	CH 2
～は [Contrast]	9	CH 11
～は～が～です : As for ～ , ～ is ～	2	CH 11
～は… にある : ～ is at / in... [The location of things and people]	2	CH 7
はい , いいえ : Yes / no [Agreement / disagreement]	3	CH 2
～ばかり : To do nothing but ～ [An extreme habit]	8	CH 14
～はずだ : I suppose that ～ [Circumstantial conclusion]	1	CH 23
はやい : Early / fast	6	CH 10
ひと (人): Other people	5	CH 21
ふるい : Old	1	CH 9
～へ : To / toward ～ [Direction]	2	CH 12

Culture

Announcing a decision	🅑	CH 21
Asking others their age	🅑	CH 4
Bowing	🅑	CH 1
Congratulating gift (おいわい)	🅐	CH 20
Describing family members	🅐	CH 3
Expressing prohibition	🅑	CH 16
Japanese currency	🅓	CH 4
Japanese food	🅒	CH 1
Japanese islands	🅔	CH 1
Japanese names	🅓	CH 1
JR パス : Japan Rail Pass	🅑	CH 24
Lucky and unlucky numbers	🅐	CH 4
Modesty	🅕	CH 1
National holidays	🅑	CH 12
New year holidays in Japan	🅑	CH 13
Polite high pitch	🅐	CH 7
Rejecting	🅒	CH 5
Repeating	🅑	CH 5
Rice	🅑	CH 6
Salesclerks and customers	🅒	CH 4
Schools in Japan	🅐	CH 14
Seasonal gifts in Japan (おちゅうげん・おせいぼ)	🅑	CH 20
Some towns in Tokyo	🅐	CH 24
Table manners	🅐	CH 6
Traditional martial arts	🅐	CH 1
いざかや : Izakaya bar	🅔	CH 5
うきよえ : Ukiyo-e	🅑	CH 19
カプセル・ホテル : Capsule hotel	🅐	CH 22

カラオケ : Karaoke	🅓	CH 5
ぎょうざ : Chinese-style dumplings	🅐	CH 19
こうばん : Police boxes	🅐	CH 10
じゅく : Tutoring school / cram school	🅐	CH 26
スリッパ : Slippers	🅐	CH 16
そろばん : Abacus	🅑	CH 26
デパート : Department store	🅐	CH 5
なっとう (納豆): Fermented soybeans	🅐	CH 21
～ねん : The year ～ [Expressing years]	🅐	CH 12
はらじゅく	🅐	CH 13
パチンコ	🅑	CH 14
ふとん : Futon mattress	🅐	CH 8
ファーストフード・レストラン	🅒	CH 6
めいし : Name cards (Business cards)	🅔	CH 4
わがし (Japanese sweets)	🅐	CH 25

Writing

Hiragana	Ⓐ	CH 1
Kanji components	Ⓐ	CH 3
Kanji strokes	Ⓐ	CH 2
New year's cards (ねんがじょう)	Ⓔ	CH 13
Punctuation and format	Ⓑ	CH 1
Reading kanji	Ⓑ	CH 2
Writing postcards to say hello	Ⓐ	CH 21
Writing styles: ですます -style, だ -style and である -style	Ⓓ	CH 15
あめかんむり	Ⓑ	CH 15
いとへん	Ⓐ	CH 19
うかんむり	Ⓓ	CH 4
うまへん	Ⓐ	CH 24

おおざと	[a]	CH 16		てへん	[d]	CH 16
おくりがな	[a]	CH 4		とり	[b]	CH 21
おのづくり	[b]	CH 7		なつあし	[a]	CH 12
おんなへん	[c]	CH 8		なべぶた	[c]	CH 4
カタカナ	[e]	CH 4		にんべん	[c]	CH 6
きへん	[a]	CH 8		のぎへん	[c]	CH 16
ぎょうにんべん	[a]	CH 18		ひとあし	[b]	CH 3
くさかんむり	[c]	CH 13		ひとがしら	[b]	CH 4
くにがまえ	[a]	CH 11		ひへん	[a]	CH 5
こころ	[a]	CH 15		ふゆがしら	[b]	CH 12
こざとへん	[a]	CH 23		ふるとり	[a]	CH 13
ごんべん	[b]	CH 9		ぼくづくり	[b]	CH 8
さかなへん	[a]	CH 17		まだれ	[a]	CH 9
さんずいへん	[b]	CH 13		むしへん	[a]	CH 22
しかばね	[b]	CH 16		もんがまえ	[a]	CH 6
しめすへん	[b]	CH 11		やまいだれ	[c]	CH 15
しょくへん	[b]	CH 6		ゆみへん	[d]	CH 8
しんにょう	[a]	CH 7		よつてん	[d]	CH 13
ちから	[c]	CH 3				